MW01483967

SCRIPTURAL TRACES:
CRITICAL PERSPECTIVES ON THE RECEPTION AND INFLUENCE OF THE BIBLE

1

Editors
Claudia V. Camp, Texas Christian University
W. J. Lyons, University of Bristol
Andrew Mein, Westcott House, Cambridge

Editorial Board
Michael J. Gilmour, David M. Gunn, James E. Harding, Jorunn Økland

Published under

LIBRARY OF HEBREW BIBLE/ OLD TESTAMENT STUDIES

586

Formerly Journal for the Study of the Old Testament Supplement Series

Editors
Claudia V. Camp, Texas Christian University
Andrew Mein, Westcott House, Cambridge

Founding Editors
David J. A. Clines, Philip R. Davies and David M. Gunn

Editorial Board
Alan Cooper, John Goldingay, Robert P. Gordon,
Norman K. Gottwald, James E. Harding, John Jarick, Carol Meyers,
Francesca Stavrakopoulou, Daniel L. Smith-Christopher

THE BIBLE, GENDER, AND RECEPTION HISTORY

The Case of Job's Wife

Katherine Low

BLOOMSBURY
LONDON • NEW DELHI • NEW YORK • SYDNEY

Bloomsbury T&T Clark

An imprint of Bloomsbury Publishing Plc

50 Bedford Square 1385 Broadway
London New York
WC1B 3DP NY 10018
UK USA

www.bloomsbury.com

First published 2013

© Katherine Low, 2013

All rights reserved. No part of this publication may be reproduced or transmitted in any form or by any means, electronic or mechanical, including photocopying, recording, or any information storage or retrieval system, without prior permission in writing from the publishers.

Katherine Low has asserted her rights under the Copyright, Designs and Patents Act, 1988, to be identified as Author of this work.

No responsibility for loss caused to any individual or organization acting on or refraining from action as a result of the material in this publication can be accepted by Bloomsbury Academic or the author.

British Library Cataloguing-in-Publication Data
A catalogue record for this book is available from the British Library.

ISBN: HB: 978-0-56723-921-1

Library of Congress Cataloging-in-Publication Data
A catalog record for this book is available from the Library of Congress.

Typeset by Forthcoming Publications Ltd (www.forthpub.com)
Printed and bound in Great Britain

CONTENTS

ACKNOWLEDGMENTS

This book is a product of a long journey. It is a version of my doctoral dissertation and I owe much to the faculty, staff, and students at Brite Divinity School, Texas Christian University, especially to Leo Perdue and Toni Craven. Brite Divinity School held me in beloved community, making it safe to explore my own identity as a biblical scholar and for that I will always be grateful. David Gunn at Texas Christian University provided guidance during my doctoral work and instilled in me a love of reception history that I will carry throughout my career.

Many others have contributed to this study as well. Christopher Rowland read the chapter on William Blake, helping me to hone in on my ideas, and C. L. Seow contributed by being open to discussing ideas with me. The journey of this book has taught me the value of the collaboration of ideas. Furthermore, my present colleagues at Mary Baldwin College in Staunton, Virginia, carry with them a passion and dedication for liberal arts education that has captured my heart. I look forward to many more years of teamwork with the wonderful people at Mary Baldwin as we build relationships together in the landscape of higher education.

The journey behind this book begins in a small Nebraska town. I have fond memories of sitting at the kitchen table across from my grandmother who helped me with my homework every day and who fostered my love of learning. I write these words a few days after my father's death and some part of him informs this work. To the living ones, though, who carry on legacies, I dedicate this book. My mother Bonnie, my husband Andy, and my daughter Lila remind me that ideas matter and that love provides a foundation for all things.

LIST OF FIGURES

The author and publisher gratefully acknowledge the permission granted to reproduce the copyright material in this book. Every effort has been made to trace copyright holders and to obtain their permission for the use of copyright material. The publisher apologizes for any errors or omissions in the following list and would be grateful if notified of any corrections that should be incorporated in future reprints or editions of this book.

INTRODUCTION

Perhaps no other words spoken by a woman in the Hebrew Bible carry more bite and bafflement than those of Job's wife in chapter 2, verse 9— "Curse God and die!" Her apparent lack of spousal commitment leaves readers wanting more, especially since she disappears from the story after uttering her infamous words. Job receives more children at the end of the book, likely by his wife, although Job's wife never again speaks. The biblical text remains silent on her whereabouts, but a reception history of Job and his wife reveals a wealth of explanatory interpretations for Job's wife's words and their lives together as husband and wife.

Two twenty-first century examples of the use of Job 2:9 in fictitious contexts of suffering and misery, one in a comedic fashion and one in a post-apocalyptic novel, attest to the enduring power of the words of Job's wife. Stephen Colbert, a comedian and political satirist, co-wrote a television series and subsequent film called *Strangers with Candy*, which takes place in an average North American high school.[1] Colbert plays a science teacher who fails to guide his students on their science fair projects. When Colbert's character, Mr. Noblet, hears a student expressing some hope, he dramatically cries before laying his head on his desk: "Hope? You fool. Don't you know death when you see it? I'm being punished. You have no idea the terrible things I've done. Curse God and die!"[2] Colbert's character humorously applies serious and tragic divine rhetoric to a seemingly minor situation, but in his character's mind, all hope is lost for his students to enter the science fair.

A desperate situation also leads to the use of Job's wife's words in a Pulitzer Prize winning novel *The Road* by Cormac McCarthy. After a cataclysmic event occurs on earth, a man and his son are left migrating on foot from a cold climate to a warmer one, hopelessly trying to avoid

---

1. *Strangers with Candy* (movie) © 2005. Directed by Paul Dinello. Produced by Stephen Colbert and David Letterman. Production Studio: Worldwide Pants Inc. and Comedy Central Films. Originally Distributed by Think Film Inc.
2. Chapter 14, "Hope," *Strangers with Candy* © 2005.

cannibalistic gangs and starvation. When the father contemplates shoot-
ing his own son in the head rather than allowing his capture by cannibals,
the father's inner thoughts ask, "Can you do it? When the time comes?
When the time comes there will be no time. Now is the time. Curse God
and die."[3]

Feelings of hopelessness and despair surround both contemporary uses
of Job's wife's phrase, stemming from an overwhelming assumption that
Job's wife wishes for Job to commit suicide by cursing God. In the
biblical book, Job's wife asks Job: "Do you still persist in your integrity?
Curse God and die" (2:9).[4] Her statement might assume a cause and
effect, that if Job curses God, he will die. The causal notion comes from
an implicit assumption that God would retaliate if Job cursed him to his
face, as the satan suggests earlier (2:5).[5] Samuel Terrien calls her suggestion a "theological method of euthanasia."[6] To curse God is to defy God,
to self-destruct, and thus violate God's creation. Leviticus 24 describes
an instance in which someone blasphemes YHWH, an offense that evokes
the punishment of stoning. Cursing God insinuates death, but only as part
of a community willing to enforce the law (cf. 1 Kgs 21:1–14).[7] Furthermore, Job ends up violating God's creation in ch. 3, which is the next
time Job speaks after addressing his wife. Leo Perdue describes Job 3 as
an "assault on creation," in that Job cursing the day of his birth and all of
God's creation calls for a reversal of creation.[8] In this light, some see
Job's wife's words in terms of their impetus for Job to start questioning
his unquestionable piety and to move him from a passive faith to an

---

3. Cormac McCarthy, *The Road* (New York: Vintage, 2006), 114.

4. All biblical quotes come from the New Revised Standard Version of the Bible
unless otherwise stated.

5. I use the form "the satan" (definite article, no capitalization) here when
referring to the role in the biblical book of Job because it is best translated as "the
adversary," a position or an office of the heavenly council (Zech 3:1–2), rather than
the postexilic personal name. Peggy L. Day, *An Adversary in Heaven: Satan in the
Hebrew Bible* (HSM; Atlanta: Scholars Press, 1988).

6. Samuel Terrien, *Job: Poet of Existence* (Indianapolis: Bobbs-Merrill, 1957),
42.

7. See also D. J. O'Connor, *Job, His Wife, His Friends and His God* (Dublin:
Columba, 1995), 34.

8. Leo G. Perdue, "Job's Assault on Creation," *HAR* 10 (1987): 295–315. See
also Leo G. Perdue, *Wisdom Literature: A Theological History* (Louisville, Ky.:
Westminster John Knox, 2007), 98–102. For more on Job 3, see Valerie Forstman
Pettys, "Let There Be Darkness: Continuity and Discontinuity in the 'Curse' of Job
3," *JSOT* 98 (2002): 89–104.

assertive one.[9] If this is the case, it seems as if the text no longer needs her to provoke response in Job because she totally disappears from the story, except for a few passing references. Job's wife exemplifies yet another biblical case of "the disappearing woman," especially when Job's children "were born to him" (1:2; see also 42:13).[10] The structure of the biblical book lends to the difficulty of interpreting her place beyond the second chapter because a prose tale (chs. 1–2 and 42) frames a large poetic dialogue between Job and his companions. The wife of Job is only referenced a few times in the poetic sections (19:17; 31:10), and, by implication, with the birth of children (1:2 and 42:13).

Given the nature of her words, Job's wife *does* theology when she speaks. Carol Newsom's feminist perspective praises Job's wife for "religious radicalism."[11] Phyllis Trible describes Job's wife as one who breaks "the bounds of orthodoxy" because she questions Job's fixed categories. If Job's wife does adhere to retributive theology, in that Job's cursing God and doing "bad" will lead to bad things, such as his death, she challenges the theology just by suggesting he carry forth with his theology.[12]

The Hebrew word *barek* literally means "bless": It is possible that scribes engage in a technique to offer a euphemism in the place of "curse" (Job 1:5, 11; 2:5, 9). The word inextricably links the satan with Job's wife. Both the satan and Job's wife assume a causal relationship between piety and prosperity because both relate Job's cursing God to the removal of God's favor (2:5, 9). In other words, both the satan and

9. Ellen Van Wolde, "The Development of Job: Mrs Job as Catalyst," in *A Feminist Companion to Wisdom* (ed. Athalya Brenner; The Feminist Companion to the Bible; Sheffield: Sheffield Academic, 1995), 201–21.

10. For Klein, Job's wife only provides "a background for the all-male enclave": Lillian R. Klein, *From Deborah to Esther: Sexual Politics in the Hebrew Bible* (Minneapolis: Fortress, 2003), 76. Contrary, when comparing Kafka's *The Trial* with Job, Halvorson-Taylor suggests that the loss of Job's wife signifies Job's misinterpretation of the events that surround him: Martien A. Halvorson-Taylor, "The Strange Case of the Disappearing Woman: Biblical Resonances in Kafka's Fräulein Bürstner," in *From the Margins.* Vol. 1, *Women of the Hebrew Bible and Their Afterlives* (ed. Peter S. Hawkins and Lesleigh Cushing Stahlberg; Sheffield: Sheffield Phoenix, 2009), 159–73.

11. Carol A. Newsom, "Job," in *Women's Bible Commentary* (ed. Carol A. Newsom and Sharon H. Ringe; Louisville, Ky.: Westminster John Knox, 1998), 140.

12. Phyllis Trible, "Biblical Theology as Women's Work," *Religion in Life* 44, no. 1 (1975): 9–10. In another way, West advocates that by speaking, Job's wife shows assertiveness, the kind of voice of faith that feminists should advocate for, as argued in Gerald West, "Hearing Job's Wife: Towards a Feminist Reading of Job," *OTE* 4 (1991): 107–31.

Job's wife function as adversaries against Job's supposed integrity. This is not such a problem if one assumes the satan's role in a non-Christian light, that of an adversary in God's heavenly court, but even Norman Habel assumes a more negative role for the satan in terms of Christian temptation when he states that "the narrator has Job's wife serve as the earthly mouthpiece for the hidden Satan."[13] Tod Linafelt complicates clear uses of the euphemism in Job, suggesting that the book means to set up constant negotiations between blessing and cursing.[14] Whereas Trible associates this relation with the satan in terms of Job's wife challenging the status quo, others circumvent the problem of associating Job's wife with the satan, and all the negative assumptions therein, by arguing that Job's wife actually means for Job to bless God, after which Job can die in peace knowing that he did all he could to maintain his integrity.[15] However, Job's response seems a bit more heated than necessary if indeed Job's wife had implied a blessing (2:10).

Job's response to his wife is unmistakably negative, but commentators disagree on the level of anger in Job's rebuke.[16] Job calls her "one of the foolish women" (2:10). When Job engages the substantive נבל (*nābāl/ nebālā*), calling her one of the foolish women, he implies her social deviance (2 Sam 3:33; Prov 17:7), bordering on denying her a place in the community.[17] Unlike how the fool functions in Ps 14:1, as someone who denies the existence of God, Job's wife keeps God in the center of

13. N. C. Habel, *The Book of Job: A Commentary* (Philadelphia: Westminster, 1985), 96.

14. Tod Linafelt, "The Undecidability of Brk in the Prologue to Job and Beyond," *BibInt* 4 (1996): 154–72. Linafelt ultimately argues that the euphemism seems less likely for Job's wife, who means to say "Still you hold fast to your integrity; continue to bless God [for all the good it has done you] and you will die" (p. 167).

15. The most extensive argument for such is found in Donal O'Connor, " 'Bless God and Die' (Job 2:9): Euphemism or Irony?," in *Proceedings of the Irish Biblical Association* (ed. Martin McNamara; Dublin: The Irish Biblical Association, 1996), 48–65; O'Connor, *Job, His Wife, His Friends and His God*, 21–38.

16. Job is "aggressively vehement" in Athalya Brenner, "On Female Figurations in Biblical Wisdom Literature," in *Of Prophets' Visions and the Wisdom of Sages: Essays in Honour of R. Norman Whybray on His Seventieth Birthday* (ed. Heather A. McKay and David J. A. Clines; Sheffield: JSOT, 1993), 198–99. On the other hand, Clines contends that Job's reply is "remarkably mild" in David Clines, *Job 1–20* (WBC 17; Waco: Word, 1989), 53.

17. In a feminist materialistic reading, Erin Runions compares the foolish reference here with Job 30:1–13, suggesting that foolish women imply socio-economic conditions, those expelled from community, noting an internal critique of Job and his wealth: Erin Runions, "Ms Job and the Problem of God: A Feminist, Existentialist, Materialist Reading," in Hawkins and Stahlberg, eds., *From the Margins*, 1:174–89.

their debate. Both Job and his wife agree that what has befallen Job has come from God. Carol Newsom points out that Job's wife constructs a moral framework different from that of Job. Her use of the term "die" expects that alienating one's self from God is an appropriate response to catastrophe. Job calls her a fool because her "obtuseness expresses itself as impiety."[18]

Job maintains acceptance of God's dealings, whether good or bad: "Shall we receive the good at the hand of God, and not receive the bad?" (2:10). Job uses the communal "we," thereby including her in his system of thought. The verse ends with an important note: "In all this Job did not sin with his lips" (v. 10). The notion that Job did not sin *with his lips*, as opposed to simply did not sin (1:22), offers some commentators evidence that Job might have been thinking about cursing God.[19] The tension remains between spoken word and possible voiceless intentions of the heart.

Unanswered questions about motivations, meanings, and messages emerge from such a small interchange between a biblical man and his unnamed wife. The interaction between Job and his wife takes up a small portion of the book itself, but it is an important mechanism in a grand Christian theological tradition to uplift Job as a model of piety. Judith Baskin demonstrates an unresolved tension in rabbinic literature concerning Job's ethnic origins and his claims to righteousness.[20] In early Christian exegesis, this tension dissipates because the Job in the prose tale represents "a model of Christian fortitude and faith."[21] The model gains greater legitimacy because it allows for a Christian predecessor, in this case Job, to face many enemies and hardships yet still maintain his piety. To take this a step further, Job "also became a type and prefiguration of the crucified and resurrected Christ."[22] Given such a model, any images of Job's wife that support her husband's piety inevitably fade into the background of Job's triumph against adversity, including the adversary Job finds in his wife, the one who should be closest to him.

18. Carol A. Newsom, *The Book of Job: A Contest of Moral Imaginations* (Oxford: Oxford University Press, 2003), 59–60.

19. Claire M. McGinnis, "Playing the Devil's Advocate in Job: On Job's Wife," in *Whirlwind: Essays on Job, Hermeneutics and Theology in Memory of Jane Morse* (ed. Jane Morse; New York: Sheffield Academic, 2001), 137.

20. Judith R. Baskin, "Rabbinic Interpretations of Job," in *The Voice from the Whirlwind: Interpreting the Book of Job* (ed. Leo G. Perdue and W. Clark Gilpin; Nashville: Abingdon, 1992), 101–10.

21. Judith R. Baskin, *Pharaoh's Counsellors: Job, Jethro, and Balaam in Rabbinic and Patristic Tradition* (BJS; Chico, Calif.: Scholars Press, 1983), 32.

22. Ibid.

A clear Christian interpretive history exists to uplift Job for his piety in the prose tale over and against more anguished complaints of Job in the poetic sections. As Christianity expands into the West, it provides biblical and non-biblical saints as models of the benefits of Christian salvation for those whom they considered "pagan." A brief look into Job's wife in early Christian interpretation provides a glimpse into this development of Job as an overwhelming example of Christian fortitude and faith.

Early Christian Versions of Job's Wife

It is in the ambiguities of Job's wife that the Greek text interpolates and expands her message to Job. The Greek Septuagint (LXX) adds extra sentences to the MT to give Job's wife expression to her loss (Job 2:9). The added words read as follows from Ziegler's LXX:[23]

> [9a] ἰδοὺ ἀναμένω χρόνον ἔτι μικρὸν προσδεχόμενος τὴν ἐλπίδα τῆς σωτηρίας μου [9b] ἰδοὺ γὰρ ἠφάνισταί σου τὸ μνημόσυνον ἀπὸ τῆς γῆς υἱοὶ καὶ θυγατέρες ἐμῆς κοιλίας ὠδῖνες καὶ πόνοι οὓς εἰς τὸ κενὸν ἐκοπίασα μετὰ μόχθων [9c] σύ τε αὐτὸς ἐν σαπρίᾳ σκωλήκων κάθησαι διανυκτερεύων αἴθριος [9d] κἀγὼ πλανῆτις καὶ λάτρις τόπον ἐκ τόπου περιερχομένη καὶ οἰκίαν ἐξ οἰκίας προσδεχομένη τὸν ἥλιον πότε δύσεται ἵνα ἀναπαύσωμαι τῶν μόχθων καὶ τῶν ὀδυνῶν αἵ με νῦν συνέχουσιν [9e] ἀλλὰ εἰπόν τι ῥῆμα εἰς κύριον καὶ τελεύτα

> [9a] Look! I wait yet a little while for the hope of receiving my salvation? [9b] Look! Your memorial is destroyed from the earth, even my sons and daughters, the pangs and pains of my womb which I labored in vain with toil. [9c] You, you, sit and spend the whole night in the open air among the rottenness of worms. [9d] And from place to place I go about from house to house as a wanderer and a maidservant, waiting for the setting of the sun. When can I take rest from the hardships and the sorrows which now oppress me? [9e] Except, speak one word against the Lord and die!

The Greek translators here show real concern for her role as mother and her role as provider for her husband, digging deeper into what kind of relationship Job had with his wife. Through her husband's misfortunes, Job's wife is forced to lower her own status to that of a domestic worker. Many have found affinities to the book of Tobit and his wife, Anna, whose status was reduced to a domestic worker as well, in particular, a

---

23. Joseph Ziegler, ed., *Iob* (SVTG; Göttingen: Vandenhoeck & Ruprecht, 1982), 218–19 (author's translation). For more critical notes, see Joseph Ziegler, *Beiträge zum griechischen Job* (Göttingen: Vandenhoeck & Ruprecht, 1985).

weaver.[24] Like Job's wife, Anna must bring whatever provisions she can to support her husband, who went blind as a result of doing charitable acts. The Vulgate of Tobit uniquely connects Job with Tobit: "the Lord thus allowed this trial to happen to him that an example of his patience might be given to posterity, similar to holy Job."[25] The Vulgate of Tobit comes closest to recalling Job's wife as well, by cutting out much of the dialogue between Tobit and Anna from the Greek text and by including another unique verse, that with "by these and other such words she excoriated him."[26] The verse insinuates that like those of Job's wife, Anna's angered words also provide hardship for her husband.

An early Christian reference to "holy Job" in the Vulgate of Tobit serves as an example of the trend to sanctify Job as saint. Early Christians adopted the Septuagint translation as a major source for interpreting Job, even though the translation consists of 75% of the word count of the Masoretic texts. The case has been made that the translators overlooked some of the Hebrew and muted Job's angry speeches containing impious remarks.[27] Over and against an affinity to cut out elements from Job, the elongated edition from the translators for Job's wife suggests a priority to insert more social expectations of gender in their marriage. Job's wife's sufferings reflect her husband's status, as well as her loss of her mother role.

The existence of names for Job's wife outside Christianity serves as another example of an early Christian move to maintain Job's wife as one of Job's challengers rather than one of Job's helpers. In the Masoretic text, it is possible that Job's wife's mysterious appearance and disappearance subverts "any definitive naming of her," but early interpreters provide her with a name.[28] The *Tales of the Prophets* of al-Kisa'i, for instance, along with other Arabic sources, give Job's wife the name of

24. Stephen J. Vicchio, *Job in the Ancient World: The Image of the Biblical Job: A History*, vol. 1 (Eugene, Ore.: Wipf & Stock, 2006), 119–22.

25. VgTobit 2:12: "hanc autem temptationem ideo permisit Dominus evenire illi ut posteris daretur exemplum patientiae eius sicut et sancti Iob." Translation comes from Vincent T. M. Skemp, *The Vulgate of Tobit Compared with Other Ancient Witnesses* (Atlanta: Society of Biblical Literature, 2000), 70.

26. VgTobit 2:23: "atque his et aliis huiusmodi verbis exprobrabat ei." Ibid., 92.

27. Stephen Vicchio and Lucinda Dukes Edinberg, *The Sweet Uses of Adversity: Images of the Biblical Job* (Baltimore, Md.: IPP, 2002), 12–14. For more on the Greek translators and their desire to present a righteous Job over and against his angry speeches, see Donald Gard, *The Exegetical Method of the Greek Translator of the Book of Job* (Philadelphia, Pa.: Society of Biblical Literature, 1952).

28. Holly Henry suggests that "her silence subverts any definitive naming of her": Holly Henry, "Job's Wife's Name," *College Literature* 18 (1991): 35.

Rahmah, in tradition of the compassion that she demonstrates in caring for Job.[29] Rabbinic traditions suggest that Job married Dinah, thus allowing an Israelite wife for Job, a place among the patriarchs, and also offering an explanation as to what happened to Dinah after the sons of Jacob slaughtered all the sons of Shechem (Gen 34).[30] The *Targum of Job*, as well as Pseudo-Philo, name Dinah as Job's wife.[31] The first century B.C.E. apocryphal text *The Testament of Job* (abbreviated as "T. Job" in this book) converges such traditions by giving Job two subsequent wives. The story begins with Job calling his seven sons and three daughters to him while Job rests on his deathbed. He tells the tale of his life with his first wife Sitidos, before he married his second wife Dinah.[32] Due to the fact that T. Job brings in a Jewish Dinah tradition, the text more than likely stems from a Jewish origin. Yet, the author relies heavily on the LXX and evidences a kind of Hellenistic Judaism that had a major influence on the New Testament.[33]

The concept of a Testament is a Hellenistic development, one that means to leave a spiritual legacy from a patriarch. Since Hellenistic culture attests to the use of legal wills and to the composition of testaments

29.   Demonstrating influence from T. Job as well in that she sells her hair. The Swahili text *Utendi Wa Ayubu* names her as Lady Rehema and continues her role in a similar fashion. See Mishael Caspi and Sara Milstein, *Why Hidest Thy Face: Job in Traditions and Literature* (Bibal Monograph Series; North Richland Hills: BIBAL, 2004), 82–198.

30.   Michael C. Legaspi, "Job's Wives in the *Testament of Job:* A Note on the Synthesis of Two Traditions," *JBL* 127 (2008): 71–79.

31.   Celine Mangan, "Some Observations on the Dating of Targum Job," in *Back to the Sources: Biblical and Near Eastern Studies in Honour of Dermot Ryan* (ed. K. J. Cathcart and J. F. Healey; Dublin: Glendale, 1989), 67–78; Mangan, "The Targum of Job," in *The Aramaic Bible: The Targums* (ed. Kevin Carthcart et al.; The Aramaic Bible; Collegeville, Minn.: Liturgical, 1991), 1–98; David M. Stec, *The Text of the Targum of Job: An Introduction and Critical Edition* (Leiden: Brill, 1994). The extant pieces of the *Targum of Job* from Qumran omit this information: B. Jongeling, C. J. Labuschagne, and A. S. Van Der Woude, *Aramaic Texts from Qumran* (Leiden: Brill, 1976). For extensive coverage of the Aramaic version of Job found at Qumran, consult David Shepherd, *Targum and Translation: A Reconsideration of the Qumran Aramaic Version of Job* (Assen: Royal Van Gorcum, 2004). See also Celine Mangan, "The Attitude to Women in the Prologue of Targum Job," in *Targumic and Cognate Studies* (ed. Kevin J. Cathcart and Michael Maher; Sheffield: Sheffield Academic, 1996), 100–110.

32.   The Job as Jobab tradition evident in LXX but not in rabbinic sources merges in T. Job. See Legaspi, "Job's Wives in the *Testament of Job*," 74–76.

33.   Michael A. Knibb and Pieter W. van der Horst, ed., *Studies on the Testament of Job* (SNTS; New York: Cambridge University Press, 1989).

for Greek philosophers, Jewish communities utilized similar conventions for their heritage. T. Job, unlike other Greek testaments, focuses more on story than on apocalyptic elements, making it more like a novel.[34] Written in Greek, T. Job's overall themes are that of a spiritual nature, over and against an emphasis on material goods and wealth. The "Testament" as a literary category presents a revered figure's last-will-and-testament. A patriarch calls his children to his deathbed to recount his life story in which he places emphasis on certain virtues. The testament ends with details of the patriarch's death and burial.[35]

Robert Kugler conjectures that Roman domination of the Jews in Alexandria lends to T. Job's sharp divergence from the biblical counterpart in terms of the origins of Job's sufferings. The text, dating somewhere between the first century B.C.E. and the first century C.E., dismisses earthly possessions and material wealth and could coincide with the time of the destruction of the temple in Jerusalem in 70 C.E.[36] T. Job opens with Job calling together his family and reminding them of a time when he was ruler over all Egypt (28:7).[37] When he lived near a popular temple, Job doubted its origins were from God, and an angel confirmed his suspicions, telling him in a dream that it originated from the Devil. After Job destroyed Satan's temple, Satan begins to attack Job and inflicts illness on him. Job's friends, the three kings, come to see Job twenty years after the onset of his illness. Job's wife, Sitidos, living a life of destitution and servanthood in order to care for Job, pleads with the kings to bury her children properly. But when Job provides them with a vision of her children in heaven, Sitidos retreats and dies peacefully of exhaustion (ch. 40).

The female characters in T. Job have received much attention from scholars because their roles, for better or for worse, are greatly expanded compared to the biblical version. First, when Satan first attacks Job, he

34. Lawrence M. Wills, ed., *Ancient Jewish Novels: An Anthology* (New York: Oxford University Press, 2002).

35. George W. E. Nickelsburg, *Jewish Literature Between the Bible and the Mishnah: A Historical and Literary Introduction* (Philadelphia: Fortress, 1981), 231–34. See also John J. Collins, "The Testament of Job," in *Jewish Writings of the Second Temple Period* (ed. Michael Stone; Compendia Rerum Iudaicarum Ad Novum Testamentum; Philadelphia: Fortress, 1984).

36. Robert A. Kugler, "Testaments," in *Justification and Variegated Nomism* (ed. D. A. Carson, Peter T. O'Brien, and Mark A. Seifrid; Grand Rapids: Baker Academic, 2001), 202–4. Kugler builds upon Collins here.

37. All references and citations of T. Job come from Robert A. Kraft, ed., *The Testament of Job: According to the Sv Text* (Texts and Translations: Pseudepigrapha Series; Missoula, Mont.: Scholars Press, 1974).

disguises himself as a beggar who comes to Job's door. Job knows the beggar is Satan but Job's maidservant does not; she gives Satan a fresh loaf of bread instead of the burnt loaf Job instructed her to give him (ch. 7). When Job left the city after Satan struck him with disease, Job sat on a dungheap for 48 years, his skin infested with worms and his eyes humbled watching his wife work as a maidservant (vv. 19–20). The situation gets so bad that Sitidos begs for bread in the market place, and Satan, disguised as a bread-seller, requires Sitidos to cut her hair in public for a loaf (v. 22). Satan figures prominently in the first section of T. Job, interacting mostly with two principle characters, with a woman or with Job.[38]

Both Sitidos and the household maidservant cannot recognize Satan in disguise, a fact that leads Kugler and Rohrbaugh to suggest that the women symbolize the uselessness of earthly honor in contrast to the kind of honor Job receives from God.[39] Others note the contrasts between knowing and not knowing, enduring and not enduring, and that Job's wife, though a faithful wife, cannot transcend "the state of deception," a testament to the weak nature of female insight.[40] In contrast, notes Maria Haralambakis, Job maintains his identity as a "man in charge," in terms of his ability to uphold the masculine ideals of control, resistance, and endurance.[41]

An underlying ideology of femininity as earth-bound and masculinity as spirit-bound exists in T. Job. Or, as Susan Garrett notes, in giving Job's daughters a spiritual inheritance, the text affirms female corporeal nature, the kind that Job's daughters give up, or transcend, through an

---

38.   Satan nearly disappears when the kings enter the story, nor is Satan mentioned in the final section of T. Job. This is discussed in Bradford A. Kirkegaard, "Satan in the *Testament of Job*: A Literary Analysis," in *Of Scribes and Sages: Early Jewish Interpretation and Transmission of Scripture* (ed. Craig A. Evans; New York: T&T Clark, 2004), 4–19. For more on Satan's role, see H. C. Kee, "Satan, Magic, and Salvation in the Testament of Job," in *Society of Biblical Literature 1974 Seminar Papers* (ed. George MacRae; Atlanta: SBL, 1974), 53–76.

39.   Robert A. Kugler and Richard L. Rohrbaugh, "On Women and Honor in the *Testament of Job*," *JSP* 14 (2004): 43–62.

40.   John J. Collins, "Testaments," in *Jewish Writings of the Second Temple Period: Apocrypha, Pseudepigrapha, Qumran Sectarian Writings, Philo, Josephus* (ed. Michael E. Stone; Assen: Van Gorcum, 1984), 352.

41.   Maria Haralambakis, "'I Am Not Afraid of Anybody, I Am the Ruler of This Land': The Portrayal of Job in the *Testament of Job*," in *Men and Masculinity in the Hebrew Bible and Beyond* (ed. Ovidiu Creangă; Sheffield: Sheffield Phoenix, 2010), 127–44.

expression of masculine ideals.[42] When it comes to expression of masculine virtues, though, Nancy Klancher has most recently argued that Job's daughters mean to mirror Job in his acceptance of monotheistic inheritance and that they characterize a right relationship with the Hebrew God.[43]

At the end of his life, Job grants his three daughters, the ones born to him through Dinah, with three golden boxes with golden bands/girdles inside, the same that Job received from the Lord. The amulets cured Job's body and will protect his daughters from the enemy as well (ch. 47). When the daughters put on the girdles they experience a change of heart, and begin to speak in the language of the angels (ch. 48), in the tradition of Christian glossolalia (see 1 Cor 13:1; 14:14–17; 2 Cor 12:4; Rom 8:26). Three days later, Job gives each daughter an instrument to play, and the daughters sing while Job ascends to heaven and his body goes into a tomb (ch. 53). Whether or not wearing the girdles and embodying spiritual gifts constitutes a masculine performance, a denial of female embodiment, or a signal of concern for heavenly riches over and against earthly riches, remains debated.

Reception History and Job

When it comes to the women in T. Job, the words of Maier and Schroer, in their feminist leanings, reveal what reception history can enlighten, especially in the midst of the gaps of the text:

> For a feminist reading of the book of Job the wife is a challenge in various respects. Through her, the patriarchal character of the book becomes dramatically apparent. Although she is inflicted by the same disasters as Job, apart from the disease, her suffering is not recognized; in fact, she

42. Susan R. Garrett, "The 'Weaker Sex' in the *Testament of Job*," *JBL* 112 (1993): 55–70.

43. Nancy Klancher, "The Male Soul in Drag: Women-as-Job in the *Testament of Job*," *JSP* 19 (2010): 225–45. When it comes to the inheritance of Job's daughters in the MT text (42:14–15) and in T. Job, see Zafrira Ben-Barak, "Inheritance by Daughters in the Ancient Near East," *JSS* 25 (1980): 22–33; Ben-Barak, "The Daughters of Job," *ErIs* 24, Avraham Malamat Volume (1993): 41–48; Rebecca Lesses, "The Daughters of Job," in *Searching the Scriptures* (ed. Elisabeth Schüssler Fiorenza; New York: Crossroad, 1994), 139–49; William S. Morrow, "Toxic Religion and the Daughters of Job," *Studies in Religion/Sciences Religieuses* 27, no. 3 (1998): 263–76; Heike Omerzu, "Women, Magic and Angels: On the Emancipation of Job's Daughters in the Apocryphal *Testament of Job*," in *Bodies in Question: Gender, Religion, Text* (ed. Yvonne Sherwood and Darlene Bird; Burlington, Vt.: Ashgate, 2005), 57–70.

herself is hardly mentioned. Contrary to all biblical role-conventions her advice is not accepted by Job: she is called foolish and dishonorable, and is removed from the story that follows. At the same time, however, the later narrative traditions show that this important gap had a stimulating effect on readers' imagination and called for more details. It is no coincidence that the *Testament of Job* devotes so much attention to this wife and to Job's daughters. A Job as devoid of relationships as the one in the Hebrew tradition was not acceptable.[44]

Biblical interpreters who engage reception history begin first with their knowledge of the biblical text and the interpretive gaps, questions, and insights that have motivated people to interpret the biblical text in their own social and political contexts. In many cases, reception history of the Bible is a method of tracing how people fill the gaps.

The amount of material that demonstrates how people use the Bible throughout history remains immense. Therefore, in numerous studies on biblical reception history, especially from the Blackwell Bible Commentaries, scholars use a guiding principle, or a specific criterion through which to disseminate, organize, and analyze a vast amount of material. It is left up to the authors to emphasize the material that they find particularly impactful or historically significant.[45] The use of, and clear explanation of, one's limits regarding the material in a reception history is helpful for both focusing and restraining any comprehensive analysis. Also, it reveals ideological choices made by the author in terms of what material he or she presents. One single volume of reception history might be able to catalog and describe all post-biblical interpretations of a biblical text, but it would lack depth to do so. On the other hand, to focus on one particular post-biblical interpretation of a biblical text might not allow for the kinds of comparative social, historical, and economic factors that can help put the interpretation in context. This book attempts to balance the general with the specific.

Reception history, as engaged by biblical scholars, assumes that texts, as cultural products, are intrinsically wrapped up in societal processes. Reception history of the Bible at its very broadest means to evaluate how people have imputed biblical sources in their cultural contexts, in other words how they depict, learn, interpret, engage, and make sense of the

44. Christl Maier and Silvia Schroer, "What About Job? Questioning the Book of 'the Righteous Sufferer'," in *Wisdom and Psalms: A Feminist Companion to the Bible, Second Series* (ed. Athalya Brenner and Carole F. Fontaine; Sheffield: Sheffield Academic, 1998), 196–97.

45. See the editorial preface in David M. Gunn, *Judges* (ed. John Sawyer, Christopher Rowland, and Judith Kovacs; Blackwell Bible Commentaries; Malden, Mass.: Blackwell, 2005).

Bible. Due to its analysis of how culture, values, social movements, power practices, economics, and technology impact biblical interpretation, this broad definition places reception history under a rubric of cultural studies. Also, at the center of this method stand the readers who interact with biblical texts in a variety of social formations. David Gunn situates reception history under cultural criticism and reader-response under literary theory. The distinction is helpful, as Gunn notes that "it is an axiom of cultural studies that texts and their readers or users are in a reciprocal relationship."[46] In other words, culture impacts the Bible and the Bible impacts culture.

One area that has impacted reception history of the Bible in terms of audiences and viewers engaging biblical interpretations and the impact on those interpretations on society has been film studies.[47] Incorporating the influential film theory of Laura Mulvey, "the male gaze,"[48] into the study of religious visual culture, David Morgan creates the phrase "the sacred gaze." Visual culture, as a mode of analysis, studies images, the practices surrounding the use of those images, and convergences of cultural meanings adapted for various contexts. Morgan defines the sacred gaze as a cultural term designating the range of seeing spiritually significant imagery in a variety of mediums. He suggests that any visual culture contains around it a "field of vision," a whole complex gamut of how images connect with viewers, audiences, subjects, and cultural conventions. The literary influences behind any image remain just one of the many influences of an image.[49] Whether one works with word or image, both are bound in textuality, which "is about message-sending and about the correct decoding of the message," whether that message be encoded in the medium of text, artistic canvas, or on the television screen.[50]

J. Cheryl Exum and Ela Nutu note the rich complexities that emerge from an analysis of the relationships between the Bible and canvas, again with attention to the gaps in the text:

46. David M. Gunn, "Cultural Criticism: Viewing the Sacrifice of Jephthah's Daughter," in *Judges and Method: New Approaches in Biblical Studies* (ed. Gale A. Yee; Minneapolis: Fortress, 2007), 204.

47. For an effective example, see David M. Gunn, "Bathsheba Goes Bathing in Hollywood: Words, Images, and Social Locations," in *Semeia 74: Biblical Glamour and Hollywood Glitz* (ed. Alice Bach; Atlanta: Scholars Press, 1996), 75–101.

48. Laura Mulvey, *Visual and Other Pleasures* (Theories of Representation and Difference; Bloomington: Indiana University Press, 1989).

49. David Morgan, *The Sacred Gaze: Religious Visual Culture in Theory and Practice* (Berkeley: University of California Press, 2005).

50. Ibid., 89.

> Staging a meaningful dialogue between the text and the canvas is often a matter of identifying an interpretive crux—a conundrum, gap, ambiguity or difficulty in the text, a stumbling block for interpretation or question that crops up repeatedly in artistic representations of it—and following its thread as it knits the text and painting together in complex and often unexpected ways.[51]

Furthermore, Mieke Bal advocates that one can "read" art. From a semiotics perspective, reading images is similar to reading printed text; a reader or viewer attributes meaning to a visual work through encoded signs and thus engages in an interpretive process. The meanings of signs come from one's socio-historical context. The important part of Bal's work for this context is her idea that a reader or viewer frames an interpretation in a socio-historical cultural context.[52]

Similarly, Choon-Leong Seow speaks of reception history of the Bible in terms of consequences, meaning "*what comes after*" and "*impact and effects*" of "all types of engagements of and encounters with the Bible."[53] The work of Seow, which has enlightened and contributed to the reception history of Job in meaningful ways, provides an example of attempts to recover positive meanings for Job's wife. In considering two pieces of art that he argues portray Job's wife in a positive light, Seow means to recover alternative representations because "her place in the history of interpretation and reception" has been skewed in a harsh misogynistic and negative tradition.[54] Similarly, Seow gives Job's wife "due respect" by offering positive, sympathetic readings of Job's wife alongside antifeminist, "extremely negative perceptions."[55]

Seow poignantly reveals the tensions involved in a variety of viewpoints on Job's wife. And, such a variety continues to challenge readers: "The minority position can challenge the exegesis of the majority,

---

51. J. Cheryl Exum and Ela Nutu, *Between the Text and the Canvas: The Bible and Art in Dialogue* (Sheffield: Sheffield Phoenix, 2007), 2.

52. Mieke Bal, "Reading Art?," in *Generations and Geographies in the Visual Arts: Feminist Readings* (ed. Griselda Pollock; New York: Routledge, 1996), 25–42.

53. C. L. Seow, "Reflections on the History of Consequences: The Case of Job," in *Method Matters: Essays on the Interpretation of the Hebrew Bible in Honor of David L. Peterson* (ed. Joel M. LeMon and Ken Harold Richards; Atlanta: Society of Biblical Literature, 2009), 563.

54. C. L. Seow, "Job's Wife," in *Engaging the Bible in a Gendered World: An Introduction to Feminist Biblical Interpretation in Honor of Katherine Doob Sakenfeld* (ed. Linda Day and Carolyn Pressler; Louisville, Ky.: Westminster John Knox, 2006), 141–50.

55. Choon-Leong Seow, "Job's Wife, with Due Respect," in *Das Buch Hiob und seine Interpretationen* (ed. T. Krüger et al.; Zurich: Theologischer Verlag, 2007), 351–73.

thereby pointing to the ambiguity of the text to which the reader is invited to return."[56] Thus, Seow takes a reception history of Job's wife within art and word, ending up full circle into a textual reading of Job's wife, suggesting that "the interpreter may realize that the role of Job's wife in her single contribution in the book is to give voice on earth to Job of divine confidence as well as divine doubt."[57]

Seow's analysis of art informs his analysis of the biblical book and he credits reception history of the Bible with bringing fresh perspectives to reading the Bible. This book follows his form. However, I am cautious of labeling any interpretation of Job and his wife "positive" or "negative." In a response to the proliferation of positive positions on Job's wife, Victor Sasson warns biased "politically correct" critics not to take lightly the harmful blasphemy Job's wife insinuates; she deserves the verbal reprimand from her husband. She remains a minor character, no matter whether one wishes to view her negatively or positively.[58] While this textual point may ring true, it is in the reception history of Job's wife, in which Seow works, that Job's wife remains more than a simple minor character.

Sasson's concern for unwarranted positivity on behalf of interpreters relates to a by-product of feminist interpretation, that of dichotomies. In an attempt to cast Job's wife in an either/or, negative/positive light, commentators tend to polarize themselves against one another, taking oppositional stances. If one takes a wider approach, a "wider lens" of gender, then the dichotomies of hero/villain become more complex. Even postcolonial feminists note how a Western Christian "emphasis on inno-cent victim and oppositional relationship between good and evil," cannot completely address the complexity of both "positive" and "negative" components of women's lives.[59] For instance, an "Asian way of problem solving has *esthetic direction* rather than *ethical direction*," meaning that differentiating between "good and evil" is less important than seeking restoration through balance and harmony.[60] Furthermore, representations

56. Ibid., 574.
57. Ibid.
58. Victor Sasson, "The Literary and Theological Function of Job's Wife in the Book of Job," *Bib* 79 (1998): 86–90. See also Mayer Gruber, "The Rhetoric of Familiarity and Contempt in Job 2:9–10," *Scriptura* 87 (2004): 261–66.
59. Asian feminists in particular have brought up this problem. See Chung Hyun Kyung, "Your Comfort Vs. My Death," in *Women Resisting Violence: Spirituality for Life* (ed. Mary John Mananzan et al.; Maryknoll, N.Y.: Orbis, 1996), 138.
60. Ibid. Kyung references the keynote address by Rita Nakashima Brock here. For more on Asian biblical hermeneutics, see Kwok Pui-lan, *Discovering the Bible in the Non-Biblical World* (Maryknoll, N.Y.: Orbis, 1995). For a consideration of

of women in terms of ideological splits between victim or heroine, between positive or negative, create contradictory categorizations.[61] This aside is to say that, given the complexity of Job's wife's situation and the rich dynamics involved in the reception of Job and his wife, I avoid labeling any interpretation as "positive" or "negative" in this book. In my opinion, the work of reception history is served best when such categorizations are avoided because of the cultural contexts out of which biblical receptions occur. In discussing the use of biblical ideas in the lives of biblical readers, labeling any interpretation as "positive" or "negative" reduces the complexities involved in human interpretation, especially in terms of how social, historical, economic, and ethnic factors influence interpretation.

The method of reception history as part of a larger area of cultural studies contains broad scopes and those involved in the method must make choices concerning what material they include and why. In an attempt to remain transparent about why I chose the material presented in this book, I suggest that reception history of the Bible need not be a single, sole, method. In this light, the adoption of a secondary method, or lens, through which to choose material remains helpful. The benefit of a reception history with a clearly delineated guiding/secondary principle is that it allows for the author to track particular trends of interpretation and to investigate the factors surrounding those trends. The guiding principle I use in this book comes from gender theory. Ultimately, through the main ideas of gender, a reception history of the marriage of Job and his wife reveals ways in which people consistently negotiate how to relate gender roles to Christianity with biblical backgrounds.

Gender Theory

Few female biblical scholars write commentaries on Job. So Victor Sasson indicates in a footnote in his brief article on Job's wife.[62] Since the late 1990s, only a handful of women have written full commentaries

---

"dialogical imagination" as a method of biblical interpretation, see Kwok Pui-lan, *Postcolonial Imagination and Feminist Theology* (Louisville, Ky.: Westminster John Knox, 2005).

61. This has also been pointed out by an Asian feminist in terms of the ways antithetical images of women help support hierarchal claims of national identity in Wai-Ching Angela Wong, *"The Poor Woman": A Critical Analysis of Asian Theology and Contemporary Chinese Fiction by Women* (New York: Lang, 2002), 44.

62. See Sasson, "The Literary and Theological Function of Job's Wife in the Book of Job," 87 n. 2.

on the book of Job.[63] My response to Victor Sasson in regard to a lack of female commentators on Job comes from the historical development of feminism in biblical studies. The political and social women's movements of the 1960s and '70s, deemed Second Wave Feminism, faced challenges of sexual discrimination and inequality. Feminists of all kinds engaged institutions that held women in ideological subordination—an assumption of the natural inferiority of women. The burgeoning challenges to male hegemonic control of Western society and woman as "other" ranged from radical, reformed, literary, psychoanalytical, to egalitarian theories.[64]

In the 1980s, feminist biblical scholarship slowly emerged as an "acceptable" category in the mainstream field of biblical interpretation.[65] During the 1980s, one of the major goals of feminist scholarship was "to uncover positive portrayals of women in the Bible."[66] Traditionally, a feminist interpreter centralizes women's voices and experiences.[67] The editorial preface to *Women in Scripture* summarizes a feminist perspective: it "seeks to understand a text specifically for the way it functions as a representation of women's lives and experiences and also to evaluate whether sexism is encoded in the text..."[68] Generally, feminists acknowledge that biblical literature comes from patriarchal contexts. Patriarchy (rule of the father) as the main structure of home, state, Church, education, and workplace serves as the central ideological challenge to feminist

63. Including Katharine J. Dell, *The Book of Job as Sceptical Literature* (ed. Otto Kaiser; BZAW 197; New York: de Gruyter, 1991); F. Rachel Magdalene, *On the Scales of Righteousness: Neo-Babylonian Trial Law and the Book of Job* (BJS 348; Providence, R.I.: Brown Judaic Studies, 2007); Newsom, *The Book of Job*; E. J. van Wolde, *Mr and Mrs Job* (London: SCM, 1997).

64. Ginette Castro, *American Feminism: A Contemporary History* (trans. Elizabeth Loverde-Bagwell; New York: New York University Press, 1990).

65. Phyllis Trible, "The Effects of Women's Studies on Biblical Studies: An Introduction," *JSOT* 22 (1982): 3–5.

66. Cheryl Exum, "Second Thoughts About Secondary Characters: Women in Exodus 1.8–2.10," in *A Feminist Companion to Exodus to Deuteronomy* (ed. Athalya Brenner; Sheffield: Sheffield Academic, 1994), 76.

67. Ruth Robbins, "Introduction: Will the Real Feminist Theory Please Stand Up?," in *Literary Theories: A Reader and Guide* (ed. Julian Wolfreys; New York: New York University Press, 1999), 49–58.

68. Carol L. Meyers, Toni Craven, and Ross Shepard Kraemer, *Women in Scripture: A Dictionary of Named and Unnamed Women in the Hebrew Bible, the Apocryphal/Deuterocanonical Books, and the New Testament* (Boston: Houghton Mifflin, 2000), x.

theory.[69] Therefore, a form of a feminist canon has emerged in which feminist biblical scholars can engage their agendas to centralize women in light of a history of patriarchal subordination. Deborah Sawyer lists texts in a "feminist canon," including those in which women are central characters, victims of patriarchal structures, and active participants in their own destiny.[70] Most likely due to the scant presence of women in the book, the book of Job is not on Sawyer's list.

One major consequence of feminisms is the correlation between the construction of female behavior and the construction of masculine behavior. Feminisms drew attention to the many ways women's experiences have been naturalized; the idea of men as gendered beings was largely left uninvestigated. By the time a prominent scholar of gender, Judith Butler, began writing her now influential *Gender Trouble: Feminism and the Subversion of Identity*, published in 1990, one of the wider known by-products of feminism dismissing masculinity as a binding oppressive system began to cause concern.[71] In 1985, Eve Sedgwick called attention to homosocial bonds that maintain heterosexual patriarchal power; men learn about masculinity, since the seventeenth century anyway, through their relationships with other men in culturally sanctioned ways.[72]

Sedgwick's account of heterosexuality is situated in a structuralist position, Levi-Strauss's theory of the exchange of women, because she accounts for implicit homosocial bonds that are formed through a man desiring a woman. Women, essentially, come "between men" in that they act as material rewards for male relationships. In her essay from 1975, "The Traffic in Women," Gayle Rubin draws heavily from Lévi-Strauss's *The Elementary Structures of Kinship*. She argues that in an economic system humans modify raw material into goods to exchange those goods. Rubin argues for the existence of a kinship system, as part of a political economy, that exchanges women like "biological raw material of human

69. Robbins, "Introduction," 50.

70. Deborah F. Sawyer, "Gender Criticism: A New Discipline in Biblical Studies or Feminism in Disguise?," in *A Question of Sex? Gender and Difference in the Hebrew Bible and Beyond* (ed. Deborah W. Rooke; Sheffield: Sheffield Academic, 2007), 2–17.

71. Judith Butler, *Gender Trouble: Feminism and the Subversion of Identity* (10th Anniversary ed.; New York: Routledge, 1999). One of the most succinct discussions I have found on this topic is Toby L. Ditz, "The New Men's History and the Peculiar Absence of Gendered Power: Some Remedies from Early American Gender History," *Gender & History* 16 (2004): 1–35.

72. Eve Kosofsky Sedgwick, *Between Men: English Literature and Male Homosocial Desire* (New York: Columbia University Press, 1985).

sex and procreation [that is] shaped by human, social intervention."[73] The traditional social institution of marriage in terms of "giving" a bride away is a prime example of the exchange of women among men, keeping them relegated to social commerce that solidifies kinship systems. Rubin warns against universalizing and fixing the idea of this exchange, but she engages structuralist kinship theories to reveal a symbolic meaning behind male-dominated societies that subordinate women. It is in a social system, and not in biology, that the oppression of women takes place.[74]

An overall goal of Judith Butler's work is to challenge the culturally fixed constructions of gender present in a Levi-Straussian model, a model picked up by Jacques Lacan and used by both Rubin and Sedgwick. Butler believes that a Levi-Straussian model turns sexuality into a symbolic reality that essentially locks males and females into rigid categories. Butler highlights the work of Monique Wittig here, who brings to light the question of whether binary notions of biological "male" and "female" might actually be cultural constructions themselves.[75] Furthermore, in a reaction to the impact of Sedgwick's work, Butler notes that "the Lacanian feminist insistence on the primacy of the phallus" maintains sexual difference in an inescapable heterosexual position. Granted, Sedgwick's *Between Men* has had lasting implications for queer theory because it complicates desire and calls into question how desire affects identity.[76] Butler's work emerges out of feminism, but widens its lenses and challenges established lines of interpretation within

---

73. Gayle Rubin, "The Traffic in Women: Notes on the 'Political Economy' of Sex," in *The Second Wave: A Reader in Feminist Theory* (ed. Linda Nicholson; New York: Routledge, 1997), 32.

74. Ibid., 37–38.

75. Monique Wittig, *The Straight Mind: And Other Essays* (Boston: Beacon, 1992).

76. Judith Butler, "Capacity," in *Regarding Sedgwick: Essays on Queer Culture and Critical Theory* (ed. Stephen M. Barber and David L. Clark; New York: Routledge, 2002), 113. See also Judith Butler, *Antigone's Claim: Kinship Between Life and Death* (Wellek Library Lectures; New York: Columbia University Press, 2000); Butler, "Is Kinship Always Already Heterosexual?," in *Going Public: Feminism and the Shifting Boundaries of the Private Sphere* (ed. Joan W. Scott and Debra Keates; Urbana: University of Illinois Press, 2004), 123–50; Butler, *Undoing Gender* (New York: Routledge, 2004). For Sedgwick's work in queer theory, see Eve Kosofsky Sedgwick, *Epistemology of the Closet* (Berkeley: University of California Press, 1990). Sedgwick's later works have complicated notions of performance. See, for instance, Sedgwick, *Touching Feeling: Affect, Pedagogy, Performativity* (Durham, N.C.: Duke University Press, 2003).

feminism.[77] This "wider lens"[78] does not exclude previous feminist analyses but positions the ideas of "man" and "woman" in an unfixed and complicated process of relations.

Gender is an unfixed cultural process. Gender is what any given culture constructs as "man" and "woman" based on social assumptions of masculine and feminine behavior and performance. Cultures encode the concepts of "man" and "woman" with specific meanings. The foundational work of Judith Butler rejects symmetry between the concepts of "man" and "woman"; the terms do not represent split limitations and boundaries, instead they represent negotiated terms in a fluid cultural process.

Gender remains performative, but Butler warns "performative is not simply to insist on a right to produce a pleasurable and subversive spectacle but to allegorize the spectacular and consequential ways in which reality is both reproduced and contested."[79] In other words, performances of gender create the reality of gender. Repetitive acts give the illusion of substance and it is when "male" or "female" acts defy or contradict a constructed identity of "manhood" or "womanhood" that gender destabilization occurs.

One point of unease from Butler's work on gender is her heavy-handed theoretical and philosophical position that tends to ignore some realities of biology, which puts many in danger of polarizing biology/culture. Butler's concept of gender performance allows for the possibility of queer dissections and gender crossings because she highlights that gender formation is mediated through culture and resists any account that frames "gendered characteristics in either biological or psychic structures."[80] Therefore, Butler removes links between biological processes such as menstruation, childbirth, or the production of semen to conceptualizations of masculinity and femininity as performances. Butler means to "unfix" references between biological sex and the uniformity that structures of power impose upon the body in order to regulate sexuality. The next section introduces the importance of body in terms of gender, power, and regulatory impositions of cultural institutions.

---

77. I have also struggled with inescapable sexual identifications and Butler's advocacy to rid feminism of the primacy of the phallus in Katherine Low, "The Sexual Abuse of Lot's Daughters: Reconceptualizing Kinship for the Sake of Our Daughters," *Journal of Feminist Studies in Religion* 26, no. 2 (2010): 37–54.

78. To borrow the phrase from Sawyer, "Gender Criticism," 5.

79. Butler, *Undoing Gender*, 30.

80. Rachel Alsop, Annette Fitzsimons, and Kathleen Lennon, *Theorizing Gender* (Cambridge: Polity, 2002), 166. This is a valuable discussion and organization of gender theory.

The Gendered Body and Job

Theorists are now starting to take note of the importance of body in terms of how gender plays out in society. In her book on Tobias Smollett, Aileen Douglas poignantly points out that "If you prick a socially constructed body, it still bleeds."[81] The body remains critically attached to culturally perceived "natural" boundaries of gender. Paul Goring points out, "cultural representations gain power by their association with the body precisely because the flesh can bestow authority through the persuasive rhetoric of 'nature.'"[82] One example comes from the common way to illustrate the book of Job in medieval art—Job's nude, marked body lies on a dung pile while his tormentors stand over him. Rather than displaying Job's bodily restoration that takes place at the end of the book, the medieval artist focuses on Job's nudity, and his suffering (see Fig. 2.1 as an example). Why do medieval artists make the choice to perpetuate images of Job's anguished body?

One answer comes from the text itself, for Job relinquishes his hold on possessions and uses the word "naked" (Job 1:21) to note a kind of "vulnerability of exposure."[83] The idea of Job's naked body full of sores presents a theological message concerning the trials God imparts on Job's body. In her study on how Job reflects a trial based on Neo-Babylonian law, Magdalene suggests that God tortures Job to test his faith, as a result of the prosecuting role of the satan bringing a charge against Job's piety.[84] Job's body remains important here, for after God allows for his physical infliction, Job begins to lament his situation, and his friends enter to elicit a confession for some unknown sin. The physical torture of Job means to bring him to confession so that the powers-that-be can maintain their control.[85] The body in pain affects the mind. Basing her observation on Elaine Scarry's *The Body in Pain*, Magdalene observes that "if one controls the body through pain, one can control the mind. If one controls the mind, one can construct a new

81. Aileen Douglas, *Uneasy Sensations: Smollett and the Body* (Chicago: University of Chicago Press, 1995), xxii.

82. Paul Goring, *The Rhetoric of Sensibility in Eighteenth-century Culture* (Cambridge: Cambridge University Press, 2005), 19.

83. Newsom, *The Book of Job*, 58.

84. For another argument that the satan targets not just Job's piety, but "Job's skin" in terms of Job's wife, see David Shepherd, "'Strike His Bone and His Flesh': Reading Job from the Beginning," *JSOT* 33 (2008): 81–97.

85. In this way, argues Magdalene, Job's friends act as God's witnesses in the trial. See Magdalene, *On the Scales of Righteousness*, 199–223.

world."[86] She also suggests that "God is not an agent of mercy in the minds of these people; rather, he is an abuse perpetrator. Mrs. Job is actually exhorting Job to provoke his abuser to the point of death."[87]

In Scarry's *The Body in Pain*, pain functions as the ultimate reality. Scarry calls pain an "interior state" that takes no object. Pain is pain, and trying to describe it often defies or shatters language. The inexpressibility of pain makes it a prime weapon in war because the institution of pain empties "the body of cultural content."[88] In torture, for instance, the torturer collapses a person's world-consciousness through continual contraction of the body's inner state and can thus reinsert his or her own worldview. This is why words of confession often come after torture; the tortured expresses the confession that the torturer wants to hear only so that he or she might end the pain. Carol Fontaine applies this notion to Job, in which God acts as the Divine Warrior and Job his captive: through the torture of his body, Job is "being deconstructed by God just as the bodies of victims are taken apart by the warrior in order to inscribe new boundaries under his own complete control."[89]

In her discussion of biblical texts, Scarry describes humans as permanently wounded creatures of a divine creator, a creator that consistently engages in the act of wounding because inflicting pain brings the human into divine reality. The difference in power is in that God has no body while humans have bodies.[90] God remains outside of the ability to feel pain. Therefore, as Fontaine has noted about Scarry's point of view, "the ability to inflict pain [on the body] becomes a structural sign of power."[91] In this light, Fontaine has also argued for an ideology at work in representations of the captured in the ancient Near East, an ideology that feminizes the captives. Given the association of warfare with masculinity, "feminizing the enemy serves to both shame the foe and hearten one's own troops."[92]

86. F. Rachel Magdalene, "Job's Wife as Hero: A Feminist-Forensic Reading of the Book of Job," *BibInt* 14 (2006): 229 n. 80.

87. Ibid., 213.

88. Elaine Scarry, *The Body in Pain: The Making and Unmaking of the World* (New York: Oxford University Press, 1985), 118. For more contextual applications of pain, see David Morris, *The Culture of Pain* (Berkeley: University of California Press, 1991).

89. Carole R. Fontaine, *With Eyes of Flesh: The Bible, Gender and Human Rights* (Sheffield: Sheffield Phoenix, 2008), 106.

90. Scarry, *The Body in Pain*, 209. Scarry mostly focuses on Genesis and Christian scriptures here and does not mention Job.

91. Fontaine, *With Eyes of Flesh*, 39.

92. Ibid., 56.

Despite some of the ways Job's body may invite inquiry into the nature of God and evil, Job's body in art of Christianity as presented in this book means to send a different message. In commenting on Job's ubiquitous, barely covered body on a dunghill, Marina Warner notes that his temporary nudity, or *nuditas temporalis*, symbolizes the rejection of earthly goods and wealth. But, this rejection coincides with Job's natural nudity, or *nuditas virtualis*, that reminds the viewer of the resurrection of flesh. An artistic focus on Job's temporary nudity only reinforces the Church's spiritual ambitions for the viewers, that one day nakedness will culminate in heavenly nudity rather than symbolize the shortcomings of the flesh.[93] The sanctity of Job's suffering body visually contrasts with skin blemishes of socially marginalized figures in art, those categorized by Ruth Mellinkoff as Jews, blacks, mockers, and evil figures like Satan. Her study reveals that in the late Middle Ages, people categorized skin blemishes more as outside evidence of inner sin rather than signs of divine grace, as in the case of Job.[94] Furthermore, the emergence of Satan as a primary figure torturing Job in Christian art relieves some theological tensions that may surface from viewing Job's naked body with the existence of sores and suffering that are allowed by God.

Theologians from early Christianity through the early modern period focus more on Job as a Christian saint who successfully battles Satan. The more trials artists can compound on Job the more saintly he appears. Therefore, Job's wife comes to represent a whole package of assumptions about marriage, female vulnerability to Satan, and religious expectations of gendered behavior. Job's body helps to reinforce such a theology prevalent in the Church during the Middle Ages. Michel Foucault notes that discourses on sex during the Middle Ages were "organized around the theme of the flesh and the practice of penance," which Job emulates.[95]

The body, as it is represented, exhibits a society's view of gendered constructions. As noted about Butler's work, gender comes in the form of performativity, the sense that cultures produce expectations of gender through repeated sets of acts that appear to provide the substance of gender.[96] People "do" gender, in that they "see" gender played out in

93. Marina Warner, *Monuments and Maidens: The Allegory of the Female Form* (Berkeley: University of California Press, 1985), 304.

94. Ruth Mellinkoff, *Outcasts: Signs of Otherness in Northern European Art of the Late Middle Ages*. Vol. 1, *Text* (Berkeley: University of California Press, 1993), 113–17.

95. Michel Foucault, *The History of Sexuality*, vol. 1 (trans. Robert Hurley; New York: Vintage, 1990), 33.

96. Butler, *Gender Trouble*, 44.

their societies and they themselves "play out" gender in their corporal existence. Performativity relates to an entire gamut of cultural expectations for "proper" masculine behavior and "proper" feminine behavior. In this sense, polar genders (male and female) are cultural fictions, created to keep the body regulated in its behaviors. Butler moves gender as far away from essence as possible. In other words, gender remains a set of unfixed attributes given or assigned to one's sex based on culture, not based on natural categories of biological sex.[97]

Butler relates a binary system of conceptualizing gender—man and woman—to power relations. Such gender categories depend on the stabilization of behavior in society; a destabilization of gender, then, includes acknowledging that there "are the myriad 'bodies' that constitute the domain of gendered subjects."[98] The body does not engage in one single cultural drama but rather takes part in numerous social spaces and in numerous societal regulatory grids. The challenge becomes, for Butler, how to speak of "the body," not as a passive entity, but as a location of multiple cultural exchanges "in which identity itself is ever shifting, indeed, where identity itself is constructed, disintegrated, and recirculated only within the context of a dynamic field of cultural relations."[99]

To engage Butler with embodiment, or, to mediate a gap between the body as a biological mechanism that dictates gendered experience and social impositions upon the body that inscribe behavior (sex/gender distinction), many authors, including Butler, have turned to Michel Foucault, who has imparted a legacy of the "social body" and its relation to power structures. Foucault has challenged a mind/body dualism and has maintained the view that the body is both a site of political struggle and an area of subjectivity. The complexity of Foucault's claims come from the idea of power and its oscillating forms because the body becomes a site of both societal inscriptions of gendered norms and a material subject that resists and destabilizes those norms.[100]

Any social system imparts prescriptions for particular behavior onto the body and uses the body to "regulate and shape society."[101] The body

97. Ibid., 179.

98. Ibid., 13.

99. Ibid., 161–62.

100. See Chapter 4, "Foucault and the Body: A Feminist Reappraisal," in Margaret A. McLaren, *Feminism, Foucault, and Embodied Subjectivity* (Albany, N.Y.: SUNY Press, 2002), 81–116.

101. Lisa Isherwood, "Sex and Body Politics: Issues for Feminist Theology," in *The Good News of the Body: Sexual Theology and Feminism* (ed. Lisa Isherwood; New York: New York University Press, 2000), 20.

is involved in a dynamic process of biological and social practices. Bryan Turner's *The Body and Society* highlights how the body, as conceptualized in culture, conflates with notions of sexuality and social power.[102] The body pertains not only to the nature of a human (biological), but also to the human's situatedness in culture. The body's physical nature contains internal structures and pre-set biological determinations, but the outer surface of the body remains interpreted, represented, and situated in society. Therefore, any theoretical discussion of the body includes issues of social control.[103] In one of his main premises, Turner argues that "the body lies at the centre of political struggles."[104] By "political," Turner means the interactions of various cultural relationships. "Gender identity," Turner states, is "inserted into physiology by socialization into specific roles and identities."[105]

Turner's statement about the insertion of gender identity into physiology leaves open the question of who does the inserting. R. W. Connell has provided an answer, one that presupposes dependency of regional, economic, racial, and religious factors on gender, but an answer, none the less, that has impacted gender studies, that of "hegemonic masculinity." While recognizing the existence of multiple masculinities in Western gender orders, Connell's study on masculinities builds upon Antonio Gramsci's work on class relations and the concept of hegemony as a sustainment of power in society by a dominant group. Connell states, "Hegemonic masculinity can be defined as the configuration of gender practice which embodies the currently accepted answer to the problem of legitimacy of patriarchy, which guarantees (or is taken to guarantee) the dominant position of men and the subordination of women."[106] The

102. Although Turner builds on Foucault, he also challenges some of Foucault's premises. For instance, Turner disagrees with Foucault when it comes to the relation between discourse and socialization. Foucault assumes that discourses have social effects, but Turner argues that a plurality of discourses about the body make it impossible to present a uniform picture of the body in society. This critique comes mainly from Foucault's philosophical treatments of the body in prison. See Bryan S. Turner, *The Body and Society: Explorations in Social Theory* (3d ed.; Theory, Culture & Society; London: Sage, 2008).

103. Ibid., 41–42. Turner's primary concern when it comes to social control is to discuss how patriarchal systems in society have regulated and controlled women's bodies. See Shilling's assessment of Turner's work in Chris Shilling, *The Body and Social Theory* (London: Sage, 1993), 102–5.

104. Turner, *The Body and Society*, 40.

105. Ibid.

106. R. W. Connell, *Masculinities* (2d ed.; Berkeley: University of California Press, 2005), 77.

greatest maintainers of hegemonic masculine power are the established institutions of society, those which gain from maintaining a rigid form of gender in order to impose power over the subordinates, in this case, women. Connell emphasizes, however, that hegemonic masculinity is in constant negotiation because groups consistently challenge the dominance of rigid gendered constructions in society.[107] Furthermore, one of the side-effects of Foucault's *History of Sexuality*, with its focus on Christian confession and the denial of flesh is the calling into question established forms of Christianity that function as major agencies of power, sequester the body into limited categories, and, as a result, maintain the subordination of women.[108]

For centuries, especially before Enlightenment historical-critical analysis, Christians have largely ignored the moral ruptures and incongruencies in Job. David Clines sums up the traditional Christian view of Job: "Job has been read typically as prefiguring the sufferings of Christ, or the tribulations of the Church. And in medieval exegesis and iconography in particular the figure of Job was essentially a symbol of the Christian virtue of patience."[109] It is quite stunning that the first five centuries of Christianity focus on the image of the saintly Job, largely ignoring his angry speeches.[110] Thus, any painful reminders of God's treatment of Job remain lost on early Christian interpreters, who, like in the epistle of James, only receive Job in terms of his patience and righteousness in light of his typological connection with Christ (Jas 5:11).

Alongside a motif of the saintly Job exists the Job as Warrior/Athlete motif, according to Vicchio, which stemmed from Hellenistic times and continued on through several centuries of Christianity.[111] The idea that Job wrestles with adversity might provide a way of speaking about Job's blatant attempts to question God's justice, but early Christian commentators kept more focus on the Christian concept of the Devil and his place

---

107. See, for instance, R. W. Connell and James W. Messerschmidt, "Hegemonic Masculinity: Rethinking the Concept," *Gender & Society* 19, no. 6 (2005): 829–59.

108. Jeremy R. Carrette, "Prologue to a Confession of the Flesh," in *Religion and Culture: Michel Foucault* (ed. Jeremy R. Carrette; New York: Routledge, 1999), 1–47.

109. Clines, *The Book of Job 1–20*, liv–lv. Jewish reception study of Job is beyond the scope of this work, but it is interesting to note that rabbinic interpreters predominantly considered Job as a righteous gentile according to Baskin, *Pharaoh's Counsellors*.

110. Vicchio, *Job in the Ancient World*, 140.

111. Ibid., 4, 218–19.

in Job. In other words, early allegorists and commentators avoid facing the issue of God's actions by directing Job's anger toward Satan's inflictions, finding no contradiction in God's permission for the satan to strike Job.[112]

The fact that Job remains at the center of the book, and at the center of expanded traditions about the book of Job, provides all the more reason why the perspective of gender is valuable. This book pays attention to what authors and artists mean to convey about Job's masculinity, and, in turn, his wife's femininity. How do Christians want Job's masculinity to function with, over, or against, his wife's femininity and how do Christians understand the nature of their marriage in terms of social gender roles?

Even with a focus on gender, the amount of material available for a reception history of Job and his wife is staggering. Therefore, I have placed another limit on this study, that of geography and religion. A rich interpretive history exists for Job's wife in Judaism and Islam, but I only highlight Christian sources. Furthermore, the sources emerge from viewpoints from the West and I hope that a future study beyond the so-called "Western classics" can further enhance the findings presented here.

Outline of Chapters

Chapter 1 begins with medieval Christianity and the developing literary sources that explain the marriage of Job and his wife in terms of Eden and a verbal interaction between Adam and Eve. This common medieval tradition to recall Adam and Eve is examined within a broader cultural phenomenon, that of gendered deviant speech and the continued establishment of Church dogma.

In Chapter 2, this trend to compare Adam and Eve to Job and his wife lends itself to an analysis of medieval art. Images of Job and his wife in which Job's wife visually aligns with Satan will be considered, especially in *The Mirror of Human Salvation* (*Speculum Humanae Salvationis*), a popular and standard work of Christian theology which circulated throughout Europe during the late Middle Ages. It provides evidence of an underlying theme to relate Job's wife to a woman of deviant speech.

112. Stephen J. Vicchio, *Job in the Medieval World*, Vol. 2, *The Image of the Biblical Job: A History* (Eugene, Ore.: Wipf & Stock, 2006), 33, 41.

Chapter 3 discusses medieval concerns for Satan's role in the Job story in order to assess changes that take place in early modern art of Job. When changing notions of Satan enter artistic traditions, representations of Job's wife receive more sinister characteristics. As a result, particularly in Baroque art, Job's wife serves not to side with Satan, or to engage in a theologically challenging and deviant speech, as much as she serves as a model for a bad wife.

In Chapter 4, the image of Job's wife as a shrew in Renaissance art relates to a literary trend in early modern Europe that speaks of Job and his wife in terms of proper Christian marriage in domestic conduct literature. Marital advice for Christians from the sixteenth and seventeenth centuries provides a backdrop for the images gathered in the previous chapter. The literature addressing Job and his wife reveals the ways in which authors prescribe social gender expectations onto the marriage of Job and his wife.

Chapter 5 focuses on one artist, William Blake, because he deviates from traditional iconographical standards for Job and his wife and because his illustrations of Job continue to inspire contemporary audiences. Romantic inclinations toward sublimity and beauty inform an overall interpretation of Blake's Job, notwithstanding Blake's dissent of established forms of Christianity. Blake's system of gender, as part of his ideological move toward imaginative freedom, "brotherhood," and political deviance, remains central to why Blake depicts Job's wife in non-traditional ways.

Chapter 1

EDEN'S DUNGHILL AND THE WIFE'S
DEVIANT SPEECH

In tracing how the story of Gen 3, "the Fall," since Augustine, acted in medieval Christian culture as a central paradigm for human existence, Jager suggests that Christian-Latin authors focused heavily on the myth of the Fall because of its ideas about language and its moral consequences. They carried an anxiety for the proper transmission of scriptural tradition over and against "false teachings." In *The Tempter's Voice*, Jager compellingly argues that the grounding of religious experience in written word, rather than oral speech, remains one consequence of medieval monastic culture. Even when monks read aloud, they did so from the written word, the same word they took great lengths to preserve and reproduce. A clerical distrust of the oral poems from surrounding "pagan" cultures as rival oral traditions also comes into play. And, according to Jager, the Fall acted as the quintessential narrative warning of the dangers of unmediated oral communication and human consumption of false oral tradition.[1]

To use the Fall as an epistemological framework for engaging Christian classical tradition is to suggest that the first humans were inexperienced users of language. Furthermore, medieval scholars assumed that the differences in human languages resulted from the degeneration of the original language Adam had spoken to God.[2] God's word, or language, impinges on human understanding, and both Adam and Eve corrupt God's command by eating the fruit of the tree of the knowledge of good and evil. The convention that the Devil embodies the serpent is a later

---

1. Eric Jager, *The Tempter's Voice: Language and the Fall in Medieval Literature* (Ithaca, N.Y.: Cornell University Press, 1993).
2. Umberto Eco, *The Search for the Perfect Language* (trans. James Fentress; Malden, Mass.: Blackwell, 1997).

Christian interpolation in the biblical text,[3] one that suggests that patristic authors, and the medieval exegetes that followed them, viewed the story of Eden as "a calamitous violation of the whole divinely instituted order of Paradise. After the Serpent, Eve was the first to challenge the 'received text,' the 'tradition,' or the 'canon' as passed down to her."[4] Therefore, Eve sets a precedent for all women who follow; as a result of her speaking, Eve brought about shame upon her sex. This chapter builds upon Jager's analysis while tracing a particular medieval literary and artistic tradition of comparing Job and his wife to Adam and Eve. In the notion of the Fall as a story Christian-Latin medieval authors used to approach their anxieties over the transmission of non-orthodox teachings, Job's wife emerges as another Eve and Job as another Adam.

Early Christian art of Job and his wife reaches well into the fourth and fifth centuries, an example of which can be seen on the Junius Bassus sarcophagus from around 359 C.E. The sarcophagus features a seated Job in Roman toga attire with Job's wife standing in front of him. The wife holds a shrouded left hand up to her face; previous destruction on the sarcophagus has removed the stick that his wife holds out to Job in her right hand. A male figure stands between them, possibly echoing the Satan character in T. Job.[5] The scene may anticipate a comparison between Job and his wife and Adam and Eve, especially since Adam and Eve rest to the immediate right of the Job scene. The connection, though, remains elusive until medieval artists and authors make it substantive.

Just a few years after the creation of the Junius Bassus sarcophagus, Jerome was in Rome working on translating the Hebrew Scriptures into Latin, a translation known as the Vulgate. In 384, Jerome moved from Rome to Jerusalem. After Rome was sacked in 410, another important Christian theologian, Augustine of Hippo, was serving as bishop of Hippo and responded by writing his spiritual autobiography, *The City of God*. Augustine's leadership in the Imperial Church of the West had lasting implications for Christian thought throughout the Middle Ages. Furthermore, Augustine's writings served as the basis for Pope Gregory's commentaries. Gregory the Great, who served as pope from 590–604,

3. For a thorough listing of Christian sources equating the serpent with Satan, see Linda S. Schearing, Valarie H. Ziegler, and Kristen E. Kvam, eds., *Eve and Adam: Jewish, Christian, and Muslim Readings on Genesis and Gender* (Bloomington: Indiana University Press, 1999).

4. Jager, *The Tempter's Voice*, 38.

5. See Elizabeth Struthers Malbon, *The Iconography of the Sarcophagus of Junius Bassus* (Princeton, N.J.: Princeton University Press, 1990).

held Augustine's conjectures as infallible. In Gregory's uncertain time, Augustine's theology provided him with a stable epistemological foundation.[6] In Rome in 595, Gregory completed his *Moralia on Job*. When it comes to the book of Job, no other Christian theologian holds more influence over medieval literary interpretations of Job than Gregory the Great.

As Christianity spread throughout the Roman Empire in the 300s and as hierarchies emerged, public regulations were established, and as Roman cultural and social mores and beliefs absorbed into Christianity, ideas about marriage changed. Teachings about hierarchal marital relations and proper behaviors for husbands and wives did not change, but, as Pamela Norris notes, Christian authors debated among multiple cultural groups about the "regulation of the mind and the appropriate control of the body's pressing needs."[7] Asceticism raised new questions about marriage and celibacy, endorsing a role of humanity contrary to its biological drive to mate and procreate, and, in so doing, it put humans into spiritual conflicts that required extreme tests of will and endurance. Through their expositions on Job, Christian authors exemplify him as one who survived countless spiritual tests at the expense of his own marriage.

Medieval Christian Theological Writings on Job

In a letter to his sister from 385 C.E., Ambrose describes a conflict with the Arians over control of a new basilica. The emperor Valentinian sent soldiers to seize the basilica because his mother Justina was Arian. The public was in uproar, according to Ambrose, when he preached a sermon on Job. He called all of his audience "Jobs" because they had withstood adversity with patience and faith. Ambrose compares the great disturbances of his own time—the Goths, the armed men in their presence, and their trials—to the "accumulated tidings of evil" found in Job's wife's oppositional speech to her husband:

> You see what is asked when this command is given: Hand over the basilica—that is: 'Speak a word against God, and die,' do not merely speak a word opposing God, but make yourself an opponent of God. The order is: Hand over the altars of God. We are hard-pressed by the royal edicts,

6. Justo L. González, *The Story of Christianity*. Vol. 1, *The Early Church to the Dawn of the Reformation* (New York: HarperCollins, 1984), 201–16, 46–48.

7. Pamela Norris, *Eve: A Biography* (Washington Square: New York University Press, 1998), 166.

but we are strengthened by the words of Scripture, which answered: 'You have spoken like one of the senseless.' And that was no slight temptation, because we know that those temptations are more severe which are brought about through women. Indeed, through Eve Adam was deceived, and thus did it come about that he departed from divine commands.[8]

Ambrose uses the exchange of Job and his wife to argue against relinquishing control of the basilica to the Arians, but he also compares them to Adam and Eve. Underlying the comparison rests a distrust of heresies and a concern to maintain control. Augustine knew of Ambrose as Bishop of Milan in the years 385 to 387, but no letter exists today from Ambrose to Augustine. They held similar views about Job and his wife, sharing an emerging trend for Job and his wife that culminates in Gregory's *Moralia*.

Some early examples do not speak of Job's wife in terms of Eve. In his treatises from 251 C.E., Cyprian, Bishop of Carthage, simply suggests that Job's wife urges Job to curse God in a complaining and envious voice.[9] Tertullian makes a vague reference to Job's wife in the context of the Devil's agenda against Job, and even mentions the weariness of Job's wife.[10] A sermon on divorce by Asterius of Amasea offers a literary

---

8.   Ambrose, Letter XX: To Marcellina as to the Arian Party. Easter, 386. PL, vol. 16, 1041: "Advertitis quid jubeatur, cum mandatur: Trade basilicam, hoc est: Dic aliquod verbum in Deum, et morere. Nec solum dic adversum Deum, sed etiam fac adversus Deum. Mandatur: Trade altaria Dei. Urgemur igitur praeceptis regalibus, sed confirmamur Scripturae sermonibus, quae respondit: Tanquam una ex insipientibus locuta es. Non mediocris igitur ista tentatio; namque asperiores tentationes has esse cognovimus, quae fiunt per mulieres. Denique per Evam etiam Adam supplantatus est; eoque factum, ut a mandatis coelestibus deviaret." English translation from Ambrose, *Saint Ambrose: Letters* (trans. Sister Mary Melchior Beyenka; The Fathers of the Church: A New Translation; New York: Fathers of the Church Inc., 1954), 370. Incidentally, C. L. Seow has stated that Job is at the center of every early Christian controversy: Choon Leong Seow, "Christian Consequences of Job" (paper presented at the Ministers Week, The McFadin Lectures, Brite Divinity School, Fort Worth, Tex., 2009).

9.   *Treatises of Cyprian* VII. 10. Alexander Roberts and James Donaldson, eds., *The Ante-Nicene Fathers: Translations of the Writings of the Fathers Down to A.D. 325*, vol. 5 (American ed.; Grand Rapids: Eerdmans, 1996), 471.

10.   *Patience*, ch. 14:14: "Quale in illo uiro feretrum Deus de diabolo extruxit, quale uexillum de inimico gloriae suae extulit, cum ille homo ad omnem acerbum nuntium nihil ex ore promeret nisi 'Deo gratias', cum uxorem iam malis delassatam et ad praua remedia suadentem execraretur!" Tertullian, *Disciplinary, Moral and Ascetical Works* (ed. Roy Joseph Deferrari; The Fathers of the Church: A New Translation; New York: Fathers of the Church Inc., 1959), 218.

source that upholds Job's wife as an ideal wife. Preaching his sermons sometime around 386 as bishop, Asterius shows connection with the Antioch school and an affinity towards the Cappadocian Fathers and a cynical-stoical moral philosophy.[11] Warning his audience not to take divorce lightly, Asterius points out a wife's role as a husband's healer (ἀνδρὸς θεραπείας) who comforts him in his distress and who can manage the household. He turns to Job's wife as an example. She sat with Job on the dunghill, scraping his sores and pulling worms from them. As an inseparable friend (ἀχώριστος φίλος), Job's wife falls into the sin of blasphemy only to urge Job to end his misery so that she might not see him continue on in pain. She took no account of her state of widowhood that would follow (Τὴν γὰρ ἰδίαν λοιπὸν συμφορὰν τὴν τῆς χηρείας οὐκ ἐλογίζετο) and therefore thought not of herself.[12]

In his commentary on Job, Julian of Eclanum offers no comparison between Job and his wife and Adam and Eve. Rather, he simply describes the situation, noting that Job's wife speaks out of anger.[13] Since Julian was a follower of Pelagius, Julian and Augustine exchanged heated debates. Augustine disagreed with the followers of Pelagius who believed that baptized Christians possessed free will to make moral choices. For Augustine, a very negative view of Eden impacts his theology. Even in Augustine's last years, and after the death of Pelagius, Julian and Augustine continued heated arguments over human will and the ability of Adam's single willful act to corrupt the structure of the universe into an irrevocable state of sinfulness.[14]

Augustine suggests that the Devil did not destroy Job's wife along with Job's children so that he might bring about another Eve-incident with Job, that is, the Devil tempting a husband through his wife to deceive him into blasphemy. In his treatise *On Patience*, Augustine compares Job to Adam in husbandly terms:

11.   My appreciation to C. L. Seow for giving me this reference. Introduction in C. Datema, ed., *Asterius of Amasea: Homilies I–XIV* (Leiden: Brill, 1970), xix–xxxiii.

12.   Homily V, *On Divorce*, in ibid., 48.

13.   CCSL vol. 88, 9: "Verbis uxoris ostenditur, Iob positum in illa conuulsione membrorum, Deo iugiter gratias egisse, ac dixisse, se inter illas dolorum nimietates eius in uita miseratione seruari. Unde uelut consequenter ei ab uxore dicitur: si vitam tibi praestat tuis precibus exoratus, auferat melius est uoce tuae conquestionis iratus."

14.   Elaine Pagels, *Adam, Eve, and the Serpent* (New York: Random House, 1988), 130.

She brought no help to her husband, but went on blaspheming God. Skilled in wrong-doing, the Devil had not deserted her when he had destroyed her sons, for he learned with Eve how necessary woman was for the tempter. But, this time he did not find another Adam whom he could entice through a woman.[15]

Again, in a sermon "To the Catechumens on the Creed," Augustine elaborates on Job's wife's role:

After the pattern of the serpent, who, in Paradise, deceived the first man whom God made, so now she also thought by suggesting blasphemy to succeed in deceiving a man who pleased God. How great were his sufferings, brethren! Who can suffer so much in his possessions, in his house, in his children, in his person, yea, in his wife, the temptress who remained to him? But even her Satan would long before have taken from him if he had not kept her to be his helper. He had overcome the first man by means of Eve, therefore he had kept his Eve.[16]

Augustine goes on to say that "His wife, the Devil's helper, not her husband's comforter, would fain have persuaded him to blaspheme."[17]

For Augustine, all women are impacted by Eve's act in Eden. Therefore, Eve serves as Mary's "antitype," her exact opposite in terms of their symbolic roles. Irenaeus (ca. 130–200) makes this clear in his *Against Heresies*. Irenaeus's main concern is Christology and the progression of humankind in light of Christ's salvation. Adam and Eve acted as immature people when they expected knowledge of good and evil but

15. Augustine, *On Patience*, ch. 9, CSEL vol. 41, 673–74: "Aderat uxor nec ferebat opem aliquam uiro, sed in deum blasphemiam suggerebat. Non enim eam diabolus, cum etiam filios abstulisset, tamquam nocendi inperitus reliquerat, quji wuantum esset necessaria temptatori iam in Eua didicerat.Sed modo alterum Adam, quem per mulierem caperet, non inuenerat." English translation from Augustine, *Treatises on Various Subjects* (ed. Roy Joseph Deferrari; trans. Mary Sarah Muldowney; The Fathers of the Church: A New Translation; New York: Fathers of the Church Inc., 1952), 245–46.

16. Augustine, *A Sermon to Catechumens on the Creed* 10:235–44, CCSL vol. 46, 192–93: "Et tamen eum sua persuasion mala mulier decipere uoluit, habens et haec figuram illius serpentis, qui sicut in paradise decepit hominem primum factum a Deo, ita etiam nunc blasphemiam suggerendo putauit posse decipere placentem hominem deo. Quanta passus est, fraters. Quis potest tanta pati in re sua, in domo sua, in filis suis, in carne sua, in ipsa quae remanserat tentatrice uxore sua? Sed etiam ipsam quae remanserat, olim auferret, nisi adiutricem sibi seuasset, quia primum hominem per Euam debellauerat. Euam seruauerat." English translation from Charles A. Heurtley, ed., *On Faith and the Creed: Dogmatic Teaching of the Church of the Fourth and Fifth Centuries* (London: Parker & Co., 1886), 44.

17. 10:256, CCSL vol. 46, 193: "Voluit mulier illa, diaboli adiutrix, non mariti consolatrix, persuadere blasphemiam." Heurtley, 45.

Christ makes that knowledge possible.[18] As Eve was disobedient and brought sin into the world, God will redeem sin of humankind through a woman, who gives birth to Jesus Christ. Just as a woman causes humankind to sin, a woman brings salvation to humankind.[19] Joan Gregg Young calls this comparison a "clerical splitting of the female into saints or sinners, Eves or Marys."[20] The Eve/Mary typology was so ubiquitous that countless Middle English sermons note the Eve/Mary relationship, as well as numerous English Cycle plays that would have reached a wide variety of audiences in the Middle Ages.[21] Job's wife, as another Eve, recalls yet again Augustine's view of the autonomous woman, in general, in the words of Kim Power as being "a demonic instrument in her potential willfully to disrupt familial and social order through her pride."[22]

Another theologian in the 380s compared Adam and Eve with Job and his wife, with Satan acting as the connective entity between the couples. John Chrysostom, who calls Job an "athlete," preaches of the Devil's connection with Job's wife in a sermon "On The Power of Man to Resist the Devil." Again, a comparison between Adam and Eve exists:

> For this man will give us greater zeal, so that we may raise our hands against the Devil. There he who deceived and conquered was a serpent; here the tempter was a woman, and she did not prevail: and yet at least she was far more persuasive than he. For to Job after the destruction of his wealth, after the loss of his children, after being stripped bare of all his goods, her wiles were added. But in the other case there was nothing

18.   Thomas Holsinger-Friesen, *Irenaeus and Genesis: A Study of Competition in Early Christian Hermeneutics* (Winona Lake, Ind.: Eisenbrauns, 2009), 120, 36.

19.   Irenaeus, *Against Heresies*, Book 5, Chapter 19. Alexander Roberts and James Donaldson, eds., *The Ante-Nicene Fathers*. Vol. 1, *The Apostolic Fathers–Justine Martyr–Irenaeus* (Grand Rapids: Eerdmans, 1987), 547.

20.   Joan Young Gregg, *Devils, Women, and Jews: Reflections of the Other in Medieval Sermon Stories* (Suny Series in Medieval Studies; Albany, N.Y.: State University of New York Press, 1997), 108.

21.   Walter E. Meyers, "Typology and the Audience of the English Cycle Plays," in *Typology and English Medieval Literature* (ed. Hugh Keenan; New York: AMS, 1992), 261–88.

22.   Kim Power, *Veiled Desire: Augustine on Women* (New York: Continuum, 1996), 170. Power discusses that Augustine held several views of women. First, the "real" women of his life held positive matronly images, such as his mother and his concubine. Second, Augustine wrote of the autonomous woman in a general sense. Third, a sexual woman, represents for Augustine the locus of desire and danger in need of restraint. In the last two images, Mary functions as a "meta-symbol" who could exemplify the opposite of both his autonomous and sexual woman.

of this kind. Adam did not suffer the destruction of his children, nor did he lose his wealth: he did not sit upon a dunghill, but inhabited a Paradise of luxury and enjoyed all manner of fruits, and fountains and rivers, and every other kind of security.[23]

The connection between Satan and Job's wife comes through just as clear in Chrysostom's commentary on Job, in which he comments that the Devil formerly used the serpent, but now he uses the woman.[24]

Chrysostom considered human nature corrupt enough that wealth, power, and luxury compromised the integrity of the Church.[25] Thus, Job's example provides a means to speak to his audience about this corruption—even in paradise Adam falls victim to his wife's temptation, and dung is far worse than the luxury of paradise. Yet, Job prevails. As Vicchio notes, the popular notion of "saint Job" in the fourth century provides that Job serves as a model for spiritual fortitude.[26]

Augustine considered Eden the locus of universal human sin. Unlike Pelagius and his followers, or John Chrysostom, Augustine advocated that human nature could not bring about death by act of will, but, rather, that death was the nature of humanity. Also, as Elaine Pagels describes in Augustinian terms, "woman, although created to be man's helper, became his temptress and led him into disaster. The Genesis account describes the results: God himself reinforced the husband's authority over his wife."[27]

23. Homily III, "On the Power of Man to Resist the Devil," section 4. Joannis *Chrysostomi Opera Omnia* (Paris), vol. 2:321–22: "Ille namque majores nobis animos faciet, ut manus cum diabolo conseramus. Illic serpens erat, qui decipiebat, et vicit; hic mulier, quae non praevaluit, tametsi ad persuadendum aptior, quam ille. Ac Jobo quidem post pecuniarum jacturam, filiorum amissionem, necnon bonorum omnium, machina admovebatur; illic vero nihilerat ejusmodi: filios non amiserat nec pecunias Adam, neque in fimo sedebat, sed in paradiso voluptatis habitabat, et omnis generis lignorum copia fruebatur, fonte item, fluviis, aliisque omnibus commodis: nusquam labor, non tristitia, non moeror, non contumeliae et convicia, neque innumera illa mala, quae Job immissa sunt; attamen cum nihil adesset hujusmodi, lapsus et supplantatus est." English translation from John Chrysostom, *St. Chrysostom: On the Priesthood; Ascetic Treatises; Select Homilies and Letters; Homilies on the Statues* (trans. Philip Schaff; New York: Christian Literature Publishing, 1886), 195. Listed as Homily III under the title "Three Homilies Concerning the Power of Demons," in the 1956 repr. by Eerdmans, vol. 9:194–95.

24. See Chapter II, section 12, in John Chrysostom, *Commentaire Sur Job*, vol. 1 (Paris: Cerf, 1988), 188–89.

25. Pagels, *Adam, Eve, and the Serpent*, 104.

26. Vicchio, *Job in the Medieval World*, 9.

27. Pagels, *Adam, Eve, and the Serpent*, 114.

Two important notions emerge for Job and his wife. First, where Adam fails in his marriage, Job succeeds. Job does not give in to his wife's words. Second, both wives engage problematic speech in the presence of their husbands, due to the Devil's control over them. Augustine goes so far as to suggest that Job's wife blasphemes against God. Such Augustinian traditions were carried on well into the Middle Ages.

Even a byzantine presbyter in Constantinople during the sixth century, Leontius, preached of Job's wife as another Eve. Job stands firm, according to Leontius, and does not lose paradise because of his wife, and does not have to hide from God in shame.[28] When Leontius preached a sermon on Maundy Thursday, scolding his congregation for breaking a fast, he compares Job's wife to the woman with the alabaster jar who anointed Jesus (Matt 26:7). The woman who anoints Jesus with perfume serves as a reversal of the kind of blasphemous sin instigated by Job's wife. Job's wife served the Devil while the other woman attended to the Lord.[29]

No other text about Job has more influence on medieval traditions of Job than Gregory the Great's *Moralia*. Western Europe underwent political disunity and disharmony after the Goths sacked Rome in 410 C.E. While the Byzantine Church continued its establishment in the East for at least a thousand more years, groups known to the Roman Empire as "barbarians" began settling throughout the West. The papacy served as an institution that provided stability throughout the Middle Ages. In order to achieve such stability, Christians needed clear orthodox teachings.

Gregory's reign (590–604) anticipates the shift from the ancient world to the medieval world and signifies all the imperial efforts the old Roman Empire had left in the West. War, plague, and pestilence left Rome in shambles. In his *History of the Franks*, Gregory of Tours (539–594) upholds his faith using Job's words despite horrific loss from the plague:

> We lost dear sweet children whom we nursed on our knees or carried in our arms and nourished with attentive care, feeding them with our own hand. But wiping away our tears we say with the blessed Job: 'The Lord has given; the Lord has taken away; the Lord's will has been done. Blessed be his name throughout the ages.'[30]

28. Homily V.20 in Leontius, *Fourteen Homilies* (trans. Pauline Allen and Cornelis Datema; Brisbane: Australian Association for Byzantine Studies, 1991), 80.

29. Homily VI. 9 in ibid., 84. The translation calls Job's wife "a companion of Eve" and "a handmaid of the Devil."

30. Book 1, Gregory of Tours, *History of the Franks* (trans. E. Bréhaut; New York: Columbia University Press, 1916), 129.

Gregory the Great also looked to Job for a model of faith and endurance. In the year he was ordained pope, Gregory fell ill with fever from which he never fully recovered. His own personal life provided the impetus for his exposition on the tribulations of Job, for Gregory assumed that his sickness came as a punishment from God for sin, one that he must bear with relentless patience like Job.[31]

Gregory, who was unable to read Greek, worked with Latin transla- tions of the Church Fathers and saw Job as a patient sufferer. A plague hit Rome in 590 and raged for four months.[32] Drought affected Italy for most of 591. Due to such events, Gregory believed that the end of the world was imminent. As an active endorser of the true Christian life, he sought to liberate the mind from the flesh, to live a life of contemplation. Spiritual power resulted from disengaging the world and actively con- templating, thus providing an outward sign of God's power so to convert non-Christians.[33] Therefore, Gregory deems Job as one who overcomes diversity through spiritual contemplation.

In Gregory's commentary, Job's wife functions as just another test Job must overcome. Like Augustine before him, Gregory focuses a great deal on the mouth of Job's wife: "the old foe put in motion the tongue of his wife" (*antiques hostis linguam mouit uxoris*). The connection between Adam and Job remains evident for Gregory—Job is "Adam on a dunghill" (*Adam in sterquilinio*). When Satan attempts to defeat Job, he does so through Job's wife, knowing that as Adam was prone to be deceived through his wife Eve, so might Job's wife persuade Job to curse God. Gregory refers to Satan as the serpent who, through his wife, the one closest to Job, attempted to sway his faith (III. viii). Job rebuked her rightly, especially since he knew from the first fall of man that her "looser mind" needs "manly reproof."[34] In the same passage, Gregory uses the incident to explain why women are not worthy to instruct God's word, citing 1 Tim 2:12 as support.

31. Jeffrey Richards, *Consul of God: The Life and Times of Gregory the Great* (London: Routledge & Kegan Paul, 1980), 47.

32. Dionysios Ch. Stathakopoulos, *Famine and Pestilence in the Late Roman and Early Byzantine Empire: A Systematic Survey of Subsistence Crises and Epidemics* (ed. Anthony Bryer and John Haldon; Birmingham Byzantine and Ottoman Monographs; Burlington, Vt.: Ashgate, 2004), 118.

33. Richards, *Consul of God*, 54–57.

34. CCSL 143: "Dignum quippe era ut fluxam mentem uirilis censura restringeret cum profecto et de ipso primo lapsu humani generis nosset quod docere mulier recta nesciret." Pope Gregory I, *S. Gregorii Magni Moralia in Job*, vol. 143 (Corpus Christianorum Series Latina; Turnholti: Brepols, 1979), 122.

One common thread throughout the comparisons between Job and his wife and Adam and Eve is the menacing presence of Satan to disrupt their marriage. When Gregory began his papacy, the Devil became the vehicle through which popular superstitions concerning evil spirits were channeled. Rather than the so-called "pagan" notion of numerous spirits at work throughout the world, the Church upheld that evil came from God's judgment or from the Devil's hand. As Jeffrey Richards notes, "The Devil was everywhere and could take any form he wished in order to work his wicked ways."[35] Although two centuries of Christianity as an established religion permeated the West, people, especially in rural areas, still kept their loyalties to their gods. For the Church, these gods were known as demons. Supernatural forces still maintained their presence in holy sites across the country landscape. The Church had to deal with idol-worshipping agrarian peasants. As Augustine of Hippo before him, Gregory recommended the subtle absorption of paganism into Christianity. Therefore, holy sites were renamed and festival days taken over. The Devil had a large role to play here, for the pagan practices not so easily adaptable to Christianity became the work of the Devil.[36]

According to an early eleventh-century Anglo-Saxon English abbot and authoritative Winchester scholar, Ælfric, when preaching about the pagan custom of divination, "every blessing comes from God, and cursing from the Devil" as the Devil "is an instigator of evil and worker of falsehood, author of sins, and deceiver of souls."[37] In other sermons, Ælfric lifts up the importance of Job as a saint, who overcomes the Devil's malicious acts.[38] As a literary construction, the Devil acts less as a tempter and more as an ontological symbol that constantly challenges saints. Peter Dendle notes how the Devil acts as a prop in Old English literature, a symbol of general evil that saints must overcome. The Devil acts as a saint's shadow, a "continuous reminder of the perils of the present world."[39]

35. Richards, *Consul of God*, 17.

36. Ibid., 17–20.

37. *Kalendas Ianvarii Octabas et Circvmcisio Domini* VI: 35–39: "Ælc bletsung is of Gode, and wyrigung of deofle" and "ac he is yfel tihtend, and leas wycrend, synna ordfruma, and sawla bepæcend." See Peter Clemoes, ed., *Ælfric's Catholic Homilies: The First Series* (Oxford: Oxford University Press for the Early English Text Society, 1997), 230.

38. *Praefatio* I: 100, in ibid., 176. See also his *Sermo De Memoria Sanctorum* XVI.

39. Peter Dendle, *Satan Unbound: The Devil in Old English Narrative Literature* (Toronto: University of Toronto Press, 2001), 61. The Latin tradition carries a certain tension between internal/external sin. The Anglo-Saxons inherited such a

The emphasis on heroic moments in the history of redemption is a common theme in early medieval theology. John Damon argues that Ælfric inherited a concept of the non-violent holy martyr who reaches masculinity through struggling against spiritual temptation and yoked it with a new cultural norm of the "growing ideal of the holy warrior/ champion of Christ."[40] As Damon suggests, Ælfric, in his lives of saints, presents both the cleric and the warrior "as equally capable of achieving true Christian sainthood" but in separate sectors of society, "through the spiritual fulfillment of duty."[41]

Ælfric was a prolific author and theologian whose sermons meant to educate clergy and expound on Christ's redemption.[42] After a tenth-century English revival of monasticism, it was important for Ælfric to clearly delineate the teachings of the Church through precise sources and not just apocryphal, anonymous Old English poetry and tradition, which meant basing his teachings on the "exegetical and canonical writings of the most honoured fathers of the Latin West."[43]

From his second series of Catholic homilies, Ælfric preaches a sermon on "the first Sunday in September, when Job is read" (*Dominica I in Mense Septembri. Quando Legitur Iob*). In typical fashion in terms of the sentiments that came before him from Augustine and Gregory, Ælfric understood Job as part of the universal history of Christian salvation. Job's wife embodies Satan's temptations, in her "witlessness" (*gewitleast*), as Eve did for Adam:

> The guileful devil took to him the woman as a helper, that he might through her deceive the holy man, as he had before deceived Adam through Eve; but the same God that permitted him to be so tempted, preserved him against the devil's machinations, and against the loss of his soul.[44]

tension in dealing with the Devil and generally blur his role as internal/external source of sin.

40. John Edward Damon, *Soldier Saints and Holy Warriors: Warfare and Sanctity in the Literature of Early England* (Burlington, Vt.: Ashgate, 2003), 196.

41. Ibid.

42. For more on Ælfric, see Milton McC. Gatch, *Preaching and Theology in Anglo-Saxon England: Ælfric and Wulfstan* (Toronto: University of Toronto Press, 1977).

43. Ibid., 120.

44. "Dominica I in Mense Septembri I," 125–29: "Se swicola deofol genam þæt wif him to gefyl/stan. þæt he ðone halgan wer ðurh hí beswice. Swa swa he ær Adam purh euan beswac.ac se ylca god ðe geðafode þæt hé swa gecostnod wære heold hine wið pæs deofles syrwungum. and wið his sawle lyre". Anglo-Saxon text in Malcolm Godden, ed., *Ælfric's Catholic Homilies: The Second Series* (London: Oxford University Press, for The Early English Text Society, 1979). English

In the early thirteenth century, the case of Job and his wife remains the same. In a time in Western culture when Aristotle's writings became accessible in Latin translation, Thomas Aquinas's *Literal Exposition on Job* recounts much of the same themes as did earlier writings. Like Augustine, Aquinas notes that Satan keeps Job's wife alive so that he might attempt to bring him down through his wife like he did with Adam. Job, however, maintains his constant innocence.[45] Aquinas's commentary on Job includes Aristotelian influences and philosophical conclusions about how divine providence functions in human matters, but his view of Job's wife follows suit with his Latin predecessors.[46] Perhaps this is due to the fact that in Aquinas's time, religious reforms reinforced male clerical celibacy and stricter, more traditional roles, for married men. Furthermore, Aristotle's views provided "biological explanations and justifications for the social and cultural inequalities between men and women."[47]

Job and His Wife in Medieval Christian Texts

Evidence of a trend to compare Adam with Job and Eve with Job's wife continues throughout the Middle Ages. In twelfth-century France, Heloise makes mention of Job's wife in one her letters to Abelard. In the context of marriage, she places herself among "bad" wives of the Bible, including Delilah, the wives of Solomon, and Job's wife:

> It was the first woman in the beginning who lured man from Paradise, and she who had been created by the Lord as his helpmate became the instrument of his total downfall... Job, holiest of men, fought his last and hardest battle against his wife, who urged him to curse God. The cunning arch-tempter well knew from repeated experience that men are most easily brought to ruin through their wives.[48]

translation from Ælfric, *Sermones Catholici; or, Homilies of Aelfric* (trans. Benjamin Thorpe; 2 vols.; London: Taylor, 1844–46), 2:453–55.

45. Thomas Aquinas, *The Literal Exposition on Job: A Scriptural Commentary Concerning Providence* (ed. Carl A. Raschke; trans. Anthony Damico; Classics in Religious Studies; Atlanta: Scholars Press, 1989), 94–95.

46. Martin D. Yaffe, "Providence in Medieval Aristotelianism: Moses Maimonides and Thomas Aquinas on the Book of Job," in Perdue and Gilpin, eds., *Voice from the Whirlwind*, 111–28.

47. Sharon Farmer, "Persuasive Voices: Clerical Images of Medieval Wives," *Speculum* 61, no. 3 (1986): 520.

48. Letter III, from Heloise to Abelard: "Prima statim mulier de paradise virum captivavit et, quae ei a Domino creata fuerat in auxilium, in summum ei conversa est exitium... Iob sanctissimus in uxore novissimam atque gravissiam sustinuit pugnam,

The letter offers a unique insight into a female appropriation of the Adam/Eve—Job/Wife juxtaposition. Susan Smith discusses Heloise's use of the "Power of Women" *topos* and defines *topos* as "the representational practice of bringing together at least two, but usually more, well-known figures from the Bible…to exemplify a cluster of inter-related themes that include the wiles of women, the power of love, and the trials of marriage."[49] Here, Heloise demonstrates the instability of gender hierarchy. On the surface, her letter reads as if she accepts the ideology of patriarchal discourse that supports women as a "weaker sex." According to Smith, she does so in order to keep Abelard's guidance and love, thus claiming moral weakness to maintain power over Abelard's desire.[50] In any case, Job's wife and Eve share a basic characteristic. They bring, or attempt to bring, the downfall of their husbands through their persuasive and powerful speech.

A Benedictine monk, John Lydgate (ca. 1370–ca. 1451), who studied in Oxford and Cambridge, and who also traveled to France, was a prolific author in the Chaucerian tradition. His poem, "Examples Against Women," follows examples of biblical women, from Eve to Delilah, to suggest that Christ was wise not to marry. Job's wife qualifies as one of those examples: Wasn't it a pity that in Job's "most povert and moste myserie,/His wyf hym rebuked & on a donghyll left hym lye?"[51]

The *fabliaux*—French tales from the thirteenth and fourteenth centuries—also present stereotypes of the cuckolded husband, but in often humorous accounts.[52] The satire *Le Miroir de Mariage* written by Eustache Deschamps between 1381 and 1420, for instance, attempts to persuade the reader that a contemplative life is better than marriage because women ultimately lead men to unhappiness.[53] He mentions Job's

---

quae eum ad maledicendum Deo stimulabat. Et callidissimus tentator hoc optime noverat, quod saepius expertus fuerat, virorum videlicet ruinam in uxoribus esse facillimam." Latin from J. T. Muckle, "The Personal Letters Between Abelard and Heloise," *Mediaeval Studies* 15 (1953): 80. English translation from Peter Abelard, *The Letters of Abelard and Heloise* (trans. Betty Radice; Harmondsworth: Penguin, 1974), 77–78.

49. Susan L. Smith, *The Power of Women: A Topos in Medieval Art and Literature* (Philadelphia: University of Pennsylvania Press, 1995), 2.

50. Ibid., 39.

51. John Lydgate, *The Minor Poems of John Lydgate*. Vol. 2, *The Secular Poems* (The Early English Text Society; New York: Oxford University Press, 1961), 444.

52. Shulamith Shahar, *The Fourth Estate: A History of Women in the Middle Ages* (trans. Chaya Galai; New York: Methuen, 1983), 77.

53. Prudence Allen, *The Concept of Woman: The Early Humanist Reformation, 1250–1500*, vol. 2 (Grand Rapids: Eerdmans, 2002), 448–53.

wife as an example of wifely nastiness because if Job had listened to her advice, he would have missed paradise, just like Adam did when he listened to Eve.[54] The cultural convention of making fun of marriage lurks in the background of Chaucer's "The Wife of Bath's Tale." Chaucer writes the tale based out of, and in response to, the twelfth and thirteenth centuries of French writing.[55] Alisoun, the wife, recounts her five marriages and mentions that her fifth husband, Jankyn, reads aloud to her out of the "book of wikked wyves" (v. 685). She concludes that no clerk will speak well of wives (vv. 688–89).

Behind Alisoun's assumption about clerks rests what Michael Cherniss suggests is "a sort of model for unfortunate husbands."[56] The wife of Job carries a reputation of that as shrew or scold, defined as "the person (usually a woman) who disturbs the peace by publicly abusing family members."[57] The shrew underlies the Wife of Bath's mentioning of Job in terms of a husband's patience for his wife:

> Or so you preach of Job and his patience! Always be patient; practice what you preach, for if you don't, we've got a thing to teach. Which is: it's good to have one's wife in peace! One of us has got to knuckle under. And since man is more rational a creature than woman is, it's you who must forbear.[58]

54. LVIII, lines 5982–6019. Eustache Deschamps, *Le Miroir de Mariage*, vol. 9 (Oeuvres Complètes de Eustache Deschamps; New York: Johnson Reprint Corporation, 1966), 196–97.

55. Alain Renoir, "Eve's I.Q. Rating: Two Sexist Views of Genesis B," in *New Readings on Women in Old English Literature* (ed. Helen Damico and Alexandra Hennessey Olsen; Bloomington: Indiana University Press, 1990), 263. See also Charles Muscatine, *Chaucer and the French Tradition* (Berkeley: University of California Press, 1957).

56. Michael D. Cherniss, "The 'Clerk's Tale' and 'Envoy,' the Wife of Bath's Purgatory, and the 'Merchant's Tale'," *The Chaucer Review* 6, no. 4 (1972): 235–54. Cherniss explains the Clerk's ironic metaphor for the Wife of Bath as one who performed a spiritual service to her fourth husband by keeping him in purgatory on earth in order to pave the way for heaven after death, thus aligning her with Job's wife (pp. 244–45).

57. D. E. Underdown, "The Taming of the Scold: The Enforcement of Patriarchal Authority in Early Modern England," in *Order and Disorder in Early Modern England* (ed. Anthony Fletcher and John Stevenson; Cambridge: Cambridge University Press, 1985), 119.

58. "Wife of Bath's Tale," vv. 436–42: "Sith ye so preche of jobes pacience. Suffreth alwey, syn ye so wel kan preche; And but ye do, certein we shal yow teche. That it is fair to have a wyf in pees. Oon of us two moste bowen, doutelees; And sith a man is moore reasonable. Than womman is, ye moste been suffrable." All middle English quotes come from John H. Fisher and Mark Allen, eds., *The Complete*

The Wife of Bath subverts an allegation of inferior female rationality by requiring the husband to give in to the wife, all along keeping in line with Job's proverbial patience. In essence, she reveals the hypocrisy of clerics who call upon the patience of Job yet fail to live up to the task. Furthermore, her discourse about marriage demonstrates how both men and women fall victim to a cultural text, the book of wicked wives, which supports misogyny and wives' bitterness towards their husbands.[59]

Ann Astell compares Alisoun (the Wife of Bath) to Job's wife—a "dangerous rhetor, speaking words of bad persuasion ('verba malae persuasionis') that repeat Eve's temptation."[60] Astell goes on to suggest that Chaucer refashions Job's wife in his two characters—the Wife of Bath and the Wife of Walter. In "The Clerk's Tale," the narrator offers a picture of Griselda, the Wife of Walter, who, as Astell points out, is "Job in female form" or "Chaucer's bold reinvention of Job's wife," a "Marylike New Eve at the side of a New Adam."[61] Elsewhere, she is called "a veritable Job of the marriage bed."[62] Several different versions of the Griselda story can be found in Boccaccio and Petrarch. As Chaucer tells it, Walter chooses a peasant wife, Griselda, on the condition that she obey him unconditionally. She agrees and soon thereafter, she bears a daughter, whom Walter sends to be raised by his sister unbeknownst to Griselda, who thinks the child has been killed. Walter repeats the same scenario at the birth of their son. Then, Walter sends his wife back to her old life and requires that she make wedding preparations for him and his new bride. Upon her dismissal, she echoes Job's words from 1:21: "'Naked out of my fadres hous,' quod she, 'I cam, and naked moot I turne agayn'" (vv. 871–72). Walter disguises their daughter as the new bride-to-be. Griselda accepts both the disguised bride-to-be and her brother, whereupon Walter reveals his plot and rejoices that Griselda has proven herself worthy. The Clerk himself makes the comparison between Job and Griselda:

Canterbury Tales of Geoffrey Chaucer (Boston: Thomson Wadsworth, 2006). All modern English translations come from Geoffrey Chaucer, *The Canterbury Tales* (trans. David Wright; Oxford: Oxford University Press, 1985).

59. Ann Astell, "Job's Wife, Walter's Wife, and the Wife of Bath," in *Old Testament Women in Western Literature* (ed. Raymond-Jean Frontain; Conway, Ark.: UCA, 1991), 98.

60. Ibid., 97.

61. Ibid., 101.

62. Katherine Usher Henderson and Barbara F. McManus, *Half Humankind: Contexts and Texts of the Controversy About Women in England, 1540–1640* (Chicago: University of Illinois Press, 1985), 10.

Men speak of Job, and most of all of his humility, as scholars can well explain when they wish to speak concerning holy men. But in truth, though clerks praise women rather little, no man can behave as humbly as a woman can, nor can be half so loyal as a woman can be, unless it has happened very recently.[63]

Chaucer, through the Clerk, makes novel, and ironical, use of the patient Job legend by advocating for a patient wife.[64] In both cases, it is Chaucer's discourse of women in a culture that reinforces a gender ideology of the dangerous rhetoric of women that makes for unsettling, pleasurable, and memorable characters.[65]

Versions of Patient Griselda often circulated with the popular *Book of the Knight of the Tower* or *Livre pour l'enseignement de ses filles* written in the 1370s by Chevalier de La Tour Landry, a French aristocrat widower concerned with instructing his daughters on proper behavior.[66] It was translated into English in 1483 and in German (*Der Ritter vom Turn*) in 1493. As a pedagogical manual, it encodes gendered behavior for young women based on traditional male and scholastic expectations. Therefore, Job's wife receives a mixed review in the *Knight of the Tower* because of the strong connection with the Devil in traditional theology alongside the author's need to find a wifely redemptive value in the story to communicate to medieval young women. The *Knight of the Tower* describes Job's wife bringing him food, even in her great misery to see Job lying on a dunghill with worms on his body, until the Devil got a hold of her and tempted her: "as the deuyll tempted her/she felle in wrathe against her lord" and spoke her words out of wrath.[67] The marriage of Job

63. Verses 932–38: "Men speke of Job, and moost for his humblesse, As clerkes, whan hem list, konne wel endite,Namely of men, but as in soothfastnesse,Though clerkes preise wommen but a lite,Ther kan no man in humblesse hym acquite As womman kan, ne kan been half so trewe. As wommen been, but it be falle of newe." For discussion of this passage, see Lawrence Besserman, "Biblical Exegesis, Typology, and the Imagination of Chaucer," in Keenan, ed., *Typology and English Medieval Literature*, 183–205.

64. Lawrence L. Besserman, *The Legend of Job in the Middle Ages* (Cambridge, Mass.: Harvard University Press, 1979), 112–13.

65. As discussed in Chapter 2 of Karma Lochrie, *Covert Operations: The Medieval Uses of Secrecy* (Philadelphia: University of Pennsylvania Press, 1999), 56–92.

66. Rebecca Barnhouse, *The Book of the Knight of the Tower: Manners for Young Medieval Women* (New York: Palgrave Macmillan, 2006), 86–87.

67. Chapter 29 in Geoffrey de La Tour Landry, *The Book of the Knight of the Tower* (trans. William Caxton; Early English Text Society; New York: Oxford University Press, 1971), 110.

and his wife withstood this test. Job's wife, "a good woman as she was" received, according to de La Tour Landry, the answer of a "good man," and Job maintained exemplary patience and humility.[68]

Another fourteenth-century medieval household manual for women, *Le Ménagier de Paris* (*The Good Wife of Paris*), couches the example of Job and his wife within a section on how a wife should provide her husband good counsel. Keeping with the story of Griselda as a model example of a proper wife, the author and compiler of *The Good Wife* also tells the story of Melibee and his wife Prudence. Melibee, a rich young man, came home one day to find that his enemies had invaded his home and beat his wife and daughter. He wailed with grief, exhibiting an uncomposed display of lamentation. Prudence advises her husband that he act like Job and reserve his grief in a more dignified way. She quotes Job's response to his wife: "Our Lord gave it to me. Our Lord took it away. He did to me just as He wished. Blessed be the name of the Lord!"[69] Just as Griselda embodies the patient virtues of Job, so too does Prudence exemplify a female reversal of Job by reminding her husband of the expected gender roles required in displays of grief. Prudence's gentle words to her husband overturn the harsh words Job's wife speaks to her husband.

The characters of Job and his wife continue to make an impact on medieval audiences. The "Life of Job" from the fifteenth century resonates with medieval pageant progressions common in the Low Countries and France, where an interest in Job certainly existed.[70] The Middle English poem, "Life of Job," which survives in one manuscript, describes Satan as a serpent, reminiscent of Eden.[71] Bessermen notes that the poem emphasizes "the identity between Satan, who in the Book of Job is portrayed as a member of the Lord's heavenly assembly, and the more familiar medieval devil of hell."[72]

The "Life of Job" also recounts the conversation between Job and his wife. Job's wife suggests that he will never recover, so his patience is futile in the face of such adversity (ll. 92–98). Similar to the biblical

---

68. Ibid.

69. 9th article in *The Good Wife's Guide: Le Ménagier de Paris, a Medieval Household Book* (trans. Gina L. Greco and Christine M. Rose; Ithaca, N.Y.: Cornell University Press, 2009), 150.

70. G. N. Garmonsway and R. M. Raymo, "A Middle English Metrical Life of Job," in *Early English and Norse Studies* (ed. Arthur Brown and Peter Foote; London: Methuen & Co, 1963), 78.

71. Line 29. All references to "Life of Job" come from ibid., 89–96.

72. Besserman, *The Legend of Job in the Middle Ages*, 92.

account, Job responds: "Folysshe woman, I counsel the, be styll, for he that takyth gode thing sumtyme must take ill" (ll. 97–98). Interestingly, God appears to Job and rebukes him for speaking hastily and insolently to his wife (ll. 115–19). This departure from tradition is obscure. Besserman suggests that the poet understood that Job is not patient with his wife in the biblical account, so the poet singles it out in order to recover Job's paradigmatic patience.[73] At any rate, it becomes clear that the poem upholds Job's saintliness while, at the same time, presents his wife as one who continues to scold Job. Whereas Job receives divine guidance concerning his speech, Job's wife is left to continue without any spiritual direction, which leads to another misunderstanding.

When minstrels come to play for Job, he pays them with scabs from his body that turn to gold. After the minstrels show the gold to his wife, she accuses Job of hiding gold from her. This incorporation comes not only from the LXX rendition of her needing to continue to procure food for Job, but, also, from a Christian folk understanding of magical transformation of bodily flesh into gold, a notion of expiating "their guilt by mortification of the flesh."[74] She openly rebukes him with sharp language: "And with many seducious wordes openly/There hym rebuked with language most sharply" (ll. 130–31).

Job's wife continues her reputation for verbal chastisement of Job in a Middle French mystery play, *Patience of Job*, which survives in one manuscript from around 1475.[75] The play itself was popular, having been performed at least thirteen times between 1514 and 1651. The author and exact location are unknown. The play incorporates an entire assembly of devils in hell—Satan gets the assignment to capture Job's soul for hell.[76]

The play reflects a popular version of the tradition of Job and his wife from Latin authors; Satan in the play declares his intent to try to dupe Job through his wife like he did Adam through Eve (ll. 5525–43). As in T. Job, Satan disguises himself as a beggar, tricking Job's wife into

---

73. Ibid.

74. Garmonsway and Raymo, "A Middle English Metrical Life of Job," 85.

75. All citations of *Pacience de Job* come from Albert Meiller, ed., *La Pacience de Job* (Paris: Klincksieck, 1971). For a helpful discussion, see Besserman, *The Legend of Job in the Middle Ages*, 94–107.

76. Lines 1431–698. The costumes for Satan and various devils, according to English records, were expensive to construct and maintain with elaborate animal-grotesque faces, no doubt providing quite a visual presence on stage. See Barbara D. Palmer, "The Inhabitants of Hell: Devils," in *The Iconography of Hell* (ed. Clifford Davidson and Thomas H. Seiler; Kalamazoo, Mich.: Medieval Institute Publications, Western Michigan University, 1992), 32–35.

thinking he received gold coins from Job, which makes her suspect he is withholding his wealth. After he shows her the worms on his body, proclaiming that they are his treasure in heaven, his wife laments the curse that is her marriage and abandons Job to go to her brother-in-law's house (ll. 5609–5714). As in the "Life of Job," the disgusting things from Job's body turn into gold, and Job's wife does not seem to understand, or is not privy to, the ascetical aspects of Job's life. The external worldly motivations of Job's wife compare sharply with Job's internal spiritual motivations.

Much more could be discussed about the sources listed in this section, but they function here to place Job and his wife within a thread of tradition that relates their verbal exchange to Adam's marital weakness when it comes to his wife's words, a marital response that is weaker than Job's. Not only do theologians engage Eve and Job's wife in terms of right and wrong speech, but they also reflect a general attitude toward women and speech prevalent in various parts of medieval society. Georges Duby notes the general attitude from preachers: "'chatter' was among the foremost of the faults of women denounced by preachers."[77] The next section elaborates even more fully on the cultural convention adapted by theologians for Eve and Job's wife—the convention of gendered deviant speech, or, "the cultural coding of women as garrulous and of garrulity as feminine" that "was firmly entrenched in late medieval culture."[78]

Medieval Gendered Deviant Speech

The poem "Piers Plowman," by the fourteenth-century English poet, William Langland, depicts a series of allegorical characters that engage in conversation about morality and seek the true Christian life in the context of the medieval Christian Church.[79] The poem's narrator, at first

77. According to Duby, no records of authentic female voices exist until the end of the thirteenth century. Georges Duby, "Affidavits and Confessions," in *A History of Women in the West: Silences of the Middle Ages* (ed. Christiane Klapisch-Zuber; Cambridge, Mass.: Belknap Press of Harvard University Press, 1992), 482.

78. Sandy Bardsley, *Venomous Tongues: Speech and Gender in Late Medieval England* (Philadelphia: University of Pennsylvania Press, 2006), 66.

79. Over 50 manuscripts of this poem survive, and many in fragments. The poem is divided into three major texts—the A text, B text, and C text. The unfinished A text is the earliest (ca. 1360s) while the B text, ca. 1377, revises A and is the most complete, and the C text is a revision of B. For coverage of these issues, see James Simpson, *Piers Plowman: An Introduction to the B-Text* (New York: Longman,

Piers the Plowman, seeks the life of Do-well, Do-better, and Do-best.[80] In one section, Study, the wife of Wit, engages in an angry speech against Wit, calling out curses, and noting how "the holy prophet Job" asks why sinners prosper (cf. Job 21:7). It is a question Study lingers on in her long speech while arriving at the conclusion that one should not desire to know *why* God lets Satan lead humans astray because everything happens according to God's will.[81] At the end of the speech, Wit demonstrates "ironical deference to his wife," by stepping back, laughing, bowing, and glancing at Will, which suggests to Will to allow his attention to entirely fall on Study.[82] The exchange offers one example of a medieval play on gendered communication.

Just as the Devil provides very real situations of social deviance in the Middle Ages, so too does the act of speech, for speech represents a social act. As early as Irenaeus, the complexities of speech and gender play a role in the Eve/Mary dichotomy, as he argues that just as Eve was seduced by the speech of an angel, so too did Mary receive good news through an angel's speech.[83] In his *De Carne Christi*, Tertullian also compares Eve and Mary in terms of "the word," for the word of death

1990). For the C text, see William Langland, *Piers Plowman: The C Version* (trans. George Economou; Philadelphia: University of Pennsylvania Press, 1996). All references and quotations from "Piers Plowman" come from the B text unless otherwise stated.

80. "Piers Plowman" uses a form of personification-allegory which personifies moral types to demonstrate some aspect of human intelligence and learning. For more on this type of literature, see Robert Worth Frank, "The Art of Reading Medieval Personification-Allegory," in *Interpretations of Piers Plowman* (ed. Edward Vasta; Notre Dame: University of Notre Dame Press, 1968), 217–31. Both Augustine and Gregory the Great play large roles in the poem, being referenced numerous times for their authoritative teachings. The poem also incorporates much of Job.

81. Piers Plowman, B Passus X. For a discussion on the role of Satan in "Piers Plowman," see Chapter 6 in C. W. Marx, *The Devil's Rights and the Redemption in the Literature of Medieval England* (Cambridge: Brewer, 1995), 100–113. For more about Langland's use of the Bible, see Mary Clemente Davlin, "William Langland," in *The Blackwell Companion to the Bible in English Literature* (ed. Rebecca Lemon et al.; Malden, Mass.: Wiley-Blackwell, 2009), 116–33.

82. J. A. Burrow, *Gestures and Looks in Medieval Narrative* (New York: Cambridge University Press, 2002), 102. For a discussion on masculinity and marriage in Piers Plowman, see Chapter 1, "The Masculine Ethics of Langland's Piers Plowman," in Isabel Davis, *Writing Masculinity in the Later Middle Ages* (Cambridge: Cambridge University Press, 2007), 12–37.

83. Irenaeus, *Against Heresies*, Book 5, Chapter 19. See Roberts and Donaldson, eds., *The Ante-Nicene Fathers*, 547.

passed into Eve and brought about death, but the Word of God came into the Virgin Mary so as to bring about life.[84] Bardsley suggests that "even the most traditional binary in medieval representation of women—that of Eve versus Mary—lent itself to a moral lesson about speech."[85]

Examples from preaching and literature make up the countless cultural artifacts reiterating the stereotype of the chatty woman, a feminine performance that plays, ballads, books, paintings, and sermons repeat in the Middle Ages. Medieval pastoral sources quote the Latin text of Prov 18:21: *Mors et vita in minibus linguae*, or "Life and death are in the hands of the tongue."[86] Gender norms of speech were more solidified for women than for men because stereotypes of scolding and garrulousness belonged to wives. John of Trevisa's fourteenth-century translation of *De proprietatibus rerum* notes that an "euyll wife, cryenge and janglynge, chydynge and skoldynge" causes a husband great woe.[87] John of Trevisa, a translator and scholar trained in Oxford, carries the common association of scolding with wives all the way from Bartholomaeus Anglicus, the author of *De proprietatibus rerum*, or, *On the Properties of Things*, an English author who completed the work in 1245. The nineteen books span the physical universe, beginning with God and angels ending with weights and measures.[88]

Such notions of the gendered performance of scolding show up in a later example, a sermon by Hugh Latimer, Bishop of Worcester, in 1535, who recounts the story of Solomon and the two supposed mothers (1 Kgs 3:16–18) and explains that they "held up the matter with scolding after a womanlike fashion."[89] "Troublesome speech in general was associated with women," so that poets and sermon authors "were quick to imply

84. Ernest Evans, ed., *Tertullian's Treatise on the Incarnation* (London: SPCK, 1956), 61.

85. Bardsley, *Venomous Tongues*, 51.

86. As noted especially by Edwin D. Craun, *Lies, Slander, and Obscenity in Medieval English Literature: Pastoral Rhetoric and the Deviant Speaker* (Cambridge: Cambridge University Press, 1997); Edwin D. Craun, ed., *The Hands of the Tongue: Essays on Deviant Speech* (Kalamazoo, Mich.: Medieval Institute Publications, Western Michigan University, 2007).

87. As cited in Sandy Bardsley, "Men's Voices in Late Medieval England," in Craun, ed., *The Hands of the Tongue*, 166.

88. For more information on John of Trevisa, see David C. Fowler, *The Life and Times of John Trevisa, Medieval Scholar* (Seattle: University of Washington Press, 1995).

89. Second sermon preached before King Edward the Sixth. See Hugh Latimer, *Sermons, by Hugh Latimer, Sometime Bishop of Worcester* (London: Dent & Co., 1926), 107.

womanliness" speech upon chattering men.[90] The mid-twelfth-century "Proverbs of Alfred" warns husbands that wives cannot control their tongues so they should refrain from telling them secrets. A woman is "word-mad" (*word-wod*), having "too swift a tongue" (*tunge to swift*).[91] These proverbs circulated throughout the Middle Ages.

Inappropriate speech is identified as a female crime from various sources in various locations. A popular *exemplum* exists from as early as the twelfth century, in which a demon sits behind chattering females in church, writing their words on parchment. Though variations exist from several countries, the chattering people in church are always female.[92] Public art in parish churches sponsored by the laity visually depicts the *exemplum* of the connection between speech, the female, and the demonic.[93]

A thirteenth-century text addressed to anchoresses, *Ancrene Wisse*, holds up Mary as an example of speech for all women because she hardly speaks in scripture. The woman who "opens her mouth with a lot of chatter" will lose "spiritual strength against the Devil."[94] The concern upheld in *Ancrene Wisse* for proper speech, against the female chatterbox (*meaðelilt*), resonates with its function to provide spiritual guidance and "proper" female social behavior of the time. *Ancrene Wisse* also explains how a restrained tongue leads to a pious life. Job's friends remained silent for a week, it points out, but, "once they had begun to speak, they simply could not stop talking."[95] *Ancrene Wisse* does not mention Job's wife but instead focuses on what Denis Renevey calls "earthly

90. Bardsley, "Men's Voices in Late Medieval England," 170.

91. "Proverbs of Alfred," 280–81. The Proverbs of Alfred probably originate in the twelfth century, although the earliest surviving manuscript dates to the thirteenth century. The proverbs are attributed to King Alfred and hold close parallels to Prov 14–17 in warning men about how to choose a wife. See Elaine Treharne, ed., *Old and Middle English C. 890–C. 1450: An Anthology* (3d ed.; Malden, Mass.: Wiley-Blackwell, 2010), 451.

92. M. T. Clanchy, *From Memory to Written Record: England 1066–1307* (2d ed.; Malden, Mass.: Blackwell, 1993), 187–88.

93. Bardsley, *Venomous Tongues*, 52–66.

94. *Ancrene Wisse* 2.21: "ah heo þe openeð hire muð wið muche meaðelunge" and "leoseð aʒein þe feond gastelich strengðe." All original text quotes come from the Corpus Christi text found in Bella Millett, ed., *Ancrene Wisse: A Corrected Edition of the Text in Cambridge, Corpus Christi College, Ms 402* (Early Text Society; Oxford: Oxford University Press, 2005). All English translations are from Bella Millett, ed., *Ancrene Wisse: Guide for Anchoresses, a Translation* (Exeter: University of Exeter Press, 2009).

95. *Ancrene Wisse* 2.19: "ah þa ha hefden alles bigunnen to speokene, þa ne cuðen ha neauer stutten hare cleappe."

deprivation," which was important to anchorite communities. By recalling the texts about Job from the *Office of the Dead*, Job comes off better as a solitary, a fitting companion to the readers. In other words, *Ancrene Wisse* employs a strategy of using Job to reinforce its "dead-to-the-world motif which characterizes the anchoritic life."[96]

The sins of the tongue, however, offered a threat to both sexes, as seen in two sources of instructions to children. The fourteenth-century anonymous text, "How the Good Wife Taught Her Daughter," survives as one of the few medieval texts that speak just to women. It instructs that a good woman will attend church and avoid gossip, being of "good tongue" (*good tunge*).[97] The fact that the text begins with remarks about church attendance suggests a clerical concern for gendered social expectations of behavior through the use of the "literary device of maternal instruction."[98] In relation to her husband, the wife should answer meekly and not like a shrew, for then she will preserve his good mood: "Meekly þou him answere, And not as an attirling, And so maist þou slake his mood."[99]

Several decades later, the early fifteenth-century text "How the Wise Man Taught His Son," also warns boys to "beware of what you say, for your own tongue may be your foe."[100] In terms of marriage, it is unwise to call his wife villainous names, or as Bardsley translates, "And if you shall not your wife displease, neither call her by no villainous name, and if you do, you are not wise, to call her foul it is your shame."[101] Both

96.   Denis Renevey, "Looking for a Context: Rolle, Anchoritic Culture, and the Office of the Dead," in *Medieval Texts in Context* (ed. Denis Renevey and Graham D. Caie; New York: Routledge, 2008), 199–201.

97.   Frederick J. Furnivall, ed., *The Babees' Book, Etc.* (Early English Text Society; London: Trübner, 1868), 37. See also Tauno F. Mustanoja, ed., *The Good Wife Taught Her Daughter* (Helsinki: Suomalaisen Kirjallisuuden Seuran, 1948). For English translation, see also Edith Rickert, *The Babees' Book: Medieval Manners for the Young* (New York: Duffield & Co., 1908), 31–42.

98.   Mirian Gill, "Female Piety and Impiety: Selected Images of Women in Wall Paintings in England After 1300," in *Gender and Holiness: Men, Women and Saints in Late Medieval Europe* (ed. Samantha J. E. Riches and Sarah Salih; New York: Routledge, 2002), 101.

99.   Furnivall, ed. *The Babees' Book, Etc.*, 38.

100.   "Þin owne tunge may be þi foo; before be waar what þou doist say." Furnivall, ed., *The Babees' Book, Etc.*, 49. English translation from Rickert, *The Babees' Book*, 43. See also George Shuffelton, ed., *Codex Ashmole 61: A Compilation of Popular Middle English Verse* (Middle English Texts Series; Kalamazoo, Mich.: Western Michigan University, Medieval Institute Publications, 2008).

101.   "And þou shcalt not þi wijf displease, neiþer calle hir bi no vilouns name; And if þou do, þou art not wijs, to calle hir foule it is þi schame." Furnivall, ed., *The Babees' Book, Etc.*, 51. Translation from Bardsley, *Venomous Tongues*, 49–50.

poems may not represent social practice, but as Kim Phillips notes, they act "as attempts at engineering gender."[102] They address an urban audience yet clerics found the poems handy in pointing out proper behavior as well. Both poems mention problematic speech but "How the Good Wife Taught Her Daughter" warns women more often and in a variety of contexts, especially in the public arena.[103]

Interestingly, the sin of blasphemy belonged primarily to men, or, at least the *exempla* of the twelfth through the fifteenth centuries include a number of didactic tales of the male swearer, a foul-mouthed individual who throws away great oaths, who receives a vision from the Virgin Mary.[104] Bardsley offers an explanation as to why problematic speech belonged to women but the specific form of speech, swearing and blasphemy, belonged to men. She claims that blasphemy carried real physical results for Christ's body, as it dismembers the Church: "Contemporary aphorisms and maxims suggest that an important distinction existed in late medieval and early modern England between words (typically gendered female) and deeds (associated primarily with men)."[105] The kind of blasphemy to which Bardsley refers comes in the form of swearing by the bones of Christ or by Christ's body. As David Lawton notes in his study on blasphemy, it is "identified as an active threat to the body politic."[106]

Blasphemy, in other words, is relative to the societies that attempt to regulate it. Blasphemy defines difference. In most medieval cases, from the fourth to the fourteenth centuries, blasphemy falls under the category of heresy. Lawton connects a broader sense of blasphemy to anti-Jewish propaganda beginning in the fourteenth century.[107] Since blasphemy was a sin dishonoring the God of Christians in speech and act, "Jews constituted perhaps the earliest blasphemous archetype in the Christian West."[108] The indication here of the life/death situation of speech also reflects in the doctrinal speech-acts, creeds, of Christianity. In this era of

102. Kim M. Phillips, *Medieval Maidens: Young Women and Gender in England, 1270–1540* (Manchester Medieval Studies; New York: Palgrave, 2003), 92.

103. Bardsley, *Venomous Tongues*, 51.

104. Miriam Gill, "From Urban Myth to Didactic Image: The Warning to Swearers," in Craun, ed., *The Hands of the Tongue*, 137–60.

105. Bardsley, "Men's Voices in Late Medieval England," 170.

106. David A. Lawton, *Blasphemy* (Philadelphia: University of Pennsylvania Press, 1993), 10.

107. Ibid., 86–87.

108. David Nash, *Blasphemy in the Christian World: A History* (New York: Oxford University Press, 2007), 42–71.

Christianity, speech crosses lines between orthodoxy and blasphemy, between the marginal and those in power.[109] John Wyclif's Latin treatise *De Blasphemia* (*Of Blasphemy*) opens with a stereotype of a blasphemer—the foolish woman. Wyclif elaborates on a word-play on blasphemy: *blas-femina*, a foolish and blabbering woman.[110] He writes against the Roman Curia, because the Roman Pontiff's pride and luxury provides a discord between word and deed, which is the form of blasphemy Wyclif expounds upon in his treatise. Social constraints on speech were important because anyone who could speak on behalf of God could wield power.[111]

Lawton notes that scandalized orthodoxy gives rise to heresy and blasphemy.[112] If blasphemy, in a religious sense, is the attacking or damaging of religious orthodoxy, then it is possible that Job's rants qualify as blasphemous speeches. Therefore, it is in the best interest of orthodox writers to uphold Job's virtue, despite his problematic complaints against God. Blasphemy remains subjective not by virtue of speech but by virtue of judgment of speech. Therefore, blasphemy is constructed by those who draw the lines between the divine and human.[113] Augustine, for example, suggests that Job's wife commits blasphemy.[114] Moreover, in his sermon on Job, for instance, Ælfric notes the importance of the fact that Job did not sin with his lips (Job 2:10). He explains: "In two ways men sin with their lips; that is, if they speak contrary to right, or silently withhold the right."[115]

In the biblical book of Job, Job himself breaks a long period of silence with curses for the day of his birth (ch. 3). Gregory notes how such language borders on malediction, or "maledictio." But, for Gregory,

109.   Lawton, *Blasphemy*, 54–55.

110.   "Est autem blasfemia insipiens detraccio honoris domini. Et dicitur a blas et femina, que quasi rane blaterant, communiter nimis stulte." Michael Henry Dziewicki, ed., *Iohannis Wyclif: Tractus De Blasphemia* (London: Trübner & Co.; Johnson Reprint Corporation, 1893; repr. 1966), 1.

111.   For a discussion of early modern English contexts concerning women, see Laura Gowing, *Domestic Dangers: Women, Words, and Sex in Early Modern London* (Oxford: Clarendon, 1996).

112.   Lawton, *Blasphemy*, 86.

113.   Iain Cabantous, *Blasphemy: Impious Speech in the West from the Seventeenth to the Nineteenth Century* (trans. Eric Rauth; New York: Columbia University Press, 2002), 1–8.

114.   *On Patience*, ch. 9, CSEL vol. 41, 673–74.

115.   *Dominica I in Mense Septembri* 1: 98–99: "On twa wison men syngiað on heora welerum. Þæt is gif hí unriht sprecað. Oþþe riht forsuwiað." Godden, ed., *Ælfric's Catholic Homilies*, 263. Eng. trans. from Ælfric, *Sermones Catholici*, 453.

Job's words are problematic only on the surface, when read superficially ("si superficie tenus attenditur," IV.ii). Gregory differentiates the kind of cursing suggested by Job's wife and the kind of cursing engaged by Job. The first kind is motivated by the malice of revenge and agitated passion, while the latter kind is spoken out of right judgment (IV.ii).[116] Gregory relates Job's wife's ill-advisement to carnal thinking ("carnalis cogitation," III.xxxii), which allows Ann Astell to comment that Gregory "underscores the emotive carnality of the wife's discourse while denying altogether the carnal dimension of Job's despairing outcry," because passionate language "is marked as feminine."[117] Gregory, among others, evidences how a concern for the right kind of oral transmission in the culture impacts views of Job's wife as a deviant speaker.

Job's wife falls into the category of a problematic feminine speaker constructed by male authors. Her speech conjures up notions of what Eve did to Adam, an immature wife's use of speech to entice her husband to do something impious. This gendered notion of problematic speech for Job's wife becomes visually evident in the next chapter. Social conventions about speech and gender carry over into illustrations of Job's wife in medieval art.

116. CCSL, CXLIII, 165.
117. Astell, "Job's Wife, Walter's Wife, and the Wife of Bath," 95. In another part of *Moralia*, though, Gregory uses the carnal sense of the flesh to argue for why women "stuck" to Christ, i.e. did not run away from his tomb (XIV. 49). This lent to medieval ideas about women at the Passion. For more discussion, see Alcuin Blamires, *The Case for Women in Medieval Culture* (Oxford: Clarendon, 1997), 146–48.

Chapter 2

THE TROUBLESOME TRIO OF JOB, HIS WIFE,
AND SATAN IN MEDIEVAL ART

Like a demon lingering behind the gossiping women in church, Satan lingers behind traditions of the power of Job's wife's speech to impact Job emotionally and spiritually. Her words wield power—the power of the Devil. Female susceptibility to satanic influence, as well as social notions of the perils of marriage when wives speak dangeriously to their husbands and theological claims that Job and his wife repeat Eden, make up the background to the illustrations of Job and his wife in Chapter 20 of the *Speculum Humanae Salvationis*. Theologians writing about Job and his wife demonstrate a level of anxiety for oral transmissions of teachings and culturally encode those concerns in gendered deviant speech. Furthermore, as Joban traditions of iconography expand into the Middle Ages, Satan becomes more of a visual presence, intricately aligning himself with Job's wife.

From her perspective as an art historian, Elizabeth Sears calls attention to two main currents in "reading" images. First, a scholar can proceed with an iconographical analysis of an image, tracing artistic conventions usually in reference to written works. As Sears notes, "part of this process involves constructing prior histories of visual motifs and charting the ways that given figures and concepts were represented over time."[1] Another way to "read" images comes not from content analysis but from visual culture, in other words, the various threads that interact with the image, such as the patron, the financial arrangements, gender, class, ethnicity, and other socio-cultural contexts. An effective analysis of art will pay attention to both content and culture, illuminating "broader currents in the field."[2]

1. Elizabeth Sears, "'Reading' Images," in *Reading Medieval Images: The Art Historian and the Object* (ed. Elizabeth Sears and Thema K. Thomas; Ann Arbor: University of Michigan Press, 2002), 2.
2. Ibid., 3.

In his model of encoding/decoding, Stuart Hall applies semiotics to audience reception, especially in television. His model has its limits for biblical studies and reception history, but some concepts provide fruitful substance for the topic at hand. For instance, visual discourse, as Hall puts it, cannot completely mediate an entire concept. Bal's definition of discourses fits this situation: "Discourse implies a set of semiotic and epistemological habits that enables and prescribes ways of communicating and thinking that others who participate in the discourse can use"; it implies some "unexamined assumptions."[3] A visual representation is a discursive message *about* something, even if those messages have been naturalized to seem real in that they seem to align perfectly with that which is being represented. A visual sign of a biblical story is not the whole biblical story itself but represents a partial picture of a biblical story. Such visual signs almost become natural or *real* when they are widely distributed.[4] To illustrate Hall's main point, I introduce a standard image of Job from medieval times (Fig. 2.1).

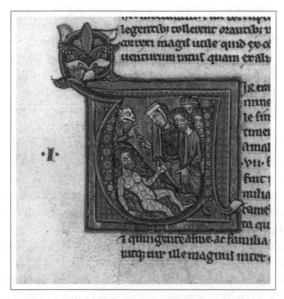

Figure 2.1. Historiated Initial, Latin Bible (Jerome, Prologue to Job). Paris, Almagest Atelier, ca. 1120–30. MS 317. Special Collections Department, University of Colorado at Boulder Libraries.

3. Mieke Bal, "Introduction," in *The Practice of Cultural Analysis: Exposing Interdisciplinary Interpretation* (ed. Mieke Bal; Stanford, Calif.: Stanford University Press, 1999), 7.

4. Stuart Hall, "Encoding, Decoding," in *The Cultural Studies Reader* (ed. Simon During; London: Routledge, 1993), 95–96.

Figure 2.1 is a historiated initial decorating the letter 'U' in a Latin Bible from Paris. The conflation of the characters in Job, including Job, his wife, the Devil, and Job's friends together in one scene, remains one of the most significant naturalized visual signs that marks the story of Job. The scene with Job, his wife, and Satan is not textually accurate and it carries assumptions about the message intended for its audience.

Figure 2.1 is a visual representation of Job that means to communicate the entire story of Job in one illustration. It is a quintessential medieval image of Job, one of many of similar form that circulated around Europe during the Middle Ages. The image is meant to be distributed among audiences. Elaborate historiated initials of the twelfth and thirteenth centuries marked the beginnings of chapters and books. Since such an initial functioned as a "visual aid to remembering," so that one could use the illustration as "a guide to lead one through the vast text," a "device to help a reader use a manuscript," as noted by Christopher De Hamel,[5] then the image also leaves a lasting impressions on the memory of the reader. Furthermore, medieval artists worked "according to a specific formula, and this most often meant using designs and compositions with a familiar precedent."[6] Medieval artists adhered to artistic tradition, visually retelling the story in the established way, through a visual *sign* familiar to an audience with its own set of social expectations.

Stuart Hall speaks of message exchange in terms of "production, circulation, distribution/consumption, reproduction."[7] The meaning of a circulated and distributed image or representation comes when people "receive" the image and frame the understanding of that image in social practice or ideology. In terms of the continuation of a dominant image, Hall states, "there exists a pattern of 'preferred readings'; and these both have the institutional/political/ideological order imprinted in them and have themselves become institutionalized."[8] When examining an image of Job through a reception history model, Hall provides a guiding principle—the ideology and the institutional mechanisms at work in certain visual patterns. In other words, what does the Church, as an institutional power, gain by keeping certain images of Job in circulation? Using gender theory to help illuminate cultural schema at work, this chapter focuses on one clearly established iconographical case of Job and his

---

5. Christopher De Hamel, *A History of Illuminated Manuscripts* (2d ed.; London: Phaidon, 1994), 101.

6. Ibid., 195.

7. Hall, "Encoding, Decoding," 91.

8. Ibid., 98.

2. The Troublesome Trio

wife in the Middle Ages—the threesome of Job, his wife, and the Devil in the "popular" medieval manuscript *Speculum humanæ salvationis* (*Mirror of Human Salvation*).[9]

Medieval Images

The *Speculum Humanae Salvationis*, or *Mirror of Human Salvation* (abbreviated as SHS), was written in the early fourteenth century in rhyming Latin verse and survives in over 400 manuscripts in Latin, Middle English, German, French, Dutch, and Czech. The general form consists of 45 chapters. Each chapter contains one hundred lines and four pictures, three of which act as Old Testament types to a New Testament antitype. Some biblical sources integrate with non-biblical sources, such as Peter Comestor's *Historia Scholastica*, *Gesta Romanorum*, and Jacobus de Voragine's *Legenda Aurea*.[10]

A comparison of the various nuances of illustrations of Job and his wife in SHS manuscripts, including to which schools, dates, and locales the illustrations belong, is beyond the scope of this chapter.[11] Space limits me from discussing, for instance, the artistic merit of illuminated manuscripts in light of the growth of the block printing processes at the middle of the fifteenth century, or how a comparison of certain manuscripts reveals artists, dates, or locations of the manuscripts.[12] Instead, in

---

9. Numerous medieval manuscripts incorporate the word "speculum" in their titles. For a general discussion on the use of the word, see Ritamary Bradley, "Backgrounds of the Title *Speculum* in Mediaeval Literature," *Speculum* 29, no. 1 (1954): 100–115.

10. Avril Henry, *The Mirour of Mans Saluacioun: A Middle English Translation of Speculum Humanae Salvationis* (Philadelphia: University of Pennsylvania Press, 1987); Albert C. Labriola and John W. Smeltz, eds., *The Mirror of Salvation [Speculum Humanae Salvationis]: An Edition of British Library Blockbook G. 11784* (Pittsburgh, Pa.: Duquesne University Press, 2002); Adrian Wilson and Joyce Lancaster Wilson, *A Medieval Mirror: Speculum Humanae Salvationis 1324–1500* (Berkeley: University of California Press, 1984).

11. For a complete list of manuscripts, see Edgar Breitenbach, *Speculum Humanae Salvationis: Eine Typengeschichtliche Untersuchung* (Strassburg: Heitz, 1930).

12. As carried out in the following: Bert Cardon, *Manuscripts of the Speculum Humanae Salvationis in the Southern Netherlands (C. 1410–C. 1470)* (Corpus of Illuminated Manuscripts; Leuven: Uitgeverij Peeters, 1996); Avril Henry, "The Woodcuts of der Spiegel Menschlicher Behältnis in the Editions Printed by Drach and Richel," *Oud Holland* 99 (1985): 1–15; Anna C. Hoyt, "The Mirror of Man's Salvation," *Bulletin of the Museum of Fine Arts* 54, no. 298 (1956): 88–92; Herbert

this chapter, a few select images from the SHS of Job and his wife act as representatives of the fundamental iconography, form, and composition of the scene, regardless of variances and revisions. In terms of illustrations in SHS, Wilson and Wilson remark, "While the artists of the Speculum created manuscript miniatures that are very different in style from one copy to the other, they are fairly consistent in the iconography and the symbolism suited to the subjects."[13] The common symbolism found in the illustrations of SHS for Job and his wife is the subject of my discussion. That form is the visual alignment of Satan and Job's wife, both book-ending Job. The image is meant to typologically coincide with the flagellation of Christ. Furthermore, the SHS belongs to a theological tradition, which excludes a discussion of Eastern iconography of Job and his wife.

In general, however, Byzantium art remains elusively tied to the form of Job and his wife from early Christianity. For instance, a ninth-century copy of the sermons from Gregory of Nazianzus, a fourth-century Cappadocian, maintains the iconographical standard of Job's wife holding a stick out to Job with food on the end while covering her mouth with her shrouded left hand.[14] Two other similar examples come from Byzantine Bibles found in Patmos (possibly from the ninth century) and Venice (from ca. 905).[15] The Venice Job offers an example of "borderline Byzantine art proper" in terms of the Greek workshops in Italy. The Eastern connection remains clear.[16] And, the Leo Bible, another

---

L. Kessler, "The Chantily *Miroir De L'humaine Salvation* and Its Models," in *Studies in Late Medieval and Renaissance Painting in Honor of Millard Meiss* (New York: New York University Press, 1977), 274–82; W. Morris, "On the Artistic Qualities of the Woodcut Books of Ulm and Augsburg in the Fifteenth Century," *Bibliographica* 1 (1895): 437–55; Kathleen L. Scott, "Four Early Fifteenth-Century English Manuscripts of the *Speculum Humanae Salvationis* and a Fourteenth-Century Exemplar," *English Manuscript Studies, 1100–1700* 10 (2002): 177–203; Evelyn Silber, "The Reconstructed Toledo Speculum Humanae Salvatonis: The Italian Connection in the Early Fourteenth Century," *Journal of the Warburg and Courtauld Institutes* 43 (1980): 32–51.

13. Wilson and Wilson, *A Medieval Mirror*, 29.

14. Paris gr. 510, fol. 71v. Fig. 13 in Leslie Brubaker, *Vision and Meaning in Ninth-Century Byzantium: Images as Exegesis in the Homilies of Gregory of Nazianzus* (Cambridge: Cambridge University Press, 1999).

15. Venice, Marciana gr. 538, fol. 23r. Fig. 154 in Brubaker, *Vision and Meaning in Ninth-Century Byzantium*, 363. For more information on Byzantine bibles, see Kurt John Weitzmann, *Die Byzantinische Buchmalerei Des Ix. Und X. Jahrhunderts* (Berlin: Gebr. Mann, 1935).

16. Vat. MS. Gr. 746, as noted by André Grabar, *Byzantium: Byzantine Art in the Middle Ages* (trans. Betty Forster; London: Methuen, 1966), 170.

ninth-century illustrated Bible named after its commissioner, a grand chamberlain, which is the highest-ranking eunuch of the court, pictures Job's wife to the right of the image with her standard pose.[17] One variation to this is found in *Sacra Parallela*, a ninth-century Byzantine codex, in which Job sits facing front with his knees drawn up, encased by an earthen hill. Often, his wife stands to his side without her usual gesture. The *Sacra Parallela* functions as a Byzantine sourcebook for ascetical teachings based on Scripture and orthodox authoritative teachings for the purpose of providing a summary of approved Christian teachings.[18] The image of Job's earthen mound with his wife by his side also appears in the sixteenth-century manuscript of the commentary on the book of Job by Olymiodorus, deacon of Alexandria in the early sixth century.[19]

Two major differences exist between an early Christian standard form for Job's wife and medieval ones, in general. First, Job's wife uncovers her mouth; she no longer holds a veiled hand to her mouth. In early Christian art, Job's wife projects a pose with a veiled hand to the face, a symbol of a modesty for a wife in early Christianity. Moshe Barasch argues that medieval art specifically adopted the motif of grieving from classical art and that "the most frequently represented gestures of sadness are the more restrained movements that late Hellenistic and Roman sculptors inherited from classical Greek art," such as the raising of the veiled hand to the face. In other words, a woman's "classical formula for depicting grief and weeping" does not "disappear in the Middle Ages."[20] The gesture, however, disappears for Job's wife in the SHS.

At Notre Dame Cathedral in Paris, on the extremities of the central portal of the western façade, known as the portal of the Last Judgment, rest four small bas-reliefs, one of which includes Job surrounded by his wife and three friends (Fig. 2.2). Purposefully chosen for the buttress flanking the central portal, the four small sculptures were probably

17. The Leo Bible, Vat. Reg. gr. I. fol. 461iv.
18. Vat. gr. 749, ff. 26r, 27r, 28v, 30r, 119r, 126r, 152r, 153v, 157r, 179v, 190r. For a discussion of the version in Paris, see Kurt John Weitzmann, *The Miniatures of the Sacra Parallela, Parisinus Graecus 923* (Princeton, N.J.: Princeton University Press, 1979).
19. The Bodleian Library, MS. Laud Gr. 86, Folio #: p. 067. For a description of this work, see Chapter XIV in Henry Chadwick, *Studies on Ancient Christianity* (Variorum Collected Studies; Burlington, Vt.: Ashgate, 2006).
20. Moshe Barasch, *Gestures of Despair in Medieval and Early Renaissance Art* (New York: New York University Press, 1976), 11, 23. Anglo-Saxon gestures also adopt Roman stage gestures, and the veiled hand certainly indicates reverence: C. R. Dodwell, *Anglo-Saxon Gestures and the Roman Stage* (Cambridge: Cambridge University Press, 2000), 106.

arranged there when the portal was modified in 1240 C.E. Though its
original placement remains unknown, the small relief of Job and his wife
is one of four similar in style and design. They are the earliest surviving sculptures in the cathedral,[21] and represent a clear example of the
medieval departure from early Christian iconography for Job and his
wife.

Figure 2.2. Job, His Friends, and His Wife. Bas-relief on central portal of
the western façade, Notre Dame de Paris Cathedral, 11–12th century.
Photo: Katherine Low.

In Figure 2.2, two of Job's friends exhibit typical mourning gestures; one
friend stands behind Job with a hand on his shoulder and the other hand
to the side of his face while the other friend, not his wife, raises one
veiled hand to his face. In the sculpture, Job's wife faces Job and with-
draws her right hand away from him towards her chest. She holds her

    21. Alain Erlande-Brandenburg, *Notre-Dame de Paris* (New York: Abrams,
1998), 104–5.

dress with her left hand. To withdraw her right hand, according to medieval gesture, is to reserve her position on a matter. When two individuals shared an oath or expressed faith for one another, they touched or clasped right hands. "Handfasting" or clasping right hands while exchanging vows was a common way for a couple to marry.[22] Touching, or body contact, demonstrates friendship. Therefore, one of Job's friends touches his back. But his wife exhibits what J. A. Burrow calls "gestures of pride, like those of scorn or anger" since she stands "aloof from any touching of other persons."[23] In Anglo-Saxon gestures, adopted from the Roman stage, the lowering of one's arm and turning the palm away from the person being addressed also indicates a sign of dissent.[24]

Even more noticeable at Notre Dame is Job's wife's open mouth, connoting the act of speech. The sculpture provides an example of tensions surrounding Job's wife's verbalization in medieval imaginations. From her feminist perspective, Katharine Rogers summarizes medieval attitudes towards Job's wife:

> The episode in which Job's wife tells her husband to curse God and die—minor in the original book—has been magnified by later writers into a general indictment of wives. Her speech, intended to show poor Job failed even by the person who should have been closest to him, has been used as evidence that women never miss an opportunity to increase their husband's misery or to lead them into sin.[25]

The use of Job's wife to make a case for the worthlessness of wives certainly existed, but, her speech exemplifies much more in the cultural and theological landscape of medieval society. In the midst of a multitude of what was deemed heretical and "pagan" behaviors, the Church set about delineating its "proper" teachings; issues of gender exist as side-notes to larger concerns for the Latin Church Fathers.[26] This leads to the second major difference between early Christian art and medieval art depicting Job and his wife—the presence of Satan. Satan

22. Burrow, *Gestures and Looks in Medieval Narrative*, 11–16, 34–35.
23. Ibid., 48.
24. Dodwell, *Anglo-Saxon Gestures and the Roman Stage*, 60–61.
25. Katharine M. Rogers, *The Troublesome Helpmate: A History of Misogyny in Literature* (Seattle: University of Washington Press, 1966), 3.
26. So argued by Tomarsz Klibengajtis, "Hiobs Weib in der Exegese der Lateinischen Kirchenväter: Ein Beitrag zur Patristischen Frauenforschung," *Analecta Cracoviensia* 38–39 (2006–2007): 195–229. Klibengajtis argues that issues of misogyny remain secondary to the concerns of the Church Fathers and one should be cautious of such a general label for the specific issues that the Church Fathers are addressing, especially when it comes to the potential blasphemy and anti-Christian behavior they saw in Job's wife.

figures more prominently in illustrations of Job and his wife in medieval art. To recall Stuart Hall's audience distribution ideas, institutional reasons exist behind the visualization of Job and his wife.

The expansion of Christianity into the West from the seventh to the twelfth centuries required appropriate teaching materials for new converts, as well as constant examination of principles in light of distinct vernacular languages. Images, then, with no clear-cut rules about how to go about using them for the spiritual benefit of the laity, led to a myriad of artistic representations of the Bible. The development of *exempla*, illustrative biblical and cultural material in the form of short didactic tales of good conduct found especially in sermons, were intended to bring teachings to the people using the everyday life of the Middle Ages as example. Although medieval preachers warned against the idolatry involved in images, their suspicion generally subsided over and against the didactic merits of art to instruct. In Italy alone during the thirteenth and fourteenth centuries, Nirit Ben-Aryeh Debby demonstrates three different ways three separate preachers dealt with the arts in their sermons, noting the complexity and ambivalence some preachers had towards art. On the whole, Debby traces a general growing historical acceptance of art among preachers in its ability to provide visual biblical *exempla*.[27]

The idea of preaching in the Middle Ages developed from Gregory the Great's *Regula pastoralis* (590–604 C.E.) and its sense of the importance of clerical preaching. But, as the Middle Ages progressed, a more complex notion of the rhetorical devices for preaching for a popular audience emerged. By the thirteenth and fourteenth centuries, preachers engaged an array of gestures and styles to facilitate the messages of their sermons.[28] If preaching, after all, was meant to present religious ideals to

27. Nirit Ben-Aryeh Debby, "The Preacher as Goldsmith: The Italian Preachers' Use of the Visual Arts," in *Preacher, Sermon and Audience in the Middle Ages* (ed. Carolyn Muessig; Leiden: Brill, 2002), 127–53. For a collection of Latin *exempla*, see Thomas Frederick Crane, ed., *The Exempla or Illustrative Stories from the Sermones Vulgares of Jacques de Vitry* (Nendeln, Liechtenstein: Kraus Reprint, 1967).

28. Phyllis B. Roberts, "The Ars Praedicandi and the Medieval Sermon," in Muessig, ed., *Preacher, Sermon and Audience in the Middle Ages*, 41–62. For a discussion of gestures and performances used by preachers, see Beverly Mayne Kienzle, "Medieval Sermons and Their Performance: Theory and Record," in Muessig, ed., *Preacher, Sermon and Audience in the Middle Ages*, 89–124. For essays on the idolatry of visual images in literature, see Jeremy Dimmick, James Simpson, and Nicolette Zeeman, eds., *Images, Idolatry, and Iconoclasm in Late Medieval England: Textuality and the Visual Image* (New York: Oxford University Press, 2002).

the popular masses in order to persuade them to repent, images and stories (*exempla*) could aid them in that manner. Joan Young Gregg suggests that during the growth and expansion of Christianity, especially in the thirteenth century, "the popular sermon did not so much address social reform directly as focus on personal spiritual conversion as the root of all social improvement."[29]

Pictures function in illustrated texts as another level of meaning for spiritual devotion. Pictures were meant to be "read," to be studied and meditated upon as any written word.[30] Medieval hermeneutics were based on what Eric Jager calls "signifying relations held to be created by God and discovered through grace to the human understanding."[31] Scripture functioned in the West as a "polysemous text" full of significations. Reading allegorically and historically at the same time means that an exegete presumes an actual biblical event occurred as recorded and, at the same time, those events, characters, and images foreshadow or prophecy occurrences in the Christian era. According to Henri de Lubac, for instance, medieval exegetes maintained a "historicality" of Scripture in that "the historical development of the revelation and the allegorical interpretation of sacred history have essentially gone hand in hand."[32] In other words, medieval exegesis functioned to illuminate biblical history in light of Christ. Four "senses" medieval interpreters gleaned from the Scriptures include historical, allegorical, troplogical, and anagogical.[33]

Speculum Humanae Salvationis

This chapter mainly concerns itself with a kind of interpretation engaged in SHS for Job and his wife. Erich Auerbach's highly influential essay "Figura" defines typology, as it functions for the Church, as a way to ground history in both type and antitype: "Figural interpretation establishes a connection between two events or persons, the first of which signifies not only itself but also the second, while the second encompasses or fulfills the first."[34] The events or persons are understood

29. Gregg, *Devils, Women, and Jews*, 9.

30. Clanchy, *From Memory to Written Record*, 191–95.

31. Jager, *The Tempter's Voice*, 12.

32. Henri de Lubac, *Medieval Exegesis*. Vol. 3, *The Four Senses of Scripture* (trans. E. M. Macierowski; Grand Rapids: Eerdmans 2009), 267.

33. Ibid.

34. Erich Auerbach, *Scenes from the Drama of European Literature* (New York: Meridian, 1959), 53.

as real and concrete historical occurrences, and, history remains spiritu-ally provisional and in constant need of interpretation. Old Testament events, for instance, point to the incarnation and the fulfillment of the gospel, and the events of the New Testament point to the promise of the end, to the "true kingdom of God."[35]

Medieval exegesis was far from rigid about typology. The idea of one medieval typological method is an invention of modern scholarship. Instead, Richard Emmerson uses the phrase "traditional yet fluid and practical nature of medieval exegesis."[36] He draws upon the pictures and text of the SHS as an example of how types and antitypes often link to one another in flexible ways. The SHS finds "connections between type and antitype" from anything that seems reasonable and convincing.[37] Rather than thinking of the SHS as a typological book for its concern for historical events as types and antitypes, Emmerson regards it as a collec-tion of visual and literary *exempla*. It engages a multiplicity of stories and images to present Christian teaching effectively, to centralize the antitype as a model for a spiritual life, and to allow one to reflect on one's salvation.

The SHS emerged out of specific religious contexts and related to a particular group of consumers. The style of SHS follows the *Biblia Pauperum*, a thirteenth-century typological book with a series of pic-tures.[38] Like *Biblia Pauperum*, SHS was probably written for the general purpose of strengthening faith through text and image, but more speci-fically for guiding preachers on particular topics.[39]

Job and his wife hold a space in the SHS as one of the three Old Testament types that prefigure, or fulfill, a moment in Christ's life—his scourging. In Chapter 20, the SHS explains how Jesus is tied to a column and scourged. Visually, Christ remains in the center of the picture surrounded by two enemies on other side holding weapons with which to lash him. The first of the three Old Testament types that prefigure Christ's flagellation is the story of Holofernes's servant who ties Prince Achior to a tree (Jdt 5:5–29; 6:7–13); as SHS puts it, "The attendants

35. Ibid., 58.
36. Richard K. Emmerson, "*Figura* and the Medieval Typological Imagination," in Keenan, ed., *Typology and English Medieval Literature*, 16.
37. Ibid., 21.
38. Avril Henry, ed., *Biblia Pauperum: A Facsimile and Edition* (Ithaca, N.Y.: Cornell University Press, 1987); Albert C. Labriola and John W. Smeltz, eds., *The Bible of the Poor [Biblia Pauperum]: A Facsimile Edition of the British Library Blockbook C.9.D.2* (Pittsburgh, Pa.: Duquesne University Press, 1990).
39. Tibor Fabiny, *The Lion and the Lamb: Figuralism and Fulfilment in the Bible, Art and Literature* (New York: St. Martin's, 1992).

of Holofernes bind Achior to a tree, and Pilate's soldiers tie Christ to a column."[40]

The prefiguration of the actual whipping of Christ comes in the form of the spousal abuse of both Lamech and Job. Such a contrastable connection puts the wives on the same ideological plane as those who flagellate Christ. Ruth Mellinkoff's study of outcasts in late medival art notes that various instances of the "configuration and context" of the male bodies of the flagellators of Christ "create a sinful ugliness that contrasts with the serene and unblemished face of sinless Christ."[41] Therefore, the bodies of both men and women carry insinuations of sin in any given context.

Figure 2.3 is a page out of the SHS that demonstrates its traditional page design and layout, with two columns of text under two images at the top of the page. In the left illustration of Figure 2.3, two women labeled Sella and Ada hold Lamech between them while Ada raises her left hand in anticipation to strike him. The SHS states clearly that Lamech's two wives, Sella and Ada, prefigure both the "pagans" who beat Christ with whips and rods and the Jews who lash Christ with their tongue. The main source of the illustration comes from Peter Comestor's twelfth-century biblical paraphrase of Genesis *Historia Scholastica*; the biblical text does name Lamech's two wives (Gen 4:18–19). In some rabbinic traditions, Lamech becomes the murderer of Cain, mostly due to his continuing to use a bow after going blind and, therefore, accidentally murdering Cain.[42] In medieval Christian commentaries, Lamech's main reputation is that of a polygamous murderer. The fact that he kills Cain comes in secondary to Comestor in his introduction of Lamech as "the worst," because he "introduced bigamy, and thus committed adultery against the laws of nature and of God."[43]

40. Unless otherwise stated, all English quotes from the *Speculum Humanae Salvationis* come from the translation from the Latin by Labriola and Smeltz, eds., *The Mirror of Salvation [Speculum Humanae Salvationis]*.

41. Mellinkoff, *Outcasts*, 125.

42. Brian Murdoch, *The Medieval Popular Bible: Expansions of Genesis in the Middle Ages* (Cambridge: Brewer, 2003), 71–72. For examples of the theme of Lamech killing Cain in Dutch art, see Sandra Hindman, "Fifteenth-century Dutch Bible Illustration and the Historia Scholastica," *Journal of the Warburg and Courtauld Institutes* 37 (1974): 131–44.

43. PL 198, 1078–80: "et pessimus, qui primus bigamiam introduxit, et sic adulterium contra legem naturae et Dei decretum commisit." For more on Comestor's influences, see James H. Morey, "Peter Comestor, Biblical Paraphrase, and the Medieval Popular Bible," *Speculum* 68 (1993): 6–35.

Figure 2.3. *Speculum Humanae Salvationis*, MS. Douce 204, fol. 020v. Catalonia, Roussillon, ca. 1430–1450. The Bodleian Libraries, The University of Oxford.

The mistreatment of Lamech by his wives shows up less frequently in medieval vernacular texts, though the SHS concentrates on it exclusively.[44] Sella and Ada remain only two of many wives who notoriously

44. Murdoch, *The Medieval Popular Bible*, 77.

nag their husbands.[45] The illustration to the right of Lamech and his wives in Figure 2.3 shows Job surrounded by his wife and Satan. Satan whips Job with actual whips, whereas her words form a bubble with which she lashes at Job. It offers a prime example of the standard icono-graphical form in the SHS for Job and his wife.[46] As discussed in the previous chapter, Job's wife offers an example of gendered deviant speech that disorients theological truth to the husband's demise. The SHS visually communicates this when Job's wife literally uses her words to whip Job.

An underlying theme for both Lamech and Job is their marital difficul-ties. The text and illustrations didactically present the perils of marriage. Though most women in medieval society were married, Shulamith Shahar conjectures that the views of marriage based on a monastic life-style made an important cultural impact on medieval society even though the monastic population itself was smaller than the general married population.[47] Chastity was a preferred Christian way of life, based on Paul's concession on marriage in 1 Corinthians (7:9), that marriage is better than living a corruptible life. A second-best option, according to prevailing Church literature, was the mutual practice of celibacy in marriage.[48]

Given the general attitudes about marriage from medieval Christian clerics, it comes as no surprise that the SHS would present similar views. Mary and Joseph, married yet celibate, offer a prime example of the most ideal marital situation. The SHS launches into a series of justifications why Mary decided to marry Joseph when pregnant: to avoid judgment, to benefit from the support of a man, to illude Satan of the Incarnation, to have a witness of her chastity, to establish genealogical lineage, to present the validity of marriage, to demonstrate the legitimacy of a celibate marriage, and to give assurance to those married that not only

45. Reiss attributes this tradition of scolding wives to popular Middle English mystery plays about Genesis, the York and Towneley Cycles, in which Noah's wife scolds him for building the ark. The over-arching theme is the perverted pre-flood condition of order that prompts a wife to question her husband's authority: Edmund Reiss, "The Story of Lamech and Its Place in Medieval Drama," *Journal of Medieval and Renaissance Studies* 2 (1972): 35–48.

46. See, also, GKS 79, fol. 50, Germany, ca. 1430 from The Royal Library, Copenhagen. Online: http://www.kb.dk/permalink/2006/manus/218/eng/50+recto/?var.

47. Shahar, *The Fourth Estate*, 65.

48. Ibid., 67–71. For an overview of an ecclesiastical view of marriage, consult Georges Duby, *Medieval Marriage: Two Models from Twelfth-Century France* (Baltimore: The Johns Hopkins University Press, 1978).

virgins are among the elect. A medieval concept of order and hierarchy compels the author of the SHS to say that "The Lord approves every state if one does his or her duty."[49] Clearly, a standard view based on Church teachings of the hierarchal make-up of marriage exists within the SHS, a testament to its ecclesiastical origins.

Several theories exist about the source of the SHS; the most common explains that around 1286 to 1324, a Dominican friar compiled the traditional teachings and lessons of the mendicant orders in order to provide a manual to take to the streets of medieval Europe.[50] Involved in this theory, explains Kimberly Vrudny, whose dissertation offers another theory of authorship, is a development in late medieval Christianity concerning negative ideas about Christ. Historical developments, such as the plague or the Black Death, led to conceptions that Christ embodied divine wrath. Therefore, the SHS evidences Mary's intercessory role. Vrudny suggests that the Dominican Nicola da Milano and his Marian lay confraternity in Imola, Italy, remains responsible for authorship of the SHS. She compares Nicola's exegetical remarks in his personal notebook with the High Marian content of the SHS.[51]

Vrudny's study of the SHS centralizes the peoples' experiences with death as a context. The SHS offered another "mirror" through which to look besides the mirror of one's death, namely, "not the mirror of life with its focus on the transience of existence, but the mirror of human salvation with its focus on escape from death's grip through the unfolding of redemption history in Christ, and, significantly, the Virgin Mary."[52] The first outbreak of the Black Death occurred in 1346, around the time that the SHS began circulating. The war between the Italians and the Tartars over access to trade routes witnessed the outbreak when the Tartars besieged the Italians in Caffa, one of the port cities of the Black Sea north of Constantinople. When the illness plagued the Tartars, they catapulted the bodies of their dead into the city. Four days later, the disease took hold. Even when people could escape, they carried infested fleas with them throughout Europe.[53] From the middle of the thirteenth

49. SHS, Chapter 6. Labriola and Smeltz, eds., *The Mirror of Salvation [Speculum Humanae Salvationis]*, 28.

50. For more on authorship, see Wilson and Wilson, *A Medieval Mirror*, 26–27.

51. Kimberly Vrudny, "Scribes, Corpses, and Friars: Lay Devotion to the Genetrix, Mediatrix, and Redemptrix through Dominican Didactic Use of the *Speculum Humanae Salvationis* in Late Medieval Europe" (Ph.D. diss., Luther Seminary, 2001).

52. Ibid., 36.

53. Ibid., 36–40.

century, the Italians set up trading posts, which eventually became populated colonies due to the silk trade connecting Europe with China. Since the rat fleas avoided the smell of horses, nomads of central Asia were less vulnerable. Complex social, political, and populated stations of missionaries and merchants were more susceptible to plague infection.[54]

Such a widespread disease with an unknown cause elicited theological reactions of God's punishment. Furthermore, the years after the outbreak brought about a change in the quality of the Church's services. "Europe at the time of plague, then, was a society reeling under repeated, powerful shocks"; states David Herlihy, "burdened with huge numbers of dependents; struggling with difficulty to maintain its occupational cadres."[55] In the face of such disaster, many clerics held on to the Church's core beliefs for stability. Yet, by the fifteenth century, the amount of young men entering the order without the quality of learning and training of previous years increased.[56] Therefore, the SHS not only served a theological need to offer hope to its readers, but it also provided a training manual in many different languages for the clerics preaching and teaching among the varied population.

In his book *From Memory to Written Record*, M. T. Clanchy argues that literacy, writing and reading, is as culturally bound in medieval England as it is in the twentieth-century Western world. Medieval readers held personal connections with their manuscripts and expected to read on many levels, including giving attention to the artistic details surrounding the text. Clanchy also calls into question a modern assumption that literacy equates to civilization, or that illiteracy leads to mental confinement. Furthermore, "literacy" in the medieval world meant that one had the ability to comprehend and engage in Latin.[57]

Beginning in 1066 with the Norman Conquest of England, Norman conquerors suppressed English in favor of French vernacular, although Latin replaced Old English in written language. The written French

---

54. Biologically, the plague had two types in this case, bubonic and pneumonic. Bubonic, the most common, comes from a flea's bite which transfers bacilli into the human system that incubates for two to eight days. After the inception of fever, vomiting and pain in the limbs, the lymph glands swell to the size of an egg or larger. Pneumonic plague occurs when the bacilli cause pneumonia which can pass from one human to another. David Herlihy, *The Black Death and the Transformation of the West* (Cambridge, Mass.: Harvard University Press, 1997), 20–23.

55. Ibid., 46.

56. Ibid.

57. Michael Camille, "Seeing and Reading: Some Visual Implications of Medieval Literacy and Illiteracy," *Art History* 8 (1985): 28.

language developed in England; the common written language in France at that time was actually Latin. In England, monks learned to write English and Latin. Nevertheless, the vast majority of rural medieval dwellers could not read or write. Clanchy argues that lay literacy grew out of ruling bureaucracy during the twelfth and thirteenth centuries in England, if not throughout medieval Europe.[58]

Besides monks preserving the Bible and the teachings of the Church Fathers through careful copying, burgeoning liturgical readings, such as illuminated liturgical manuscripts, Books of Psalms, or Gospel Books, underwent a large development over the twelfth and thirteenth centuries. Silver, gold, and silk adorned liturgical books since these books decorated the altar during formal service: "Every bishop and abbot wanted the shiniest and most advanced model of liturgical book" as a sign of status.[59] From the thirteenth century onward, the aristocracy sought personal prayer books. The emergence of the university and the medieval copying centers of the thirteenth century moved the book out of the monastic libraries and into a wider segment of the population.[60] Interactive books with large lettering and numerous illustrations allowed one to view the book even if one could not read. Repetition of the liturgy in churches allowed for textual familiarity. This led to the production of Books of Hours in the later Middle Ages, which are portable prayer manuals covering the liturgical hours for the laity which contained elaborate decorations based on the price. A gendered dimension exists in the personal liturgical books, as Clanchy notes: "through Books of Hours, ladies introduced their families and children to prayer... This domestication of the liturgical book was the foundation on which the growing literacy of the later Middle Ages was built."[61] This kind of private reading remained a luxury since a book's scarcity and cost meant that most of the time a book was read aloud to a group.

The SHS most likely circulated in such a manner, in contexts of private devotion, as early as 1350 around medieval Europe, first in Latin and then, as over 300 fourteenth- and fifteenth-century surviving manuscripts

58. Clanchy, *From Memory to Written Record*, 16–19.

59. Ibid., 110.

60. For more on secular book reproduction, see Graham Pollard, "The Pecia System in the Medieval Universities," in *Medieval Scribes, Manuscripts, and Libraries: Essays Presented to N. R. Ker* (ed. M. B. Parkes and Andrew G. Watson; London: Scolar, 1978), 145–61.

61. Clanchy, *From Memory to Written Record*, 112, 251–52. For more on women and the Books of Hours as devotional literature, see Kathryn A. Smith, *Art, Identity and Devotion in Fourteenth-Century England* (Toronto: University of Toronto Press, 2003).

attest, in several translations.[62] The need for private devotion and consolation increased after the plague. The connection between women and private devotion finds a resonance in the SHS in terms of the mass deaths of children due to the plague. Vrudny suggests that the focus on the Virgin Mary offered an empathetic image for those mourning the loss of a child because Mary herself experienced the loss of her son and would offer consolation of the reunification of loved ones after death.[63] Of course, this consolation was afforded to those who could patronize the creation of such luxuries as a personal devotional book. Wilson and Wilson note that several hundred copies of the SHS from the first part of the fourteenth century and on into the fifteenth century were produced, "nearly all illuminated," at a time "when the lessons of piety, the allegories, and all of the arts were devoted to instilling in the minds of the people the need for salvation and the dread of eternal damnation."[64]

In general, the morbidity of the Middle Ages remains an irrefutable fact.[65] A preoccupation with death shaped the very organization of the Church. Liturgical evidence from the various versions of the *Office of the Dead*, an early Christian liturgy, demonstrates a much more suffering Job, including his words of misery, despair, and loss (Job 7:16–21; 10:1–7, 8–12; 13:22–28; 14:1–6, 13–16; 17:1–3, 11–16; 19:20–27; 20:18–23). The date of the *Office of the Dead* is contested, but by the seventh century, Christian communities read it at funeral services for their loved

---

62. For those manuscripts in which pictures are not included, Kathleen Scott surmises that such copies were used in religious houses that supported private contemplation and solitary reading rather than preaching or meditating on pictures for spiritual application: Scott, "Four Early Fifteenth-Century English Manuscripts of the *Speculum Humanae Salvationis*," 197–98.

63. Vrudny, "Scribes, Corpses, and Friars," 57. Vrudny notes how the greatest level of popularity comes from the latter part of the fourteenth century, after the hit of the plague. Given the argument for consolation at the loss of children, it is interesting that the SHS does not depict, nor mention, the loss of the children of Job and his wife. SHS Chapter 25, however, depicts Mary's sorrow for the loss of her son with Jacob grieving for Joseph, Adam and Eve mourning Abel, and Naomi bewailing the death of her two sons. Shulamith Shahar notes a general ecclesiastical disinterest in children based on both experience and infant mortality rate and concepts of original sin: Shahar, *The Fourth Estate*, 103–5. For more on children in medieval societies, see Philippe Ariès, *Centuries of Childhood: A Social History of Family Life* (trans. Robert Baldick; New York: Knopf, 1962).

64. Wilson and Wilson, *A Medieval Mirror*, 10.

65. Eamon Duffy, *The Stripping of the Altars: Traditional Religion in England 1400–1580* (2d ed.; New Haven: Yale University Press, 2005), Chapter 9, "Last Things," elaborates on the theme of death in the Middle Ages.

ones.[66] The lessons from Job in the *Office of the Dead*, paraphrased and elaborated upon depending on the context, are called "Pety Jobs," or "little Jobs." Job functioned as the primary biblical figure in the *Office* as it developed throughout the Middle Ages, although the liturgy paraphrases Job's speeches, not mentioning Job's name, but keeping the words in first person so that the reader can relate to the "I" of the text.[67] Therefore, many Books of Hours illustrate Job, but, as no standard for Books of Hours existed, some do not include Job, especially since the *Office of the Dead* holds Job's anonymity in the liturgy.

Job's individual sufferings used in the *Office of the Dead*, providing for the context of individual bereavement, omits the debate with the three friends and God's wager with the Devil.[68] It is this context of individual suffering out of which a Spanish rendition of the Job texts in the *Office of the Dead* find a poetic profane parody by Garci Sánchez Badajoz from around 1516. The poem, "Las Leciones de Job," subverts the solemnity and turns it into a context for passion; it opens with the following: "Pues amore quiere que muera" ("for love wishes that I die"). His death comes from unrequited amorous passion. The work received a backlash from the Church, which suggested that the poem made a profanity out of sacred scriptures.[69]

The Church drew lines between acceptable and unacceptable ideas about Job. The SHS presents an acceptable translation of Joban tradition from Latin clerical culture for a vernacular audience. Preaching manuals of the thirteenth century, according to Claire Waters, "make it clear that the cultural difference between clergy and laity was one that had to be constructed and carefully maintained."[70] As part of the *exempla* preaching tradition, the SHS demonstrates both a concern for the learned culture of theological tradition passed down from the Latin fathers and a

66. See the chapter on Job in Medieval Christian Liturgy in Vicchio, *Job in the Medieval World*, 44–66. For a discussion of the context of the *Office of the Dead*, see Renevey, "Looking for a Context."

67. Besserman, *The Legend of Job in the Middle Ages*, 57–65, 79–84.

68. James H. Morey, *Book and Verse: A Guide to Middle English Biblical Literature*, Illinois Medieval Studies (Chicago: University of Illinois Press, 2000), 168–69.

69. Víctor Infantes, "Las Lecciones de Job en Caso de Amores, Trobadas por Garcí Sánchez de Badajoz," in *Un Volumen Facticio de Raros Post-Incunables Españoles* (Madrid: Pareja, 1999). Volume 1 of this work includes a facsimile of the poem.

70. Claire M. Waters, "Talking the Talk: Access to the Vernacular in Medieval Preaching," in *The Vulgar Tongue: Medieval and Postmedieval Vernacularity* (ed. Fiona Somerset and Nicholas Watson; University Park: Pennsylvania State University Press, 2003), 35.

desire to make a connection to the common culture. Within this connection rests a reason why SHS illustrates Job and his wife in terms of
concern for the wife's verbal abuse of the husband, alongside a satanic
spiritual crisis—the main Christian tradition of a saintly Job blasted by
spiritual foes holds no room for his wife's gender role to fluctuate to that
of loving spouse. The SHS upholds Job's wife as a mechanism of a
dangerous kind of spiritual expression, that of gendered speech.

The words in the SHS describe an external/internal contrast between
carnal and spiritual. The SHS encapsulates a long tradition of interpretation that suggests Satan made Job's wife act wickedly toward her
husband with problematic speech:

> Job was whipped two ways. Satan scourged him with whips, and his wife
> lashed him with words, the one causing pain in his body, and other
> causing pain in his heart. Satan felt the hurt that he caused in the flesh
> was not sufficient so that he instigated Job's wife to wound her husband's
> spirit.[71]

Though variances exist, illustrations in the SHS function to highlight
Job's whippings. In many cases, Satan holds an actual whip, whereas
Job's wife needs nothing in her hands because her pointing finger indicates that she engages speech. The gesture is a common one for Job's
wife in the SHS and in other sources.[72] The medieval artists engage a
Roman artistic gesture for speech, which is the presence of raised hands
or of pointing.[73]

Often, Job's wife points to a scroll floating in mid-air. In other words,
she points to her words which are encapsulated in writing. Job's wife
often points to a scroll, for in medieval illumination "scrolls were used
iconographically to indicate speech."[74] Michael Camille elaborates:

71. SHS XX, ll. 69–74: "Beatus Job fuit flagellates doubus modis/Quia Satan
flagellavit eum verberibus, et uxor verbis;/De flagello Satanae sustenuit dolorem in
carne,/De flagello linguae habuit turbationem in corde;/Non suffecit diabolo quod
flagellabat carnem exterius,/Nisi etiam instigaret uxorem, quae irritaret cor interius."

72. See GKS 80.2 *Speculum Humane Salvationis*, fol. 42v. 1400–50, The Royal
Library, Copenhagen.

73. As noted in terms of the iconography of Trajan's Column on Fig. 7 in
Lawrence Nees, *Early Medieval Art* (Oxford: Oxford University Press, 2002), 19.

74. Clanchy, *From Memory to Written Record*, 257. For an example, Job's wife
holds a scroll in her left hand and points her right index finger in front of Job as he
sits on his dungheap in the Bury Bible, a twelfth-century bible that survives in only
one volume. For a reproduction, see C. M. Kauffmann, *Biblical Imagery in Medieval
England, 700–1550* (London: Miller, 2003), 103 Fig. 71. For a detailed discussion,
consult C. M. Kauffmann, "The Bury Bible (Cambridge, Corpus Christi College,
Ms. 2)," *Journal of the Warburg and Courtauld Institutes* 29 (1966): 60–81.

> As opposed to the roll of earlier times, the codex allowed the reader to recapitulate, skim, check text against picture and refer forwards in ways not possible with the roll, which like speech itself, unfolds in one linear direction. It is probably for this reason that "speech" is signified in medieval art by scrolls held by the talkers in images.[75]

The visual incorporation of speech is a method of taking an impersonal past event and making it part of the historic present. In religious contexts, a parchment roll distinguishes a Jew from a Christian because Jews used scrolls in synagogues whereas Christians used books in churches. Furthermore, in legal proceedings, Jews swore by the roll and Christians by the book. In painting and sculpture, the God and prophets of the Old Testament hold scrolls, but Christ of the New Testament does not, for he often holds the Book of Judgment to remind the faithful of the Last Judgment.[76]

From a practical standpoint, the *bubbles* of speech communicate a real-time effect that shows influence from medieval mystery plays. Pächt argues for a correlation between the portrayal of speech and the dramas that emerged in medieval society beginning in the twelfth century: "the revival of story-telling in the twelfth century started with an enactment of spoken narrative in visual form and…it is only later that we find pictorial narrative gradually proceeding from the literal transcription of words to the visual realization of scenes and actions."[77] Furthermore, Pächt suggests that "it was the word that became flesh," and this word-image or *figure* of speech "applied to portray the real situation," so that "the mystery itself became tangible."[78]

As a tangible reality in medieval art, the power of Job's wife's words causes anxiety, especially in a culture that stifles women's voices. As Danielle Régnier-Bohler states, "Eve became the model of an arduous relation to language" because the first dialogue in which she engages "led to the expulsion from Eden and set humankind on the path of history. Women with voices, speaking for their sisters, would atone for this imprudent dialogue."[79] The SHS presents this clearly enough: "Although it is not found in the text of the Bible, it is certain that Eve had adulated Adam with flattering words. Be attentive, therefore, to the

75. Camille, "Seeing and Reading," 29.

76. Clanchy, *From Memory to Written Record*, 139–40.

77. Otto Pächt, *The Rise of Pictorial Narrative in Twelfth-Century England* (Oxford: Clarendon, 1962), 59.

78. Ibid., 56.

79. Danielle Régnier-Bohler, "Literary and Mystical Voices," in Klapisch-Zuber, ed., *A History of Women in the West*, 428.

ability of a woman to deceive."[80] Images of Job and his wife in the SHS place them in the middle of this warning. Job's wife's words visually lash Job.

Another visual indication of Job's wife's deviance is her bodily posture. The position of the gendered body sends implicit messages to the viewer. A copy of the SHS from the fifteenth century (Fig. 2.4) demonstrates how visually to present Job's wife's dominance over her husband without the clear presence of words.

Figure 2.4. *Mirror of Human Salvation*. France, 15th century C.E. Ms. 139, fol. 22 recto. René-Gabriel Ojéda at Musée Condé, Chantilly, France. Photo: Réunion des Musées Nationaux / Art Resource, N.Y.

In Figure 2.4, Job's wife is dressed in common modest fashion for a presentable married woman. Her close-fitting bodice cut to show the neck with a long skirt was a common dress. Her headdress, a padded

---

80. SHS Chapter 1. Labriola and Smeltz, eds., *The Mirror of Salvation [Speculum Humanae Salvationis]*, 19.

circlet of fabric, a *bourrelet*, rolled and worn like a turban, was common in the early fifteenth century.[81] Figure 2.4 follows blockbook illustrations but presents the miniatures in a more sophisticated Ghent-Bruges style, a Flemish style that synthesized the qualities of art from both its neighbors, England and France.[82]

The stance of Job's wife in Figure 2.4 merits attention. She stands with both hands on her hips, a gesture known as "akimbo." Both hands on the hips, or just one hand the hip, signifies a "scornful sense of superiority," for the posture "extends the amount of space claimed by a body."[83] This visual reminder of Job's wife's leads us to the next chapter, which presents Job's marriage as a form of torture to the husband because of a demanding, outspoken, quarrelsome, and scold of a wife. Furthermore, the menacing presence of Satan delineates spiritual as well as carnal challenges to a husband.

81. Joan Evans, *Dress in Mediaeval France* (Oxford: Clarendon, 1952), 50–51.

82. Wilson and Wilson, *A Medieval Mirror*, 81.

83. Burrow, *Gestures and Looks in Medieval Narrative*, 44–45. For how this extends into Renaissance art, see Joaneath Spicer, "The Renaissance Elbow," in *A Cultural History of Gesture* (ed. Jan Bremmer and Herman Roodenburg; Ithaca, N.Y.: Cornell University Press, 1991), 84–128.

Chapter 3

SATAN'S DISAPPEARANCE FROM THE DUNGHEAP
AND JOB'S WIFE AS RENAISSANCE SHREW

In line with medieval artistic tendencies to present Job, his wife, and
Satan all together at the dungheap, the troublesome trio appears on the
Chartres Cathedral. Their presence attests to the popularity, especially in
medieval French drama and literature, of visually presenting the three in
proximity to one another in order to highlight certain popular theological
messages about the book of Job. Everyday encounters with such messages took place. Chartres Cathedral dominated the town in the Middle
Ages, serving as a center not only for religious authorities but for civic
events as well. People had homes built right against the cathedral, local
festivals were held out front, and stores existed around it. Artisans and
craftspeople came from all parts of the country to serve the Church's
commission and patronage for the religious arts.[1] The present cathedral is
mostly a result of the twelfth and thirteenth centuries, which is the time
period assigned to the sculpture of Job, his wife, friends, and Satan on
the north portal.[2] The sculpture depicts Job lying down scraping his left
arm with a shard while Satan rests his right hand on Job's head. Satan's
claw-like left hand holds on to Job's left foot. Job's wife's hands extend
outwards, but the damage to the sculpture does not allow a clear idea of
her gesture. She does, however, have a small smile on her face, one that
Terrien interprets as a sign of loving and humane administration and
support of her husband.[3] The three friends look on and God sits above
Job's head.[4]

1. Robert Branner, ed., *Chartres Cathedral* (Norton Critical Study in Art
History; New York: W. W. Norton & Co., 1969).
2. Job, Satan, and his wife, ca. 1220. Chartres Cathedral, north transept portal,
right tympanum.
3. Samuel Terrien, *The Iconography of Job Through the Centuries: Artists as
Biblical Interpreters* (University Park: Pennsylvania State University Press, 1996),
76.
4. The image of God above, flanked by two angels on each side, while Job is
menaced by demons, can also be seen in "Job on the Dungheap," Rouen Book of

In similar fashion, Job and his wife appear with Satan at the Reims Cathedral, which dates from around 1220 C.E.[5] The Reims sculpture includes mourning women indicative of Roman iconography, and it remains unknown if the grieving woman at Job's head, or at his feet, is his wife.[6] For Reims and Chartres, large workshops headed by master sculptors worked for years to produce the sculptures. They retrieved the stone from thousands of limestone quarries throughout Europe. It was common in the thirteenth century for sculptors to work with separate blocks in workshops, allowing wage-workers the task of heaving the individually carved sculptures to their places. Before, in the twelfth century, artists would carve statues in *situ*. In most cases, clergy made the decisions on the kinds of subjects to be depicted, whereas the master builders negotiated the practical work of building and production.[7] Sculptors' workshops produced various forms of typological art on Job for cathedrals such as Rheims and Chartres based on popular themes, especially those recounted in the SHS.[8]

Despite the unknown iconographical issues, both the Reims and the Chartres sculptures include a devilish figure that stands among Job and Job's wife. The same holds true for a rendition of Job and his wife with Satan standing behind them, juxtaposed with Jesus being mocked by soldiers, on the Doberan Abbey altarpiece from 1360–66 in Mecklenburg, Germany.[9] The depictions of Job and his wife in the stained-glass windows of St. Patrice from the sixteenth century in Rouen include the inscription concerning both Satan's and Job's wife's torture of Job:

Hours, fifteenth century. MS Buchanen e. 3, Fol. 055r, Bodleian Library, University of Oxford. The image does not include Job's wife or friends, but, rather, a group of four demons that wields clubs in anticipation to strike Job while he reclines on a pile of dung.

   5. Tympanum of the north portal, also called the Portal of S. Remi by Arthur Gardner, "The Sculptures of Rheims Cathedral," *The Burlington Magazine* 26, no. 140 (1914): 54.

   6. Terrien believes that Elihu is presented as a feminine figure in the sculpture at Reims in the group of four people on the sculpture's right side. Therefore, he identifies the woman with the hands clasped over her mouth as his wife. Terrien, *The Iconography of Job through the Centuries*, 79.

   7. The master builder of Chartres remains unknown because of missing records. The master builder of Reims has a tomb inside the cathedral itself. For more on the roles of the master builders, see Philip Ball, *Universe of Stone: A Biography of Chartres Cathedral* (New York: HarperCollins, 2008), 139–69.

   8. Cardon, *Manuscripts of the Speculum Humanae Salvationis*, 19.

   9. For a full view of the altarpiece and discussion of its architecture, see Donald L. Ehresmann, "Some Observations on the Role of Liturgy in the Early Winged Altarpiece," *The Art Bulletin* 64, no. 3 (1982): 359–69, plate 1.

Satan réduit le bon Job en grand misère/Et sa femme en sa colère/ Insulte méchamment à sa simplicité.[10] Job's one-line lament from *Patience* sums up an entire motif in medieval art that depicts Satan on one side of Job and his wife on another: "On the one hand I am hunted by the devil,/On the other I am menaced by my wife."[11] A French manuscript of the SHS made in Bruges in 1455 features this motif (Fig. 3.1).

Figure 3.1. *Miroir de l'humaine salvation.* MS Hunter 60, fol. 29v. Bruges, 1455. University of Glasgow Library. By permission of University of Glasgow Library, Special Collections.

Medieval art of cathedrals and churches functioned as "the necessary link" between the powers of ecclesiastical commissioners and the emerging unification of political systems. The need for political unification provides reasons for why medieval exegetes connected Job's wife to issues of gendered performance concerning the power of speech and accurate transmissions. Furthermore, the centralizing of political power and monarchic government over and against the feudal and vassal systems of the early Middle Ages attributed to the formation of a clear-cut Satan in fourteenth-century art. "Art produced a very specific and highly figurative discourse" on a demonic kingdom to emphasize the power of sin that compels a Christian to confession: "the portrayal of Satan and the related pastoral message encouraged not only religious obedience, but recognition of the power of Church and State, cementing the social order by recourse to a strict moral code."[12] It need not matter to medieval artists that both Satan and Job's wife disappear in the book

10. Garmonsway and Raymo, "A Middle English Metrical Life of Job," 82 n. 3.
11. Lines 5718–5719: "D'une part le dyable me chasse,/L'aultre ma femme me mesnasse." Translation from Besserman, *The Legend of Job in the Middle Ages*, 104.
12. Robert Muchembled, *A History of the Devil: From the Middle Ages to the Present* (trans. Jean Birrell; Malden, Mass.: Polity, 2003), 24.

after the second chapter because both Job's wife and Satan serve as symbols of Job's story in terms of his ability to overcome temptation. Even if Job's wife offers a loving nursemaid presence, as argued by some,[13] she still serves as a reminder to medieval audiences, alongside Satan, of Job's spiritual struggle and physical defamation.

This chapter begins with a brief section on concepts of Satan as they pertain to bodily configurations of evil in medieval renditions of Job on the dungheap. The discussion of images of Satan relates to Job's wife in many ways. When Satan's grotesque body disappears, or takes on more generic forms in early modern art of the dungheap, the images also place less emphasis on Job's wife as part of Satan's schemes for deviant speech, and instead emphasize more general visualizations of Job's wife as a shrew.

The first section of this chapter highlights a central theme, that of Job's sore-ridden body sending a message of spiritual endurance in light of a grotesque and gendered presence of the demonic body. When humanisms, and other movements, call into question the nature of evil, images of the evil that plague Job become more subtle. This subtlety reflects a developing artistic style that de-emphasizes Satan. By the late sixteenth century, images of Job reflect a kind of sentimentalism that displayed Job in agony, and his wife as another cause of his agony. In other words, a concern to place Job's wife alongside Eve as a deviant transmitter of language subsides by the late sixteenth century and gives way to more generic forms of gendered expectations. The second section elaborates on Baroque art and its move generically to involve Satan and emphasize Job's wife as shrew. Rather than visually recall Job's wife as an actor of deviant speech, reminiscent of Eden's dunghill, Baroque artists reduce Job's wife to a simple monotone character, a "bad wife."

Medieval Bodies: Job and Satan

The physical characteristics of Satan in medieval art on Job signal common medieval messages of Job's outward signs of a spiritual struggle against Satan. In Figure 3.1, an illustration from a manuscript of the SHS, the animalistic body of Satan, including the traditional clawed feet and bat wings, also includes large breasts.

---

13. For instance, Terrien states that the presence of Satan unites the human figures in solidarity, interpreting Job's wife at Chartres as a sympathetic companion: Terrien, *The Iconography of Job Through the Centuries*, 73–74.

Figure 3.2. Untitled work of an anonymous artist, in Ulrich Pinder, *Speculum Patientie*, Nuremburg, 1509. Bayersiche Staatsbibliothek München, Beibd.1, fol. 65v.

Wilson and Wilson describe the 1455 French translation of the SHS, produced in Bruges by an anonymous artist for an anonymous patron (compare with Fig. 2.4), as "*de luxe* manuscript" with its rich touches of gold, possibly produced for Philip the Good.[14] The composite-beast Satan remains common in illustrations.[15] The warped Satan with misshaped and shriveled breasts appears in an anonymous woodcut from Ulrich Pinder's *Speculum Patientiae* from Nuremberg, 1509; Satan also whips Job while he sits in a melancholic pose (Fig. 3.2).[16]

14.   Wilson and Wilson, *A Medieval Mirror*, 19, 73. Under the influence of the Burgundian court, Bruges served as the center of *de luxe* manuscript production, which provided that scribes copied text leaving no room for illustrations. The illustrations, produced in artistic workshops, were then added later and thus were large, full-page, paintings.

15.   For instance, "The Temptation of Christ," Chapter 13 in *Mirror of Human Salvation*. France, fifteenth century C.E. Ms. 139, fol. 14 verso. At Musée Condé, Chantilly, France.

16.   Another painting of scenes from the life of Job by an unknown Flemish artist from around 1480 also incorporates bestial devils. The one that whips Job has large nipples; another devil with a penis stands amidst the group of devils behind the one

Satan's "grotesque" form, though hard to define, blurs lines between human and inhuman, between ideal and abnormal, and between control and chaos. Whereas Margaret Miles has argued that the female body in Western art has come to be associated with the grotesque because of an association between the female body and materiality,[17] it is more likely that Satan's breasts represent the Devil's monstrosity and lack of adherence to socially approved behavior. The grotesque body, Miles notes, functions "to identify, define, and thus to stabilize a feared and fantasized object."[18] David Lawton makes note of the importance of the body politic in understanding the carnivalesque Satanic body for medieval Christians. The grotesque body of the Devil counteracts the ideal body of Christian believers, or, "the carnival representation of the bad thus serves to reflect and stabilize the image of the good."[19] Lawton's notion lends itself to a medieval theological interpretation of the juxtaposition between Job's suffering body and the disgusting body of Satan in medieval illustrations. The sexualized Satan, almost pleasurable in its ambiguous masculine strength and its feminine attributes, crosses boundaries.[20] Job's body, on the other hand, stabilizes Satan's animalistic and spiritually unsound flesh.

Job's bodily suffering indicates his spiritual fortitude, over and against the grotesque demonic body and the female body of his wife that accompanies him at the dungheap. Medieval artists do not hesitate to portray Job nude with sores covering his body. His nudity, very rampant in medieval depictions, falls under the category of *nuditas virtualis*, the

whipping Job: Flemish master, *Scenes from the Life of Job*, 1480–1490. Wallraf-Ricartz Museum, Cologne. The painting is the right wing of a triptych altarpiece commissioned by an Italian merchant working in the Netherlands, Claudio Villa. His brother Pietro Villa built a chapel of Job in Chieri. The whole painting actually depicts elements from the Testament of Job and from the French mystery play. Yet another Flemish source from around 1525 by Simon Bening features Job seated, his wife standing by pointing her finger at Job, while two small devils whip him, one of which has feminine features: Simon Bening, border of illuminated manuscript of Job 1, Flemish, Bruges, ca. 1525–1530. MS. Ludwig IX 19, fol. 155, The J. Paul Getty Museum, Los Angeles.

17. Margaret R. Miles, *Carnal Knowing: Female Nakedness and Religious Meaning in the Christian West* (Vintage Books ed.; New York: Vintage, 1991), 145–68.

18. Ibid., 152.

19 Lawton, *Blasphemy*, 51.

20. Or, to put it another way, "he enfolds his victim like a woman and penetrates like a man, until the boundary between possessor and possessed is erased." In Andrew Delbanco, *The Death of Satan: How Americans Have Lost the Sense of Evil* (New York: Farrar, Straus & Giroux, 1995), 34.

nakedness that symbolizes "primordial innocence to which everyone shall return at the resurrection of the flesh."[21] In this Christian medieval tradition, the primordial innocence of nudity harkens back to Eden, as even Philippe Guillaume notes that Job, in refusing the fruit of his wife (her suggestion to curse God and die), Job also rejects the coverings God provided for the first humans (Gen 3:21), maintaining his Eden-like innocence. Whether his nudity in the MT provides a cue to sapiential wisdom and the discarding of illusions of earthly protection, as suggested by Guillaume, medieval minds would have understood the *nuditas virtualis* message in representations of Job's body.[22]

The body, according to Mary Douglas, serves as the primary instrument through which societies communicate their limits and beliefs.[23] The main belief echoed in portraying Job naked (or almost naked) comes from Vrudny's observation that the Church "combated a fatalistic view of the world with its promise of redemption," especially in terms of the soul's resurrection despite what the body might suffer.[24] Therefore, when sores cover Job's body in medieval art, they function as external signs inviting the viewer to reflect on human failings of sin indicative of Satan's work. "In the manner of Job's 'agew,'" remarks Margaret Healy, Job's visual sores "verify the presence of man's inner corruption through original sin, and...bring the elect to timely repentance."[25] As Carol Walker Bynum states about the body in the Middle Ages, "the cultivation of bodily experience" meant that the body was "a place for encounter with meaning, a locus of redemption."[26]

The proliferation of demonic presence in scenes depicting Job in the Middle Ages attests to an increase in the Devil's intensity to frighten, an increase Jeffrey Burton Russell attributes to the "terrifying famines and plagues" of the fourteenth and fifteenth centuries.[27] An illustration found in a rare book written by an Alsatian army surgeon Hans von Gersdorff

21. Warner, *Monuments and Maidens*, 304.

22. Philippe Guillaume, "Job le Nudiste ou la Genèse de la Sagesse," *BN* 88 (1997): 19–26.

23. Mary Douglas, *Natural Symbols: Explorations in Cosmology* (New York: Pantheon, 1970).

24. Vrudny, "Scribes, Corpses, and Friars," 48.

25. Margaret Healy, "'Seeing' Contagious Bodies in Early Modern London," in *The Body in Late Medieval and Early Modern Culture* (ed. Darryll Grantley and Nina Taunton; Burlington, Vt.: Ashgate, 2000), 157–67.

26. C. W. Bynum, "Why All the Fuss About the Body? A Medievalist's Perspective," *Critical Inquiry* 22, no. 1 (1995): 15.

27. Jeffrey Burton Russell, *Lucifer: The Devil in the Middle Ages* (Ithaca, N.Y.: Cornell University Press, 1984), 208.

demonstrates how a demonic form of the Devil gets blamed for causing illness. Gersdorff's *Feldtbuch der Wundartzney* acted as a "Field Manual for Wound Doctors" in the early 1500s. The section illustrating skin diseases, such as leprosy and sexually transmitted diseases, features Job, his wife, and a hovering Satan (Fig. 3.3).

Figure 3.3. Untitled work of an anonymous artist, in Hans von Gersdorff, *Feldtbuch der Wundartzney*, Augsburg, ca. 1532. Bayersiche Staatsbibliothek München, 4P. lat. 1175.

Numerous examples exist that include Job as an illustration of skin disease,[28] such as a woodcut image of Job sitting on his dungheap, resting

28. Martin Jan Bok's (1597–1671) painting of a scene of inmates at the St. Job hospital in Utrecht, witnesses to the existence of medical Job traditions. The painting, at Utrecht's Centraal Museum, is but one of many given to the hospital. Another hospital was established near the San Giobbe church in Venice. Hamburg also had a St. Job's hospital for smallpox patients founded in 1505. Apparently, Job's relation to skin diseases also relates to his connection with music in terms of the role musicians play in soothing the sick. See Kathi Meyer, "St. Job as a Patron of Music," *The Art Bulletin* 36, no. 1 (1954): 21–31. For an analysis of the wider

his left hand on his chin in a melancholic pose, being whipped from the Devil standing behind him, while musicians play in his presence.[29] Another example comes from the monogrammist "Bos with a Knife" (possibly Michiel van Gemert), who depicts Job on his dungheap with his arms crossed on his chest, with three musicians playing in front of him and a grotesque devil standing behind him raising a whip above his head.[30] A broadside of the text *On the Pox Called Malafrantzosa* from around 1500 depicts Job inflicted with sores while sitting on the dungheap in melancholic fashion, with Satan appearing in grotesque form similar to that in Figure 3.2, accompanied by two musicians.[31]

An artistic concern to portray Satan as the cause of Job's illness remained strong in the early sixteenth century. For Christians who needed "a hero exemplary for a wide Christian audience," according to Ann Astell, Job provided the basis.[32] To do so, a loss of attention toward the poetic sections of Job in favor of the prose tale takes place, especially evident in Gregory's *Moralia*.[33] Milton reaches a climatic point in terms of engaging the tradition of Job as Christian heroic poetry in *Paradise Regained* from 1671. *Paradise Regained* consists of a series of dialogues between Satan as Christ, as Satan tempts Christ in the wilderness. Like many exegetes before him, Milton recalls Job's dungheap trials as an unsuccessful repeat of Eden: God suggest that Satan "might have learned...since he failed in Job" (I, 146–147).[34] Jesus also remarks that Satan misdeemed Job, "his patience won" (I, 426). Like Job, Christ acts as a young warrior laying down his "great warfare" in order "to conquer Sin and Death the two grand foes,/By Humiliation and strong Sufference" (I, 155–160).

Neil Forsyth suggests that before 1700 Satan's role within Christian theology fit into "the combat myth." In other words, "separate devil-tales

cultural condition in England, including the body politic, see Sarah Covington, *Wounds, Flesh, and Metaphor in Seventeenth-Century England* (New York: Palgrave Macmillan, 2009).

29. For examples, consult Meyer, "St. Job as a Patron of Music."

30. See Fig. III.44, *Job Consoled by Musicians*, 's-Hertogenbosch, 1500–25, at Oxford, Ashmolean Museum, in Jos Koldeweij, "Hieronymus Bosch and His City," in *Hieronymus Bosch: The Complete Paintings and Drawings* (ed. Jos Koldeweij, Paul Vandenbroeck, and Bernard Vermet; New York: Abrams, 2001), 47.

31. Anonymous, *On the Pox Called Malafrantzosa*, ca. 1500, Bayerische Staatsbibliothek, Sign.: Einbl. VII, 9f, Munich.

32. Ann Astell, *Job, Boethius, and Epic Truth* (Ithaca, N.Y.: Cornell University Press, 1994), 98.

33. Ibid., 85.

34. All quotes from *Paradise Regained* come from Stephen Orgel and Jonathan Goldberg, eds., *John Milton* (New York: Oxford University Press, 1991).

were all seen as cases of one basic opposition, that of Christ and Satan," and Forsyth refers to that basic opposition in terms of "one of the most widespread of Near Eastern narrative patterns, the combat myth."[35] The Christian combat myth reads like the following: "A rebel god challenges the power of Yahweh, takes over the whole earth as an extension of his empire, and rules it through the power of sin and death."[36] In his discussion on the character of Satan as hero-villain in Milton's *Paradise Lost*, Harold Bloom highlights Milton's Satan as a climactic rendition of the combat myth.[37] Satan reaches his monumental peak through Milton's mid-seventeenth-century portrayal in *Paradise Lost*. Yet, Milton's rendition of the character Satan blurs the line between human and non-human because of Satan's empathetic emotional character. Jeffrey Burton Russell calls Milton's character of Satan "the epic hero" in which "the reader could see the emptiness of loveless heroism in a world governed in reality by love."[38] In *Paradise Regained*, however, Milton renders Satan worthless in light of Christ's ability to resist his temptations, still maintaining his focus on "the only direct confrontation between Christ and Satan reported in the Bible."[39]

Despite the prolific writings, theological nuances, and socially situated thoughts of Martin Luther, and Reformed theologians Calvin and Zwingli, the issue at hand—cultural notions of diabology and the Job story—does not change much in Christian tradition for Protestant leaders.[40] Forsyth notes that the Devil plays a large part in Luther's ideas of the atonement, keeping with medieval tradition, because Satan continues to play an adversarial role for humankind until his defeat at the end of history. "Luther clearly identifies the Satan of Job with the devil," remarks Vicchio; "It is just as clear that he sees Satan as a demonic force."[41] In other words, Satan was very real for Luther, and the Devil presented threats to his faith for which proper spiritual weapons to battle those threats were needed. Luther even suggested that Satan daily

35. Neil Forsyth, *The Old Enemy: Satan and the Combat Myth* (Princeton, N.J.: Princeton University Press, 1987), 6.

36. Ibid., 6–7.

37. Harold Bloom, *Ruin the Sacred Truths: Poetry and Belief from the Bible to the Present* (Cambridge, Mass.: Harvard University Press, 1989), 98.

38. Jeffrey Burton Russell, *Mephistopheles: The Devil in the Modern World* (Ithaca, N.Y.: Cornell University Press, 1986), 99.

39. Ibid., 127.

40. The variances of their understanding of sin, human will, and salvation belong to another study. Russel notes that for Luther, Calvin, and Zwingli, their diabology remained similar: Russell, *Mephistopheles*, 46–50.

41. Vicchio, *Job in the Medieval World*, 181.

disrupted his life with the stench of feces and even made his home in Luther's bowels.[42] Luther held a strong view of the Devil and scatology; he believed that Satan smelled of excrement, representing a kind of no-good "shit." "After all," notes Heiko Oberman, "the monks knew all about the Devil's affinity to cesspool and toilet," so "Luther's scatology-permeated language has to be taken seriously as an expression of the painful battle fought body and soul against the Adversary, who threatens both flesh and spirit."[43]

In his *Lectures on Genesis*, Luther expounds on the ways Satan afflicts and torments humans and offers Job as an example of faithful endurance. Job's wife, however, acts as an example of hopelessness, disbelief, and despair, engaging in blasphemous words, the kind of words that represent Satan's slanderous ways. She encourages him to die in the Devil's name![44] God allows Satan to engage people in such afflictions and temptations so as to allow men to pledge their certainty that they are faithful.[45] Elsewhere, Luther refers to Job's wife in terms of Job's "carnal mind" in time of temptation.[46] Alcuin Blamires writes of the medieval model of head and body in terms of gender, noting that a head/body polarity exists in patristic theology based on ideas in Ephesians (5:22–23) and 1 Corinthians (2:3–15). In sum, a gender hierarchy continues: "God is head of Christ who is head of man who is head of woman," while the hierarchy also extends to the Church so that the following results: "Christ, head; Church, body; (in turn compromising) husband, head; wife, body."[47] Men who think carnally are morally depraved of their ideal masculinity. Since Luther assumes that a pious life attracts the Devil, Job's afflictions result from Satan's schemes.

Both Satan and Job's wife figure into a theological scheme to render Job as hero, a prefigurement of Christ's suffering and ultimate victory.

42. Russell, *Mephistopheles*, 37–40.

43. Heiko A. Oberman, *Luther: Man Between God and the Devil* (trans. Eileen Walliser-Schwarzbart; New Haven, Conn.: Yale University Press, 1989), 108–9.

44. Luther takes Job's wife and the wife of Tobias as examples, although he quotes Job entirely. Gen 41, Martin Luther, *Luther's Works*. Vol. 7, *Lectures on Genesis, Chapters 38–44* (trans. Paul D. Pahl; Saint Louis, Miss.: Concordia, 1965), 132–33.

45. Ibid., 133.

46. *Fourteen Consolations*, Martin Luther, *Luther's Works*. Vol. 42, *Devotional Writings* (trans. Martin H. Bertram; Philadelphia: Fortress, 1955), 146–47.

47. Alcuin Blamires, "Paradox in the Medieval Gender Doctrine of Head and Body," in *Medieval Theology and the Natural Body* (ed. Peter Biller and A. J. Minnis; Rochester, N.Y.: York Medieval, 1997), 14–15. This metaphor is not without its vague and underdeveloped definitions, which Blamires explains well.

By the end of the fourteenth century, Satan is a ubiquitous presence in art, frightening believers into repentance. As the sixteenth century winds down, however, and humanism, along with religious reformations, show effects in European societies, more subtle demonic cues appear in art of Job and his wife. This is because the role of Satan undergoes development in early modern theology. At the same time that satanic presence becomes more generic, complex, or even invisible in art of Job, a less subtle message emerges for Job's wife. In general, Job's wife in early modern art represents a shrew, a "bad wife," in a more generic form than she does in medieval art.

Early Modern Changing Views of Roles at the Dungheap

In his cultural study of right and left in Western art, James Hall traces a medieval convention to parse right and left as spirit and flesh. The left side of the body held a reputation as the "worldly" side, the physical fleshy side. Medical myths of the left side having more blood, less heat, and a large vein leading from the heart to the ring finger come into play as well as symbolic theological notions of the right hand as "good" and the left hand as "bad."[48] St. John Cassian (ca. 370–ca. 435), a founding monastic father and influential author on the organization of monastic life, wrote his *Conferences* to train the inner man against temptation. He speaks of "left-sided" trials facing a monk, such as deep sorrow, carnal lust, vanity, and the loss of spiritual warmth—all trials that come from the Devil.[49] According to Cassian's Sixth Conference, Job triumphed on this left side because he did not blaspheme God even after the Devil took away everything, leaving Job sitting on a dunghill and gouging his fingers into his sores and retrieving large masses of worms from his body.[50] The fact that Job wards off the Devil's advances from his left side, the weaker side of his body, attests to Job's spiritual fortitude. The worst of Job's trials are represented by the strength of his uncorrupted soul in light of his corrupted flesh. Therefore, Cassian provides a clear example of traditional concern for Job's heroism, beginning in early Christianity and continuing on in the Middle Ages. However, as the Middle Ages unwind and the early modern period emerges, the importance of Job's ability to "fight" Satan's temptations wanes.

48. James Hall, *The Sinister Side: How Left–Right Symbolism Shaped Western Art* (Oxford: Oxford University Press, 2008), 44–67.

49. Ibid., 43–44.

50. John Cassian, *The Conferences* (trans. Boniface Ramsey; Ancient Christian Writers; New York: Paulist, 1997), 225–26.

Particularized portraits of Job emerge, especially in Italian art, as early as the mid-thirteenth century when Nicola Pisano paints St. Sebastian on a tree, with Joseph and Job standing on opposite sides.[51] Around 1518–1521, the school of Dosso Dossi puts Job alongside Sebastian, with John the Baptist on the other side, in an altarpiece of St. Sebastian.[52] Giovanni Bellini places Job separate from his common dungheap in two separate paintings and in both cases alongside St. Sebastian as well. St. Sebastian offers a youthful and traditionally nude counterpart to Job's aging body. Furthermore, they both "were considered efficacious intermediaries against the plague" of 1478.[53] In the San Giobbe altarpiece, Job stands beside the Madonna on the throne in an altarpiece for a church of the hospital of San Giobbe in Venice between 1483 and 1495. The traditional iconography of Job on his dungheap with sores on his body accompanied by his wife and Satan disappears for Bellini. For Bellini, Job's important role comes with his ability to recognize God incarnate in the Redeemer passage of Job (19:25–27). The relevance for this passage in terms of changing Joban iconography is immense because of the reception of the Redeemer passage in the Christian West pertaining to the idea that Job, in resurrected flesh, shall see God (v. 26). As a result, Job leaves no doubt that there will be a resurrection of the flesh, a true corporeal restoration.[54]

In the Uffizi, Florence, in another of Bellini's paintings *Sacred Allegory*, from around 1504, Job stands with his hands in prayer by St. Sebastian at the extreme right of the painting. Terrien interprets both paintings in terms of Venetian tradition, in light of a syphilis outbreak in Europe in 1505, to call upon Saint Job to intercede on behalf of those afflicted with sexually transmitted diseases. Most art historians suggest a Christological message at work in the paintings; that is, Job's prefiguration of the suffering of Christ and the ultimate resurrection of Christ in the flesh. No overall agreed-upon interpretation of *Sacred Allegory* exists, but the basic idea that it reflects the redemption of humankind through Christ's incarnation and passion holds.[55]

51.   Nicola Pisano, ca. 1220–1287. *Saint Sebastian, Joseph, Job and Devotees*, Pinacoteca Nazionale, Ferrara, Italy.

52.   Dossi, Dosso, ca. 1518–1521. *Altarpiece of St. Sebastian*. Duomo, Modena, Italy.

53.   Rona Goffen, "Bellini, S. Giobbe and Altar Egos," *Artibus et Historiae* 7, no. 14 (1986): 59, 65.

54.   For more on ideas about resurrection at this time, see Caroline Walker Bynum, *The Resurrection of the Body in Western Christianity, 200–1336* (New York: Columbia University Press, 1995).

55.   Meinolf Dalhoff, "Trouble at the Hermitage: A Note on Giovanni Bellini's 'Sacred Allegory'," *The Burlington Magazine* 144, no. 14 (2002): 22–23.

A growing blatant connection between Christ and Job in Renaissance art removes Job from the dungheap. A student of Bellini, Vicctore Carpaccio, also created two paintings of Job. In *Job and the Death of Christ*, Carpaccio has Job leaning against a tree, resting his chin on his hand while holding a cane in the other.[56] Earlier, Carpaccio seats Job on a cement block inscribed with the Hebrew from Job 19:25–27 in *Meditation on the Passion* from around 1495.[57] Job's aged body is a significant trademark of this style, with Brigit Blass-Simmen commenting that Job's body means to communicate the morbidity of the scene, or to reflect how Carpaccio took several motifs from the study of nature and assembled them to provide an example of death and decomposition.[58] However, in all the cases of interpretations of Job by Bellini and Carpaccio no visible sores appear on Job's skin.

The lack of sores indicates a developing Italian motif that has widespread implications for artistic renditions that follow—a connection with Job and Christ in the context of renewal, reconciliation between humanity, and traditional Christian interpretations of the "Redeemer lives" passage in Job (19:25). Fra Bartolommeo's 1516 triptych, called *Salvator Mundi*, for the chapel of Salvatore Billi in SS Annunziata in Florence, depicts Christ and the four evangelists; Job and Isaiah flank the sides.[59] Hendrick Goltzius, in 1616, has Job sitting alone on straw holding a potsherd with no visible sores on his skin.[60] He holds his right hand to his chest and looks off into the distance; Job's clutching both hands together and looking up to heaven becomes a standard form for Job in the early modern period.[61] Goltzius, a Dutch painter, connects Job with the iconography of *Christ in Distress*, which begins to develop strongly in

56. Vittore Carpaccio, *Job and the Dead Christ*, ca. 1505–10. Staatliche Museen zu Berline, Preussischer Kulturbesitz Gemäldegalerie.

57. Vittore Carpaccio, *Meditation on the Passion*, ca. 1495. Metropolitan Museum of Art, John Steward Kennedy Fund, 1911, New York.

58. Brigit Blass-Simmen, *"Studi Dal Vivo E Dal Non Più Vivo*: Carpaccio's Passion Paintings with Saint Job," *Metropolitan Museum Journal* 41 (2006): 75–90.

59. The triptych is now at Florence: Galleria dell'Accademia.

60. Hendrick Goltzius, "Job in Distress," 1616. New York, Trade Art Investments. Given the nature of a solo Job, with no sores, art historians took a great deal of time identifying the man as Job. For more, see Lawrence W. Nichols, "'Job in Distress,' a Newly-Discovered Painting of Hendrick Goltzius," *Simiolus: Netherlands Quarterly for the History of Art* 13, no. 3/4 (1983): 182–88.

61. See also Jusepe de Ribera, *Job in Prayer*, ca. 1640, Parma Pinacoteca, another individualized portrait of Job with clasped hands, no sores, and gazing toward heaven. See Fig. 96 in Terrien, *The Iconography of Job Through the Centuries*, 184.

the mid-fourteenth century. The idea of Christ's "distress" owes its form to the tradition of the mourning Job in art.[62]

Job's suffering changes from medieval heroic endurance of Satan's blows as God's athlete to early modern attention toward controlled introspection of Christ-like patience in assurance of restoration. Job continues to display outward suffering, but his sores no longer simply foreshadow Christ's sufferings. Through displays of Job's introspective suffering, Renaissance art visually communicates the emulation of the life of faith for the individual Christian and the promise of resurrection.

The notion of an individual's ability to triumph in Christian life, though trials abound, as reflected in Renaissance art, comes from a male perspective. The marriage of Job and his wife signifies another way Job emulates controlled patience in his Christian life, as opposed to his wife, who comes to represent the failing to uphold good Christian marital ideals. An artistic trend develops at the same time. Terrien notes this when he states that "Religious painters in the Low Countries during the Baroque Age stressed without restraint the motif of the cantankerous wife," but he fails to posture reasons for the clear presentation of Job's wife in such a fashion.[63] The next section of this chapter will provide a survey of such Baroque Art. The next chapter will provide an analysis of why Job's wife comes to this role. The reason for Job's wife's visual presentation as a "bad wife" relates both to changing views of evil and to a widespread literary category in Europe, domestic conduct literature, addressing how an ideal Christian marriage should function. In the meantime, the necessary fading of satanic influence over Job in favor of Job's triumph remains another important factor.

Baroque Trends for Job and His Wife
Martin van Heemskerck joins Job in artistic form with the genre of Triumph, which comes from Francesco Petrarch's influential Italian poetry on Triumphs (*Trionfi*) that he began writing in the mid-fourteenth century.[64] One of van Heemskerck's many engravings of Job from 1559

62. Von der Osten argues that it matters not whether Job's wife, his friends, or the Devil accompany Job in the illustrations, but that Job's attitude and gesture indicate his pious suffering. G. Von der Osten, "Job and Christ: The Development of a Devotional Image," *Journal of the Warburg and Courtauld Institutes* 16, no. 1/2 (1953): 153–58.

63. Terrien, *The Iconography of Job Through the Centuries*, 187.

64. Van Heemskerck applies the genre of Triumph to biblical characters here. For Petrarch's poetry, see Petrarch, *The Triumphs of Petrarch* (trans. Ernest Hatch Wilkins; Chicago: University of Chicago Press, 1962).

displays his triumph in terms of slow and steady patient suffering (Fig. 3.4). In the left background, Job sits with the typical mourning gesture, resting his chin on his hand, while his friends sit on the ground in front of him. His wife holds her arms wide open in emphatic gesture. In the foreground, Job rides upon a tortoise—he holds a shackled entourage of his wife, friends, and the Devil trailing behind him in his left hand. In keeping with traditional iconography, the Devil holds whips. Van Heemskerck visually lumps all of Job's trials in one group, with Job the clear victor. He clearly shows Job's wife as one of the menacing characters in Job's story.[65]

Figure 3.4. Martin van Heemskerck, *Triumph of Job*, 1559. Auckland Art Gallery Toi o Tamaki, purchased 1981.

Traditional notions of "Patient Job" still exist for early modern artists, but artists include more characters and more elaborate scenes, often at the expense of clear demonic presence and filthy dung in Job's story. The Dutch Northern Renaissance artist Jan Mandyn (ca. 1500–1560) depicts a mocking scene for Job (Fig. 3.5). On the right side of the painting, the townspeople have gathered to gaze upon Job, while musicians

---

65. In another engraving, Heemskerck places Job on a seat in the midst of ruined stone structures. His wife stands behind him, holding her hands, one shrouded, up to her face. Here, echoes of early Christian art exist but with early modern adaptations.

play among the crowd. Job's wife stands next to Job holding keys that are attached to her belt. Mandyn imitates the style of Dutch painter Hieronymus Bosch, making a clear interpretation of the painting difficult. The workshop of Bosch also painted the life of Job on a triptych in Bruges from 1507, which uses similar groupings of musicians and townspeople but omits Job's wife.[66] The mocking tone is quite apparent in both paintings, yet the exact functions of the characters remain a mystery, especially in terms of why Mandyn places keys in the hands of Job's wife.

Figure 3.5. Jan Mandyn (1500–1560). *Les épreuves de Job*, Musée de la Chartreuse-Douai. Photothèque—Musée de Douai.

In Christianity, keys symbolize ecclesiastical authority. Depictions of St. Genevieve often include keys on her belt or girdle, as patroness of Paris and the holder of the keys to the city. In Flemish art, Martha of Bethany, patroness of housewives, often holds household items in her hands, including cooking utensils and keys.[67] Sixteenth- and seventeenth-century sources that uphold female virtue cite Martha as exuding Christian hospitality, and Karel van Mallery, after Maarten de Vos, in a series on exceptional New Testament women from the 1590s, illustrates her

66. See Fig. III. 80b, *Job Consoled by Musicians*, at Bruges, Groeningemuseum, in Koldeweij, Vandenbroeck, and Vermet, eds., *Hieronymus Bosch*, 109.
67. Diane Apostolos-Cappadona, *Dictionary of Christian Art* (New York: Continuum, 1994), 200, 29–30. Keys can be found in a grouping of household items in the foreground of a painting by Peter Aertsen, *Christ in the House of Mary and Martha*, 1552, Kuntshistorische Museum, Vienna. See Margaret A. Sullivan, "Aertsen's Kitchen and Market Scenes: Audience and Innovation in Northern Art," *The Art Bulletin* 81, no. 2 (1999): 239 Fig. 4.

holding a ladle and wearing a girdle on which keys hang.[68] Furthermore, Martha's story of sainthood relates to an instance of her tying a dragon to her girdle so that townspeople could stone it to death.[69]

To complicate matters, however, popular theological assumptions about Martha include a dichotomy between her domestic action and her sister Mary's contemplation (Luke 10:38–42), with Martha's domesticity representing concern for worldly affairs. An example comes from the Flemish 1569 *A Theatre for Voluptuous Worldlings* by Jean vander Noot. After citing Jesus' words to Martha, that she is "troubled aboute many thingses, but one thyng is necessary," vander Noot editorializes: "Whereby sheweth Christe unto us, that it is not good to be musyng and studying upon worldely affaires, wherein is nothyng else but trouble and unquietness of minde."[70] The example from van der Noot represents a trend, based on northern humanist ideals, to criticize materialistic values, to "look beyond these objects of daily life, beyond present concerns, one's daily bread and acquisition of properties and money" and instead "be reminded of the duties required of a Christian."[71] Given Mandyn's context as a northern painter around this time, it seems more likely that Job's wife's keys function as a signal of her concern for temporal things, contrasting with Job's spiritual nature. For instance, Job also holds a gold coin as he faces the musicians in the tradition that the scabs from his skin turn into gold with which he pays the musicians in the medieval "Life of Job." Similarly, the worms from his body turn to gold in *Patience of Job*. The transcendence of Job's earthly flesh contrasts with his wife's accusation that he was hiding gold, indicative of her concern for worldly treasures. Mandyn instigates keys as a gendered symbol of his time to communicate this tradition.

A scene by Albrecht Dürer shares similarities with Mandyn's painting in terms of the presence of musicians, and in terms of enigmatic depictions of Job's wife, in an altarpiece known as the Jabach altarpiece because of its use in a private chapel of the Jabach family in Cologne. The Jabach altarpiece supposedly has three parts. One wing depicts Job's

68. Yvonne Bleyerveld, "Chaste, Obedient and Devout: Biblical Women as Patterns of Female Virtue in Netherlandish and German Graphic Art, Ca. 1500–1750," *Simiolus: Netherlands Quarterly for the History of Art* 28, no. 4 (2000–2001): 235–36 Fig. 17.

69. Jacobus de Voragine, *The Golden Legend: Readings on the Saints* (trans. William Granger Ryan; 2 vols.; Princeton, N.J.: Princeton University Press, 1993), 2:23–26.

70. Jan van der Noot, *A Theatre for Voluptuous Worldlings* (New York: Scholars' Facsimiles & Reprints, 1569), 6r.

71. Sullivan, "Aertsen's Kitchen and Market Scenes," 254–55.

wife pouring a bucket of water over Job's head, or the back of his neck, while Job sits on the ground, looking down at the ground, resting his chin in his left hand. The other wing of the painting includes two musicians, one of which bears a likeness to Dürer himself. The third piece with Job and his wife can be found at the Städel Institute in Frankfurt. Since Fredrick the Wise, Duke of Saxony, commissioned a painting of the *Adoration of the Magi*, now at the Uffizi in Florence, and the size and period match the Job painting, art historians debate whether the three pieces actually belonged to the same altarpiece.[72] Nevertheless, the supposed commissioner, Frederick the Wise, like Giovanni Bellini, probably accepted the incorporation of Job because of Job's role in intercessory healing. Dürer traveled to Venice several times in his life and could have encountered Job's saintly status in Venice as a local saint and protector from the plague.[73] Paul Bacon takes Dürer's use of Job in terms of the plague a step further considering Frederick the Wise and the liturgical context of his Wittenburg Castle Church, which enacted memorial masses and vigils on a daily basis, including monthly recitations of the *Office of the Dead*. In the Jabach altarpiece, Job functions as a prophet of Christ's resurrection.[74]

Like other early sixteenth-century renditions of Job, many traditional iconographical elements are omitted or gain more complexity. For one thing, artists remove Job from his dungheap to make a Christological point about ultimate redemption. They also take away Satan's presence. For another thing, Job's wife takes on more enigmatic functions. Mandyn includes Job's wife with keys (Fig. 3.5). Another example comes from Albrecht Dürer's rendition of Job and his wife; critics remain divided on whether the act of Job's wife pouring water on Job's head constitutes, for Dürer, "cruel action"[75] or one of "therapeutic explanation."[76] Though

72. This theory was first developed by Hans Kauffmann, and is explained in further detail in Paul M. Bacon, "Mirror of a Christian Prince: Frederick the Wise and Art Patronage in Electoral Saxony, 1486–1525" (Ph.D. diss., University of Wisconsin-Madison, 2004), 175–88.

73. Erwin Panofsky, *The Life and Art of Albrecht Dürer* (Princeton, N.J.: Princeton University Press, 1955), 93.

74. Bacon, "Mirror of a Christian Prince," 186.

75. Panofsky, *The Life and Art of Albrecht Dürer*, 94.

76. Terrien, *The Iconography of Job Through the Centuries*, 143. For an argument of Job's wife's positive portrayal, see Seow, "Job's Wife." On the other hand, another interprets Job's wife in negative terms: Zefira Gitay, "The Portrayal of Job's Wife and Her Representation in the Visual Arts," in *Fortunate the Eyes That See: Essays in Honor of David Noel Freedman in Celebration of His Seventieth Birthday* (ed. Astrid Beck et al.; Grand Rapids: Eerdmans, 1995), 516–26.

destruction looms in the background, Dürer does not include any rendition of Satan, which leaves the viewer to speculate on how Job's wife functions.[77] Job's pose, supporting his head by one hand with one knee bent, is echoed in one of Dürer's most mysterious and complex engravings, *Melencolia I.*[78] The similarities in form suggest Dürer wishes to communicate Job's melancholy state, which, in its widest sense, emphasizes one's search for wisdom, even when an ability to search for higher knowledge and creative genius leads one to depression.[79] The presence of the musicians also signals medieval melancholy ideas at work, such as the soothing power of music.[80] With one of the musicians acting as a self-portrait for Dürer, the representation references the state of being an artist, displaying the melancholic effects of a sage's life.[81]

With the emergence of Baroque art, appeals to direct and dramatic Joban iconography, with less ambiguous gestures and meanings of Mannerist art, exist. Compared to the early sixteenth-century paintings

77. I am more likely to agree with art critics who note another wife of a patient sufferer who pours water on her husband's head—Xantippe, the wife of Socrates. Chaucer's Wife of Bath mentions the popular story of when Xantippe pours filthy water on Socrates' head (lines 735–738), as noted earlier by Jerome. Jerome, in 393, makes mention of a time when Socrates opposed his abusive wife, Xantippe. Xantippe responded by dousing him with dirty water, after which he remarked that rain follows thunder ("Letter Against Jovianus," I. 48; *PL* 23: 278–279). Though somewhat later than Dürer, in 1607, a Flemish artist Otto van Veen (or Vaenius) published *Emblemata Horatiana* in which he depicts Socrates in his melancholic pose, sitting outdoors, while Xantippe pours liquid over his head from the interior of an above-story structure. The theme comes up again in Joost van den Vondel's *Gulden Winckel* from 1613, which reproduced the illustrations from the emblematic work about philosophers' stories from 1579, Laurent van Haecht's *Microcosmos* or *Parvus Mundus*. One electronic source, incorporating the work of numerous art critics, notes a connection between Xantippe in Reyer van Blommendael's painting and Dürer's painting of Job's wife: Emil Krén, "Web Gallery of Art," online: http://www.wga.hu/frames-e.html?/html/b/blommend/xantippe.html (accessed May 2010).

78. From 1514, now at the Herbert F. Johnson Museum of Art, Cornell University. For more on this subject, see Patrick Doorly, "Dürer's 'Melencolia I': Plato's Abandoned Search for the Beautiful," *The Art Bulletin* 86, no. 2 (2004): 255–76.

79. Heinz Lüdecke, *Albrecht Dürer* (trans. Richard Rickett; New York: G. P. Putnam's Sons, 1972), 37. For a more detailed discussion of the role of melancholy in art at this time, see Piers Britton, "'Mio Malinchonico, O Vero…Mio Pazzo': Michelangelo, Vasari, and the Problem of Artists' Melancholy in Sixteenth-Century Italy," *Sixteenth Century Journal* 34, no. 3 (2003): 653–75.

80. Panofsky, *The Life and Art of Albrecht Dürer*, 93.

81. Given Job's sage-like appearance, a possible connection between Job and Socrates might be at work for Dürer. Both men become celebrated for their patience, especially in Flemish traditions.

of Job and his wife discussed above, a Baroque trend emerges in the late sixteenth century that clearly gives Job's wife a shrewish presence. Furthermore, Satan's presence in Baroque art takes on more nuanced forms.

By the late sixteenth and early seventeenth centuries, a more meditative nature of the human frailty of Job and the often hidden realms of sin and evil which befall humanity are reflected in many images of Job and his wife. In general, Frederick Hartt notes a change in the meaning of Job's suffering as expressed artistically:

> In Gothic art Job's verbal cudgellings at the hands of his wife and the devil appear on cathedral portals as prefigurements of Christ's own afflictions, but by the Renaissance they are merely examples of the sufferings and heroism of a perfect Christian.[82]

Job's wife and the Devil still torment Job, but, they do so for a different purpose. A shift in portraying Job and his wife with Satan himself, to presenting them with more generic forms of evil, results from cultural attitudes concerning Satan and the inner-person that developed at this time. It became the duty of a Christian to ponder inwardly sin and salvation: "But now it was you versus the Devil; you alone, the individual, who had the responsibility for fending him off" because of a "new introspection placed upon the individual."[83] Furthermore, the ubiquitous image of a saint battling against Satan, a hero of faith and an "athlete of God," as seen with ideas about Job, gives way to less triumphant notions of facing the power of temptation.[84] Artists reflect such trends; Job's suffering becomes more poignant, dark, elaborate, dramatic, and introspective. The 1631 painting by Jan Lievens, a Baroque Dutch painter contemporary to Rembrandt, anticipates Russell's point that by the end of the seventeenth century, demonic evil reflects not so much an external figure known as Satan, but, rather, the dark recesses of one's soul. The National Gallery of Canada contains a painting called *Job in His Misery* which depicts a cave-like interior and a slumped, elderly, almost sleeping, Job. Over his left shoulder appear two demonic heads, one spewing out

82. Frederick Hartt, "Carpaccio's Meditation on the Passion," *The Art Bulletin* 22, no. 1 (1940): 29.

83. Russell, *Mephistopheles*, 31.

84. See, for instance, the triptych at Musées Royaux des Beaux-Arts, Brussels, by Bernaert van Orley, a Flemish artist with Italian style. His 1521 triptych, possibly commissioned by Margaret of Austria, the governor of the Low Countries, is meant to communicate the triumph of patience. In the central panel, a dark ominous demonic cloud above threatens his children, while in the background to the right, Job's wife gestures wildly at a naked Job.

fire. Over Job's right shoulder stands his wife. She is holding a flaming lamp with her right hand and gesturing to something outside the painting with her left palm out. Rather than picture Satan, Lievens chooses to paint animalistic, horrifying, yet generic forms of evil creatures.

Both Lievens and Rembrandt competed for the patronage of Constantijn Huygens, secretary to the Prince of Orange and promoter of Dutch art in the court in The Hague. By this time, Lievens was demonstrating influence from Peter Paul Rubens, a contemporary Flemish Baroque painter. Between 1628 and 1631, Rembrandt and Lievens painted parallel themes. Rembrandt's old man in *Jeremiah Lamenting the Destruction of Jerusalem* shows similar expressions to Job as Lievens's *Job in His Misery*.[85] Rembrandt, around 1648–1650, also sketched Job, his wife, and his friends, in which he shows Job resting his right hand on his forehead in similar melancholic expression.[86] Both Rembrandt's Jeremiah and Job wear robes in the depictions. Lievens, however, paints a nearly nude Job with the flaccid body of a defeated man. An aging body in the early modern period communicated the natural and inevitable process of living life, but, in religious and didactic contexts, it also represented the transience of life, the need for introspection, and the vanity of pursuing worldly things.[87] As Petrarch muses in "The Triumph of Time": "I followed then my hopes and vain desires, but now with mine own eyes I see myself as in a mirror, and my wanderings, considering the brevity of life, and striving to make ready for the end."[88]

A few years after Lieven's dark painting, around 1650, the French artist Georges de La Tour renders Job and his wife in a dark, cavernous space with Job's wife also holding the light which illuminates the region.[89] La Tour and Lievens differ in terms of what La Tour excludes. He does not include devilish figures. His exclusion of demonic elements, alongside his portrayal of Job's wife as a comforter, gazing into Job's eyes, with her left hand delicately touching Job's forehead palm-up, diverges from a norm for Job and his wife at the dungheap, and led to the mislabeling of his painting as *Saint Peter Delivered from Prison by an Angel*. It was not until the 1930s that Werner Weisbach developed an

85. Arthur K. Wheelock, *Jan Lievens: A Dutch Master Rediscovered* (New Haven: Yale University Press, 2008), 11–12.

86. Otto Benesch, *The Drawings of Rembrandt* (6 vols.; London: Phaidon, 1973), 3:169.

87. Shulamith Shahar, "The Middle Ages and Renaissance," in *A History of Old Age* (ed. Pat Thane; London: Thames & Hudson, 2005), 71–111.

88. Petrarch, *The Triumphs of Petrarch*, 97.

89. Georges de La Tour, *Job and His Wife*, ca. 1650. Musée Départemental des Vosges, Épinal, France.

argument for a title change to *Job Mocked by His Wife*, so that what was once an angelic female presence changed to fit the iconography of the time, Job's wife as a problematic presence.[90] However, as many have noted, La Tour strays from a stylistic presentation of Job's wife as a hostile woman.[91] La Tour follows a trend of his time, however, in presenting Job as a depleted old man, devoid of his sores and his large dung pile. In his use of light, La Tour follows chiaroscuro style of light and dark contrasts. As seen in the paintings discussed above, a Baroque style of painting, with its dramatic use of light and movement and the reality of human condition, heralded by Caravaggio and extended by Georges de La Tour and Rubens, brings with it a sense of the "mystical force" of light countered by intense shadows. But, as more and more artists incorporated such themes in the seventeenth century, light (and by contrast, shadows) became simply a "powerful stylistic device" rather than a symbol of transcendence.[92]

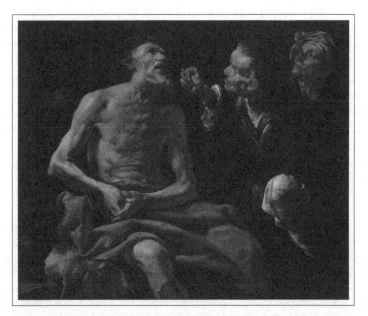

Figure 3.6. Gioacchio Asserto, *The Mocking of Job*, Museum of Fine Arts, Budapest, 1635.

90. W. Weisbach, "L'histoire de Job Dans les Arts: A Propos du Tableau du Georges de La Tour au Musée d'epinal," *Gazette des beaux-arts* 78 (1936): 102–12.

91. La Tour's departure from the tradition led to the mislabeling of his painting. See Terrien, *The Iconography of Job Through the Centuries*, 166–69.

92. Marco Bussagli and Mattia Reiche, *Baroque and Rococo* (trans. Patrick McKeown; New York: Sterling, 2009), 24.

A painting from 1635 by Gioacchino Asserto, an Italian Baroque painter of the Genoese school in Genova, who had contact with Flemish artists, puts Job in a cavernous setting with lurking demonic presence in the background and a shrewish wife (Fig. 3.6).[93] Job's wife is old in appearance. Her left hand rests on her hip or lifts her skirt in akimbo fashion. The akimbo gesture, one or both hands on one's hips with the elbow sticking out, communicates disassociation or disagreement, an "anti-social sign."[94] With her left hand, she makes the "fig sign," a gesture in which the thumb partly pokes out of the middle and index finger of a clenched fist, also known as *mano fica.* It seems that even the demon in the background is horrified at her gesture. Amulets of the "fig sign" have been found in ancient Greece and more than likely functioned to ward off the evil eye with its offensiveness because of the gesture's sexual symbolism of a penis inserted into a vagina. Cross-culturally, though, the gesture has many derivations, including a gesture meaning "I'll give you nothing," since the fig represents a fruit of low value. Or, according to Italian legends, the gesture communicates derision or degradation.[95] Images of Christ's mockers and tormentors in art using the sign hold to this interpretation; Mellinkoff calls it an "ancient obscene gesture."[96] As with many gestures, complex usages develop over time and come with cultural differences. Florio's 1611 Italian/English Dictionary helps illuminate possible functions of the gesture for Asserto's cultural background. At this time, the gesture was given in disgrace, as a symbol for a woman's vagina, and *fáre le fica* meant "to bid a fig for one," also used by Italian women as a means to "swear by," as Florio's dictionary compares the phrase to "our Englishwomen say by my apronstrings."[97]

93. Gioacchino Asserto, *Job im Elend*, 1635, Museum of Fine Arts, Budapest. See A. Pigler, ed., *Barockthemen: Eine Auswahl Von Verzeichnissen Zur Ikonographie Des 17 Und 18 Jahrhunderts* (3 vols.; Budapest: Akadémiai Kiadó, 1974), 3:79, Fig. 83.

94. Desmond Morris, *Bodywatching: A Field Guide to the Human Species* (New York: Crown, 1985), 195–96. A gendered study of this gesture, in terms of cultural use for females, has not been undertaken to the best of my knowledge.

95. Desmond Morris et al., *Gestures: Their Origins and Distribution* (New York: Stein & Day, 1979), 148–60.

96. Mellinkoff, *Outcasts*, 199.

97. John Florio (1553–1625) was born in London, a son of an Italian ex-friar who converted to Protestantism and moved to England to avoid persecution. John Florio, "Fica," in *Queen Anna's New World of Words, or Dictionarie of the Italian and English Tongues* (London: Blount & Barret, 1611), 186. The 1611 version is expanded from the 1598 edition; the latter does not include the mention of a woman's swearing.

Figure 3.7. Gaspard de Crayer, *Job's Adversity*, 1619. Toulouse, Musée des Augustins. Photo: Daniel Martin. Courtesy of Toulouse, Musée des Augustins.

Another source which supports the idea that Job's wife gives Job the fig out of defiance and vulgarity comes from the fourteenth-century Dante's *Inferno*, in Canto XXV when, in the eighth circle, seventh pit, the thief, Vanni Fucci, made his fists into figs, raising them to God, a profane gesture especially disapproved of in Italian provinces.[98] It is possible that Job's wife gives the fig gesture to the demonic figure that stands behind Job, in which case Job's wife supports him and the satanic presence shows dismay. However, given the Italian backgrounds of the

98. Anthony Oldcorn, "Notes to Canto XXV," in *Dante: Inferno* (Indianapolis, Ind.: Hackett, 2009), 240–42.

gesture in terms of its relation to God, the general attitude of Job's wife in Asserto's painting (Fig. 3.6) does not promote nurturing wifehood. The gesture relates to her urging Job to "curse God," a suggestion Asserto interprets as directed toward God in a blasphemous, theo-logically defiant way.[99]

Asserto's painting of Job and his wife shares similarities with an earlier rendition by Gaspard de Crayer from 1619 (Fig. 3.7).[100] In both cases, Job clasps both hands while looking toward heaven. His body shows no visible marks. Job's wife, who also looks elderly, puts one hand on her hip while gesturing with the other hand.

Gerard Seghers, a Flemish artist, continues Job's pensive mood and dark surroundings in *The Patience of Job* now in the National Gallery in Prague.[101] Again in a typical scene, Job, an old man, sits on straw with a white drape to cover his genitals. His wife stands to his left pointing with her right hand and resting her left hand on her left hip. Seghers visited Italy around 1620 and became a noteworthy Flemish Caravaggesque painter, but by the late 1600s, he demonstrated influence of Rubens in his work. His painting of Job from the late 1600s is an example. Rubens himself painted Job around 1612. A copy of his lost painting exists in the Louvre and demonstrates, in torment of St. Anthony fashion, the drama of the demonic (Fig. 3.8). Around 1620, the School of Vlaamse rendered Job in a way similar to that of Rubens in a painting of Job, his wife, and demons for the Chapel of Beguines, Louvain. Job's wife, an old woman, has both hands on her hips, glaring at Job, while three demons, one holding a snake, grasp at Job in an attempt to drag him away.[102]

---

99.   Oldcorn points out that a town near Florence, Prato, in 1297, put a law in effect that imposed a fine or flogging against one who would make the fig sign toward heaven or toward God. Anthony Oldcorn, "The Perverse Image: Canto Xxv," in *Lectura Dantis, Inferno* (Berkeley: University of California Press, 1998), 333.

100.   An almost exact repeat of her gesture and that of Job's gazing to the heavens sitting among ruins can be found in the anonymous painting of Job and his wife in the Institut Royal du Patrimoine Artistique, Brussels, from around 1635. See Fig. 101 in Terrien, *The Iconography of Job Through the Centuries*, 190.

101.   Similarly, Job's wife points at Job in a painting by Mattia Preti (also known as Il Calabrese) in which Job and his friends sit among columned ruins and no sores show on Job's skin. Job's wife stands beside him and points at him while she looks at his friends. To the right of her feet lays a shadowy human figure on the ground, a man, though, with horns, the Satanic presence becoming more human. He holds himself up with his right elbow, pointing and sneering at Job. See Fig. 100 in ibid., 189.

102.   See Fig. 101 in ibid.

Figure 3.8. Rubens (after), *Job Tormented by Demons*, Louvre, Paris.
Photo: Réunion des Musées Nationaux/Art Resource, N.Y.

The eighteenth century embraces an eventual fading, or complicating, of traditional Christian notions of Satan.[103] A poignant example of the disappearance of satanic presence at the dungheap, while dramatically emphasizing the anger of Job's wife, appears in an engraving from around 1630 (Fig. 3.9a) in *Icones Biblicae* by Matthaeus Merian the elder, a Swiss engraver who settled in Frankfurt. The *Icones Biblicae* (1625–1630) contained 230 engravings of the Bible, with accompanying descriptions in German, Latin, and French. In his engravings, Merian captured the form of seventeenth-century European landscapes while maintaining piety without sentimentalism.[104] His engraving of Job captures the tradition of Job's sore-covered body on the dungheap, as well as a form of Satan which dawns female characteristics.

103. Russell, *Mephistopheles*, 128–67.
104. Matthaeus Merian, *Great Scenes from the Bible: 230 Magnificent 17th-Century Engravings* (Mineola, N.Y.: Dover, 2002).

Les amis de Iob le Vindre trouuer lors quil desploroit Iob conuenerunt eius amici cum suam calamitate
se miseres en ils disputerent sauoir sil estoit   deploraret ibi que disputarunt vtrum propter sua
tourmente pour ses pechez ou non   peccata Vexaretur aut propter aliquid aliud. Iob. 4.

Figure 3.9a. Matthaeus Merian, ca. 1630, in *Icones Biblicae*. Photo:
Katherine Low.

As customary with engravings, publishers reprinted them in many
other works. Other engravers copied Merian's representation as well,
such as in the case of anonymous reproductions found in Nicolas
Fontaine's *L'Histoire du Vieux et du Nouveau Testament* published in
1670 and again in 1699.[105] The same engraving shows up in a German
Bible history from around 1765 published by Raspischen Handlung, only
the reproducer of the image omits the hovering bat-winged demonic
force, leaving behind just Job's wife and friends, also emphasizing more
of the landscape and taking away the other mourners behind them. Job's
wife remains defiant in her demeanor (Fig. 3.9b).

105.   1670Font and 1699Font, Pitts Theology Library, Candler School of
Theology, Emory University. And, also, Nicolaus Visscher copied the image in
Afbeeldingen...Soo van het Oude als Nieuwe Testament, Fig. 96, in Bo Lindberg,
William Blake's Illustrations to the Book of Job (Abo: Abo Akademi, 1973).

Figure 3.9b. Matthaeus Merian, ca. 1630, in *Icones Biblicae* as published in a German bible history by Raspischen Handlung, ca. 1765. Photo: Katherine Low.

As in the case of Merian's engraving, by omitting devilish presence, the evil presence in Job's story seems visually to transfer to Job's wife. By 1700, Bernard Picart had engraved over 50 biblical scenes for the Mortier Bible, published concurrently in Antwerp and Amsterdam, which depicted scenes from both the Old and New Testaments. Like the artists before him, Picart maintains Job's clasped hands and sore-less body, and the demonic presence hides in the shadows, behind a tree, and points to Job (Fig. 3.10). The devilish crouching figure does not have traditional satanic features, such as bat wings; he appears more like a sinister human. Job's wife furrows her brow and emphatically gestures at Job.

Figure 3.10. Bernard Picart, late seventeenth century. As reproduced in an
English family Bible printed by Henry Galbraith between 1763 and 1764.
Photo: Katherine Low.

During his years in Paris, 1698–1710, Picart became highly successful
in printmaking; his images were reproduced and copied in many different
volumes throughout Europe. Picart also worked during the emergence
of tension between "moderns" and their adherence to Descartes and the
"ancients" who maintained the superiority of Greek and Roman Antiq-
uity. Picart illustrated an academic thesis that supported Descartes in
1707, and he owned Descartes' literary works, so it follows that Picart's
emphasis on the limitations of the traditional iconography for Satan puts

emotions back into the human mind, the area in which Descartes centered his philosophical work.[106] Picart's engraving of the dungheap, the human face expressing the deformity of evil and de-emphasizing the grotesqueness of Satan himself, stresses what Russell names as "the demonic immanent in the human mind."[107] Russell also points out that new philosophies, like those of Descartes, paved the way for the weakening and eventual fading of traditional Christian ideas about the Devil during the eighteenth century.[108] The fading of traditional ideas about the Devil also put Job's wife in a precarious position.

From the sixteenth and seventeenth centuries, though the presence of the Devil stays strong, gradual changes concerning transcendent evil begin to take hold, as reflected in many paintings of Job. Artists relegate Satan to the shadows, and the Devil fades under the influence of humanism and other movements. The human struggle against evil, dramatically represented with lavish and expensive devilish costumes in mystery plays of the Middle Ages, gives way to the kind of struggle found in the human heart evident in Elizabethan theater.[109]

When it comes to Baroque art, especially from Italian and Flemish provinces, Job's wife does not help her husband with his struggle. Her akimbo gestures, or, "hands upon her hips" is "the pose of the legendary shrew."[110] Along with scowled faces, older visages, and domineering physical presence, another underlying theme for the artists, besides relegating Satan to generic demonic presence or shadowy manifestations, is the portrayal of Job's wife as a shrew. The evil that was clearly embodied by Satan now transfers to Job's wife. Her ugly features do not demonstrate a form of piety, and in her case, her old age is associated with reprehensible behavior, expressing a principle that "being ugly in old age can point to culpability."[111] At the same time that artists diminish Satan's demonic role, they demonize Job's wife as a dangerous old woman.

106. Lynn Hunt, Margaret C. Jacob, and Wijnand Mijnhardt, *The Book That Changed Europe: Picart and Bernard's Religious Ceremonies of the World* (Cambridge, Mass.: Belknap, 2010), 45–70.

107. Russell, *Mephistopheles*, 91.

108. Ibid., 128.

109. Ibid., 76.

110. Terrien, *The Iconography of Job Through the Centuries*, 188.

111. Anouk Janssen, "The Good, the Bad, and the Elderly: The Representation of Old Age in Netherlandish Prints (Ca. 1550–1650)," in *Old Age in the Middle Ages and the Renaissance: Interdisciplinary Approaches to a Neglected Topic* (ed. Albrecht Classen; New York: de Gruyter, 2007), 453.

Figure 3.11. Caspar Luyken, as published in *Historia Celebriores Veteris Testamenti* by Christopher Weigel, 1712. Photo: Katherine Low.

Sixteenth- and seventeenth-century artists overwhelmingly represent Job's wife in the guise of an aged woman. Caspar Luyken, a Dutch engraver (1672–1708), visualizes Job's wife walking with a cane (Fig. 3.11). Luyken emphasizes her elongated chin and nose, another stereotype of what happens to the body as one gets older.[112] Functioning for Luyken, like for Asserto, who makes Job's wife give Job the "fig sign" (Fig. 3.6), is a seventeenth-century idealization and symbolization of an

112. Lynn A. Bothelho, "The 17th Century," in Thane, ed., *A History of Old Age*, 113–73.

old woman as threatening because she fits outside ideal gendered boundaries. Older women were tried more often as witches than younger women.[113] Among other factors, a woman's aging body signified a lack of her ability to fulfill her "natural" role as wife and mother.[114]

Whether or not artists think his wife bears Job's children at a period of restoration (Job 42:10–17), the art depicts Job's wife as an old woman who reminds the viewer, in Renaissance iconography, of an old crone, bordering on acting as a harbinger of destruction. The artists use the iconography to express a popular idealized view of marriage in the Renaissance and Job's wife's place in contrast to that ideal—she acts outside the confines of how a proper wife should act. As the next chapter will demonstrate, popular literature of the age offers even more elaboration on her role.

113. Reasons for this remain complex. For a detailed discussion, see Edward Bever, "Old Age and Witchcraft in Early Modern Europe," in *Old Age in Preindustrial Society* (ed. Peter N. Stearns; New York: Holmes & Meier, 1982), 150–90. See also, Alison Rowlands, "Witchcraft and Old Women in Early Modern Germany," *Past & Present*, no. 173 (2001): 50–89.

114. Bothelho, "The 17th Century," 127. See also, Jeanne Addison Roberts, "Types of Crone: The Nurse and the Wise Woman in English Renaissance Drama," *Renaissance Papers* 2000 (2000): 71–86.

Chapter 4

JOB'S WIFE'S PLACE IN THE WOMAN QUESTION,
SIXTEENTH AND SEVENTEENTH CENTURIES

This chapter sheds more light on the role of Job's wife for the artists of the sixteenth and seventeenth centuries mentioned in the previous chapter by examining cultural attitudes about Job and his wife reflected in popular religious discourse on the proper nature of Christian marriage. The art of the sixteenth and seventeenth centuries reflects the place of Job and his wife in an explosion of didactic domestic manuals throughout Europe. Martha Peacock states that the "*topos* of a shrewish and overbearing woman enslaving a man through marriage occurs early in Netherlandish literature and art but reaches a high point in the mid-sixteenth century that continues through the first half of the seventeenth century."[1] Rather than providing the Church Fathers with an example of deviant speech and another Eden, the story of Job and his wife provides a prooftext, as the Bible reached the hands of many readers, for those with concern for reformations and puritan ideals and, more specifically, for those who wanted to provide men and women with examples of socially appropriate marital behaviors.[2] In the artistic pieces discussed above, Job and his wife offer a visual metaphor for tensions about the place of husbands and wives in marriage and the dominant ideology of gender in early modern Europe.

Issues of gender remain complex in the sixteenth and seventeenth centuries. The witch craze reached its height during the Renaissance and Reformation periods for both Catholics and Protestants, peaking,

1. This *topos* reflects clearly in humorous representations of the cuckold, or the husband whose wife is cheating on him. Martha Peacock, "*Hoorndragers* and *Hennetasters*: The Old Impotent Cuckold As "Other" in Sixteenth-and Seventeenth-Century Netherlandish Art," in Classen, ed., *Old Age in the Middle Ages and the Renaissance*, 493.

2. For a compilation of medieval marriage sermons, in which Job and his wife are not mentioned, see D. L. D'Avray, *Medieval Marriage Sermons* (New York: Oxford University Press, 2001).

according to Russell, from 1550 to 1650.[3] In 1487, Job presented a significant problem for Heinrich Kramer and his assistant Jakob Sprenger, Dominican authors of a major and influential work on witchcraft, *Malleus Maleficarum* (*The Hammer of Witchcraft*). Both men acted as "successful" inquisitors in that they convicted many people of witchcraft in the name of papal supremacy and monastic reform in southern Germany. In *Malleus Maleficarum*, Kramer and Sprenger describe, in much detail, elements of witchcraft. Writing in terms of an encyclopedic entry of verifying the existence of witches, they discuss the harms of witchcraft, remedies, and methods to exterminate witches. Overwhelmingly, they assume witches are women and, explicitly, women who make sexual pacts with the Devil.[4]

Job's wife, according to Kramer and Sprenger, was not a witch. The text states clearly that Satan himself caused the suffering of Job (I, Question 2, 16A-B, 110).[5] Yet, by mentioning Job's wife, Kramer and Sprenger bring her in line with devilish practices. The Devil used his wife to vex him (II, Chap. 15, 144D, 380). Then, why do witches exist if the Devil can do his tormenting without the use of other humans, as evident in the book of Job? Kramer and Sprenger suggest that witches make Satan's work easier, and women, especially, with their weak and vulnerable nature, are more susceptible to the Devil (I, Question 3, 40A–46A, 159–173).[6] Early modern English readers would have inherited such a notion for Job's wife, since, for example, a translation, published in London, from the French of John Calvin's sermons on Job in 1574, calls Job's wife an "instrument of Satan" (*organum satani*).[7]

3. Russell, *Lucifer*, 301.

4. European women accused of witchcraft were the poorer among the community, more likely single than married, and more likely older than younger. On some level, those who accused them were "upholding women to conventional standards of female conduct": Brian P. Levack, *The Witch-Hunt in Early Modern Europe* (3d ed.; London: Pearson, 2006), 141–63.

5. All references from *Malleus* come from Jacobus Sprenger, *The Hammer of Witches: A Complete Translation of the Malleus Maleficarum* (trans. Christopher S. Mackay; New York: Cambridge University Press, 2009).

6. For more on the gendered implications of women as witches in *Malleus*, see Sigrid Brauner, *Fearless Wives and Frightened Shrews: The Construction of the Witch in Early Modern Germany* (Amherst: University of Massachusetts Press, 1995), 31–49.

7. Calvin preached 159 sermons on Job in 1554–55, recorded and translated in 1549. The ninth sermon on Job is the second sermon on the second chapter: a facsimile copy of a 1574 English edition attests to the circulation of Calvin's sermons in England. John Calvin, *Sermons on Job* (trans. Arthur Golding; 16th–17th Century Facsimile ed.; Carlisle, Pa.: The Banner of Truth Trust, 1993). For further

Job's wife's connection with the Devil, alongside her traditional Christian reputation, makes her what Sigrid Brauner translates as a "bad wife"; though not a witch, the notion of a "bad wife" (*böses wîp*) functioned in early modern Germany as a way to speak about married women who violated gendered social behavioral codes. Brauner argues that often the lines between categories for female unruliness blurred, so that by sixteenth-century vernacular literature, "the bad wife increasingly comes to resemble the modern witch" because of an increase in depictions of bad wives violating social codes that extended beyond marriage.[8] The topos of a "bad wife" coincides with the topos of the "slacker husband" (*der lose man*) who drinks, gambles, or engages in other gluttonous pursuits to the detriment of the family wealth and sustainability.[9] Such a gendered marital code extends beyond early modern Germany throughout Europe.

A similar type of married woman who violated social codes, the "scold" or the "shrew," is visually captured for Job's wife in the art discussed in the previous chapter. A brief discussion of the shrew's place in the broader culture here will further the analysis. From the 1560s onward, historians note an increasing concern on behalf of ecclesiastical authorities for those who disrupt early modern order. Lisa Jardine revisions the nature of the female scold within a broader context of gender roles; the questionable acts of a woman being a scold "have in common her intervention outside the home, as a woman, in public social relations, in a way that causes tensions in which her femaleness is at once recognized, and is the source of difficulty."[10]

At the same time that European societies defined social borders of witchcraft and feminine shrewish activity, issues of marriage surfaced as well.[11] The tensions involved do not simply take the form of men writing

discussion of Calvin's sermons, see Susan E. Schreiner, *Where Shall Wisdom Be Found? Calvin's Exegesis of Job from Medieval and Modern Perspectives* (Chicago: University of Chicago Press, 1994).

8. Brauner, *Fearless Wives and Frightened Shrews*, 73.

9. Ibid., 97. Also echoed in Lyndal Roper, *Oedipus and the Devil: Witchcraft, Sexuality and Religion in Early Modern Europe* (New York: Routledge, 1994), 107–24.

10. Lisa Jardine, "Unpicking the Tapestry: The Scholar of Women's History as Penelope Among Her Suitors," in *Attending to Women in Early Modern England* (ed. Betty S. Travitsky and Adele F. Seeff; Newark: University of Delaware Press, 1994), 132.

11. For a six-volume collection of early modern conduct literature, see William St. Clair and Irmgard Maassen, eds., *Conduct Literature for Women, 1500–1640* (6 vols.; Brookfield, Vt.: Pickering & Chatto, 2000).

misogynistic ideas about women; authors of marriage manuals, or conduct literature, reacted to shifting models of gendered behavior. The witchcraft trials of early modern Europe represent just one example of the phenomena of societal instability of sexual identities. The debate concerned what Joy Wiltenburg names as "the place of women and gender in cultural thinking about authority, order, and individuality."[12] With cultural value leaning toward rational individualism, a growing early modern emphasis on what Wiltenburg describes as "a conception of society as a collection of self-sufficient individuals" began to take root.[13] Joan Kelly states it this way: "Early modern Europe was in the process of state formation. Princely rule, rank, and hierarchy coexisted with bourgeois modes of life and work and with a developing republican (liberal) ethos."[14] Fragmentations of religious beliefs that took place under various Reformations confused and complicated issues of identity. Such a complication led to "a new emphasis on inwardness," because one's performance in public did not always match one's private convictions.[15]

Gender plays a large role in the experience of the self, and, as John Jeffries Martin explains, "it becomes clear that in the Renaissance the boundary that divided an internal sense of experience—one's thoughts, and memories—from the outside world and that brought the internal and external in relation to one another was a locus of danger."[16] Deep anxieties about masculinity and femininity emerged during the Reformation because when reformers called into question religious foundations, they also brought about the instability of the ideal roles of masculine and feminine behavior. Lyndal Roper states, "there was certainly a period of intense flux in gender relations in sixteenth-century Europe," for masculine as well as for feminine performance, because "a movement which changes the sexual status of its clergy, turning models of chastity into exemplars of matrimonial harmony, clearly transforms the meaning of manhood."[17] Therefore, in order for society to function in order, not

12. Joy Wiltenburg, *Disorderly Women and Female Power in the Street Literature of Early Modern England and Germany* (Charlottesville: University Press of Virginia, 1992), 19.

13. Ibid.

14. Joan Kelly, *Women, History and Theory: The Essays of Joan Kelly* (Chicago: University of Chicago Press, 1984), 67.

15. John Jeffries Martin, *Myths of Renaissance Individualism* (New York: Palgrave Macmillan, 2004), 48.

16. Ibid., 86.

17. Roper, *Oedipus and the Devil*, 37–38.

disorder, determinate teachings about marriage as a serious undertaking, especially for reformers from Lutherans to Anglicans, emerge.

Although many areas of European society and culture experienced transformations due to religious reforms, this section focuses on one key area—marriage. During the sixteenth and seventeenth centuries, a widespread literary concern for women, marriage, and education spread throughout Europe.[18] The debate began in Latin and French literature over the education of women, a "literary quarrel known as the *Querelle des femmes*" (the woman question, dated by Joan Kelly as taking place from 1400 until 1789) in which one woman took part, Chrstine de Pisan, author of *Book of the City of Ladies* from 1405.[19] In England, the *Querelle des femmes* took on heated forms because of the question of women rulers. Juan Luis Vives's *Instruction of a Christian Woman* (1523), for instance, centered on the education of Catherine of Aragon's daughter, the future Mary I, queen of England. When it came to publications about and for women, such domestic manuals basically acted like catalogues of famous and infamous women and men, with authors using biblical and classical examples to make their cases about the ideal type of husband, wife, and marriage.[20] The conduct manuals construct prescriptive, rather than descriptive, modes of behavior. Yet, they witness to the tensions and pressures undergoing gender relations in the midst of continuous traditional understandings of the social customs involved for the household.[21]

18.   Wiltenburg, *Disorderly Women and Female Power in the Street Literature of Early Modern England and Germany*.

19.   Shahar, *The Fourth Estate*, 166. See also Joan Kelly, "Early Feminist Theory and the *Querelle des Femmes*, 1400–1789" reprinted in Kelly, *Women, History and Theory*, 65–109.

20.   Space does not allow for a discussion of the links between marriage and sexuality in the Renaissance. For an introduction to the subject, see Todd W. Reeser, "Moderation and Masculinity in Renaissance Marriage Discourse and in Rabelais's Tiers Livre," *The Romanic Review* 90 (1999): 1–25. See also Roper, *Oedipus and the Devil*. For thorough anthologies, and sourcebooks, consult Kate Aughterson, ed., *Renaissance Woman: A Sourcebook* (New York: Routledge, 1995); Aughterson, ed., *The English Renaissance: An Anthology of Sources and Documents* (New York: Routledge, 1998); Lloyd Davis, ed., *Sexuality and Gender in the English Renaissance: An Annotated Edition of Contemporary Documents* (New York: Garland, 1998); Suzanne W. Hull, *Chaste, Silent and Obedient: English Books for Women, 1475–1640* (San Marino: Huntington Library, 1982). For a more specific discussion of Shakespeare and sources, see Frances E. Dolan, ed., *The Taming of the Shrew: Texts and Contexts* (Boston: Bedford Books of St. Martin's Press, 1996).

21.   As suggested in the introduction to Davis, ed., *Sexuality and Gender in the English Renaissance*, xii–xxiii.

Taking part in a shared ideal presentation of proper gendered behavior for marriage, European household manuals borrowed heavily from one another. Therefore, this chapter focuses mainly on English sources and publications of European literature, partly because of the availability of such literature and because England's reformations built upon the reforms that began earlier in Germany and Switzerland. Furthermore, functions of marriage became a public issue, religiously and socially relevant in England, with the controversy of the divorce of Henry VIII from Catherine of Aragon and his subsequent break from the Catholic Church, and his declaration that he was the head of the Church of England in 1536.[22]

This chapter also focuses on English sources because of their abundance and availability during the peak of the Renaissance. In Germany, the existence of popular literature attests to the spread of literacy in the sixteenth century. The advance of literacy declined throughout the seventeenth century, due to the outbreak of war in Germany. In terms of the availability of literature, England held the advantage, especially in the seventeenth century, with London as a single center which contained a sustained print industry.[23] Among that industry, women acted as consumers, and if not more importantly, women began to author printed works as well. Margaret King states, "In England from 1475 to 1640, 163 titles were produced specifically for women, of whom 800 were explicitly named."[24] The bestselling books of the sixteenth and seventeenth centuries in Britain were kinds of self-help manuals directing readers on how to live a godly and proper life. Men wrote most of these conduct books, but some women engaged the genre, especially between 1604 and 1624 in England.[25] Even more striking is the acceleration of vernacular books for Englishwomen in the sixteenth and seventeenth centuries: "From 1570 through 1640, assuming a press run of 1,500 and counting multiple editions, there were printed perhaps 400,000 volumes targeted for a female audience."[26]

The first chapters of this book covered gendered deviant speech as a platform for medieval art concerning Job's wife in the SHS; the idea that a woman can use her tongue as a weapon, as part of a gendered behavior

22. Dolan, ed., *The Taming of the Shrew*, 161.
23. Ibid.; Wiltenburg, *Disorderly Women and Female Power*.
24. Margaret L. King, *Women of the Renaissance* (Chicago: University of Chicago Press, 1991), 174.
25. Valerie Wayne, "Advice for Women from Mothers and Patriarchs," in *Women and Literature in Britain 1500–1700* (ed. Helen Wilcox; Cambridge: Cambridge University Press, 1996), 56.
26. King, *Women of the Renaissance*, 175.

placed upon women, carried through medieval times. What remains noteworthy is an increase in popularity of the generalized image of woman as "shrew" in the early modern period. The shrew stereotype grew, and persisted, in popularity.

One short-lived controversy during the end of King James's rule in the 1620s helps to illuminate possibilities for why the shrew stereotype gained popularity. Two pamphlets, *Hic Mulier* and *Haec Vir*, were published in 1620 accusing women of dressing like men. The rhetoric introduced a unique spin on an old concern for women dressing like men, that of "masculine" women.[27] Masculine behavior conferred upon men in *Hic Mulier* includes short hair, pants, and carrying weapons. God created females, according to *Hic Mulier*, as separate from males, created not out of earth (and slime) like males, but in a more "refined" way that keeps sexual differentiation part of creation.[28] What remains at stake, then, is the moral obligation to uphold "natural" sexual distinctions, the kinds of distinctions socially evident in gendered performances.

While a greater emphasis on individuality characterizes the "Renaissance," it remains questionable whether women engaged in such autonomy because historical data on everyday women remains scarce. Englishwomen were authoring their own defenses of their sex and therefore expressing their opinions in a public print arena. Perhaps the explicit emphasis on the shrew may come from a widespread male concern for female rebellion.[29] Women who "defied the authority of their husbands," for instance, "threatened the entire patriarchal order."[30] More precisely, a threat existed to the godly social order accepted in the society. This is the case when a "notion was forming that women as women were devoid of power and authority by their very nature."[31]

When reformers advocated for lay and clerical marriage, they called for a reconsideration of marriage. Many of the authors of the conduct books were the first to herald a generation of married clergymen. If sexual renunciation no longer served as a sign of holiness, then theologians had to reconfigure how a hierarchal marital relationship brought with it sanctification.[32] In her analysis of the engagement of Christian

---

27. Sandra Clark, "'Hic Mulier,' 'Haec Vir,' and the Controversy Over Masculine Women," *Studies in Philology* 82, no. 2 (1985): 159.

28. *Hic Mulier* (sig. B4), see ibid., 169. For a full text, consult Henderson and McManus, *Half Humankind*, 272.

29. Henderson and McManus, *Half Humankind*, 52.

30. Underdown, "The Taming of the Scold," 127.

31. Kelly, *Women, History and Theory*, 87.

32. King, *Women of the Renaissance*, 40.

humanism by protestant reformers, Margo Todd notes that the Bible served as a means to transform society, to aid in the achievement of human potential and godly behavior for prince and commoner alike. Todd applies "Christian humanist social thought" to the Renaissance household. Christian humanists engaged classical domestic ideas, such as from Xenophon's *Oeconomicus*, and combined them with biblical examples to form household religious instruction.[33]

Job and His Wife in Sixteenth-
and Seventeenth-Century Literature

Religious ideas about the household directed toward women begin as early as the fourteenth century with the *Book of the Knight of the Tower* (*Livre pour l'enseignement de ses filles*), translated into English in 1484 by William Caxton, which mentions Job and his wife in the context of their marriage. Chevalier de La Tour Landry's work comes out of the medieval courtesy literature genre. Landry fits Job and his wife into his scheme of a "successful" marriage, one in which "women should be models of morality and patience whose virtues compensate for the faults of men."[34] Therefore, he pictures Job's wife as a sympathetic wife, who brings him food and shares in his misery, until she has a temporary lapse under Satan's temptations and verbally demonstrates anger.[35]

The 1541 anonymous poem "Schole House of Women" heralded an entire trend of circulating sixteenth- and seventeenth-century pamphlets about marriage in England, whether in instructional manuals, sermons, or in satirical poems and ballads. "Schole House" seems to be based on an old French poem, "un poëme des tourmens de Mariage."[36] As part of the usual form, the author launches into scripture for proof texts, beginning with Adam and Eve, and picks up biblical examples again beginning in line 742. In some cases, according to the author, a husband must ask the

33. Xenophon, *Oeconomicus: A Social and Historical Commentary* (trans. Sarah B. Pomeroy; Oxford: Clarendon, 1995). See also, Margo Todd, *Christian Humanism and the Puritan Social Order* (Cambridge: Cambridge University Press, 1987). One important contribution made by this work is Todd's reconfiguration of Puritanism as part of protestant mainstream England, thus tracing the development of Puritanism within a broader religious and intellectual context of the sixteenth and seventeenth centuries.

34. Diane Bornstein, *The Lady in the Tower: Medieval Courtesy Literature for Women* (Hamden, Conn.: Archon, 1983), 52.

35. Chapter 29 in Landry, *The Book of the Knight of the Tower*, 110.

36. Edward Vernon Utterson, ed., *Select Pieces of Early Popular Poetry* (2 vols.; London: William Pickering, 1825), 2:53–54.

Devil to show his wife's true nature, because if a husband thinks that all is well in his marriage, it is certainly Satan's job to show a woman's true self (ll. 574–94). Job's wife fits in with the other biblical examples of troublesome wives. The author elaborates on her speech:

> The wife of Job, the man elect,/Saluted him with scornes and mocks,/And ful unseemly oft his chect,/Saying, thou fool, ful of the pocks,/Ful like a fool thy brest thou knocks;/Weenest thou for thy fair speech/God wil come the for to seech./Thy prating leue, foule thee befall,/Trust me he wil thee neuer heale;/Thy beasts, thy goods, and thy children all,/Be dead and brent, now euery deale,/And thou liest heer with many a bile/Prating and praying to the deuine,/And wurse thou stinkest then a dead swine. (ll. 776–90)[37]

The "Schole House of Women" fits with the cultural focus on the "moral education of girls and woman in higher urban circles" which led to using classical and biblical sources to present "gender-specific virtues" on how to be a good wife and mother.[38] Biblical women remained at the heart of heated debates on the nature of womanhood. For instance, the "Schole House of Women" did not go unchallenged, especially in the case of Edward More in his "The Defence of Women" in 1560. More, an Oxford scholar and minor poet, notes that Lucifer lies at the heart of human problems. The serpent, after all, tempted Eve (ll. 43–44), and Eve just repeated what the serpent said (l. 48).[39] More offers Susanna and Judith as examples of good wives, as are Lot's daughters in terms of their desire to multiply their descendents upon the earth (ll. 178, 198). He also sprinkles in various comments about Venus being a good wife and mother. More's counter-argument against "Schole House of Women" was only printed once, as opposed to the many printings of "Schole House of Women."[40]

Also in 1541, the Swiss reformer Heinrich Bullinger's *The Christen State of Matrimonye* was translated into English.[41] By 1575, the English translation went through nine printings. Although he lists Job as a biblical married man, the particular details of Job's marriage do not concern Bullinger. Rather, he uses Job 31 several times to make arguments against the shame of defiling virgins and the consequences of adultery.[42]

---

37. Ibid., 2:83–84.
38. Bleyerveld, "Chaste, Obedient and Devout," 220.
39. Utterson, ed., *Select Pieces of Early Popular Poetry.*
40. Ibid., 2:96.
41. Heinrich Bullinger, *The Christen State of Matrimonye* (trans. Miles Coverdale; The English Experience Facsimile ed.; Norwood, N.J.: Johnson, 1974).
42. In the case of defiling virgins, p. 24 and in the case of adultery, p. 37.

Bullinger warns a husband not to touch another man's wife; the "words of Job does acknowledge that adultery is such a vice" that is "by right to be grievously punished."[43] Ultimately, Bullinger concludes, those who have struggles with marriage have "consolations out of scripture to comfort them," including the example of Job.[44]

Joannes Ludovicus Vives (Juan Luis Vives), a Spanish scholar and humanist, first wrote his *Instruction of Christen Woman* (*De institutione feminae christianae*) in Latin in 1523. His concern of the education of women came from his role as adviser to Queen Catherine of Aragon on matters concerning her daughter's education. Queen Catherine's daughter, Mary, became Queen Mary I in 1553. After its appearance in English around 1529, Vives's *Education of a Christian Woman* became influential. It appeared in at least 40 editions translated into English, Dutch, French, German, Spanish, and Italian.[45] As part of an early sixteenth-century humanist movement that supported education and the value of reading for most women, creating a "middle path" between advocating for complete subordination of women in society and total equality of women to men, Vives granted that women had intellectual capacity for education. But, that education should be just enough to center on a woman's chastity, her religious duty (made even more central by Protestantism ideals that all must learn to read the scriptures), and her future as a leader of a household.[46]

The *Education of a Christian Woman* surfaced on the edges of the development of basic education for women of the elite, who, by the fourteenth century, could read vernacular books, though many were not trained to read Latin.[47] Vives also includes a section on marital instruction, in which Job's wife fairs badly:

> I think Job's wife was the only possession left to him so that she could add to his misery and with her malicious tongue make his burden even greater. O detestable and impious woman! You reproach your husband for his holiness as if it were a crime! Not even devils would dare to do this. The devil destroyed all of Job's fortunes, slew all his servants, took away his children, covered him with ulcerous sores, but he never reproached him for persevering in his original purity of soul. His wife reproached him, showing that she was more shameless than the devil.[48]

43. Bullinger, *The Christen State of Matrimonye*, 37.
44. Ibid., 47.
45. King, *Women of the Renaissance*, 164.
46. Hull, *Chaste, Silent and Obedient*, 56–57.
47. King, *Women of the Renaissance*, 172–73.
48. Juan Luis Vives, *The Education of a Christian Woman* (trans. Charles Fantazzi; Chicago: University of Chicago Press, 2000), 198–99.

Vives offers an interesting twist from medieval concerns to demonstrate that Satan used Job's wife to tempt her husband like Satan used Eve against Adam. Vives makes it clear that Job's wife acted on her own accord and her words did not come from Satan. Despite the fact that Vives disapproves of her behavior, Vives grants a level of autonomy to Job's wife. This is perhaps due to the nature of the discussion; it behooves the authors to maintain a more realistic interpretation of Job and his wife than that of Job and his wife as another Adam and Eve tempted by Satan. In this way, they maintain a humanistic lean toward personal values and responsibility, and they can continue to use biblical couples as models for proper or improper marital behavior.

Another point of unrest during the sixteenth and seventeenth centuries comes from concern over women's bodies and the prescriptions of chaste apparel, pious activities within the home, and their modesty in expressing their desires. What follows, then, is that Satan nearly disappears from the discussions concerning the marriage of Job and his wife. Edmund Tilney, in *A Brief and Pleasant Discourse of Duties in Mariage, Called the Flower of Friendshippe* from 1568, includes Vives as a dialogue partner in the text. Tilney dedicated the book to Queen Elizabeth I and was not married when he wrote his treatise, but married later in 1583.[49] Tilney's message gave husbands the task of displacing the desires of their wives to those desires of God and her husband. Marital love may join two bodies together, but through the husband, marriage should erase the inward will of the wife so that her desires, mostly sexual ones, will be appeased and controlled.[50] In Tilney's case, "the pacience of Job" was "all to [*sic*] little" because an ideal husband suffers the matters of his wife, no matter how trifling (764–765).[51] Tilney's advice shows concern for a masculine ideal, that of master, but that a man must also master himself. Tilney presents Job's ability to maintain his patience and thereby sustain his authority with "rational discretion," like that of many other husbands, as a "constant and extremely challenging labour."[52] The Church of England puritan pastor William Whately released his *A Care-Cloth* to the streets of London in 1624, and he also uses Job's patience as a model for husbands, even when all the comforts of marriage do not exist for them. Whately does not mention Job's wife, but instead quotes

49. Alexandra Shepard, *Meanings of Manhood in Early Modern England* (New York: Oxford University Press, 2003), 71.

50. Wayne, "Advice for Women from Mothers and Patriarchs," 67–68.

51. Edmund Tilney, *The Flower of Friendship: A Renaissance Dialogue Contesting Marriage* (ed. Valerie Wayne; New York: Cornell University Press, 1992), 121.

52. Shepard, *Meanings of Manhood in Early Modern England*, 78.

Job's words to her: "Job said, Shall we receive good at Gods hand, and not evil? Lo, the speedy remembrance of what prosperity he had enjoyed enabled him to be quiet in his present tribulation: so must the married persons do in their estate, for Job is our president for patience."[53]

The harmony of society depends on a quiet and orderly household, so advocate John Dod and Robert Cleaver, in *A Godly Form of Household Government*, one of the most popular household instruction manuals of the period, first published in 1598. Dod and Cleaver, presumably the authors, often quote Tilney's *Flower of Friendshippe* verbatim and were both dissenters of the Anglican Church and puritan in their ideals.[54] They suggest that a wife maintains silence when her husband begins to complain because once a husband begins to chide, the wife begins to scold: "now and then, most unnaturally, they come to handy-gripes, more beast-like then Christian-like, which their so doing is both a great shame, and foul discredit to them both." Therefore, the answer to such a dilemma is for the wife to support her husband's anger or pain in silence and obedience.[55]

Mutual support remains an overwhelmingly important goal of marriage in conduct manuals. Companionship in marriage, after all, for both Catholics and Protestants, reflects the humanist ideal based on the Aristotelian notion that marriage is natural and leads to a harmonious commonwealth.[56] William Gouge's popular and comprehensive work *Of Domestical Duties* from 1622 turns to Job and his wife to point to the issue of both husband and wife supporting one another in times of need. They both failed at their marriage because they did not maintain one of the most principal components of marriage,

> which is to be a continual comfort and help each to other, and to ease the burdens of one another: in which respect they are made yoke-fellows. Job's wife by her unnatural carriage towards him in his affliction did much aggravate his misery when he stood in most need of her help, she afforded least unto him it appears by Job's complaint of her, in these words, my breath is strange to my wife, that she altogether neglected him in his misery.[57]

---

53. Chap. II, William Whately, *A Care-Cloth, or the Cumbers and Troubles of Marriage* (Norwood, N.J.: Johnson, 1976), 82.

54. Dolan, ed., *The Taming of the Shrew*, 201–2. See also Wayne, "Advice for Women from Mothers and Patriarchs," 68.

55. From the excerpt of *A Godly Form of Household Government* in Aughterson, ed., *The English Renaissance*, 450.

56. Todd's chapter, "The Spiritualized Household," is particularly relevant here: Todd, *Christian Humanism and the Puritan Social Order*, 96–117.

57. The second treatise, part II: "Of Common-Mutual Duties Betwixt Man and Wife," in William Gouge, *Of Domestical Duties* (ed. Greg Fox; lulu.com, 2006), 176.

Still, Gouge affords Job's wife a "shrewish disposition" in how she disgracefully spoke to her husband.[58] Henry Smith, a puritan minister in London, preached *A Preparative to Marriage*, first published in 1591. He also uses the term "yoke-fellow" when it comes to Job's wife's failings to support her husband in his illness. The Devil sent Job's wife to torment him, to tempt him to blaspheme, according to Smith, "when he [the Devil] took away all beside."[59] Smith's publication went through four editions in its first year; in the 1580s, Smith gained the title of "silver-tongued Smith" because of his successful preaching career in London. Smith never married.[60]

George Swinnock, another English Puritan concerned with living a godly life, warns his male readers that a wife can be "next to thyself" a "best friend or worst foe that godliness can have in thy family." According to Swinnock, many biblical men were defeated by their wicked wives, including Job, when Satan spared his wife in order that she may, on Satan's behalf, "cross him," because "the devil knew that none was so fit to present that poisonous potion with success to Job, as his wife; that if he ever took it, her fair hands must give it, and her sugared words sweeten it."[61] Richard Baxter's *A Christian Directory* was first published in 1673. In a section on the "Mutual Duties of Husbands and Wives Toward Each Other," Baxter, an influential puritan theologian, alludes to Job and his wife in terms of one partner hindering the holiness and salvation of the other (II. v.8).[62]

In his *The Golden Grove*, William Vaughn takes up a revival of economic writing in 1608 in the fashion of pseudo-Aristotelian *Economics*. A marriage that runs smoothly reflects the harmonious nature of society as a whole. In terms of the roles expected of them as husband and wife, in the words of Alexandra Shepard, "conduct writers insisted that it was not only the terms of manhood that were at stake, but the entire social order."[63] Therefore, a husband holds several duties toward his wife, such as putting up with her hastiness and feebleness. This sentiment shows through in Tilney's *Flower of Friendshippe* from 1568 as

58. The third treatise, paragraph 15, "Of Wives' Particular Duties," ibid.

59. Aughterson, ed., *Renaissance Woman: A Sourcebook*, 82.

60. Shepard, *Meanings of Manhood in Early Modern England*, 71.

61. First published in 1662 in London, *The Christian Man's Calling* (Part I, Chap. XXVII) in George Swinnock, *The Works of George Swinnock*, vol. 1 (London: James Nisbet & Co., 1868), 336.

62. II. vi.I. Richard Baxter, *The Practical Works of Richard Baxter* (4 vols.; (Morgan, Pa.: Soli Deo Gloria, 1673), 1:434.

63. Shepard, *Meanings of Manhood in Early Modern England*, 73.

well. A husband must also keep his wife happy by sharing a bed with her and remaining faithful. Vaughn cites Job's wife as an example of what not to do: "the wife must not forsake her husband in adversity, or deride him as Job's wife did when she bade him, *curse God and die*, but she ought to comfort and cherish him as a part of her own body."[64]

The motivation behind Job's wife's speech to her husband became another topic of interest for commentators, especially when it concerns her attempt to get Job to blaspheme. One of the most popular books in the printed debate came from Joseph Swetnam, *The Arraignment of Lewd, Idle, Froward, and Unconstant Women* in 1615, with ten editions to follow by 1637. When a man marries "a woman of evil report," it reflects negatively on his character. For example, "Job's wife gave her husband counsel to blaspheme God and to curse him (chapter 1)."[65] Rachel Speght, a daughter of a Calvinist minister in middle-class London, challenged Swetnam's accusation of blasphemy in her line-by-line direct reinterpretation of the biblical passages used by Swetnam in *Certaine Quaeres to the Bayter of Women*.[66] Speght responds: "you misconster the Text; for the true construction thereof will shew it to bee a Sarcasmus or Ironicall speech, and not an instigation to blasphemie" (ll. 34–36).[67] Speght's main critique of Swetnam is his uneducated statements and general use of biblical examples to make his point about the depravity of women. F. W. Van Heertum's critical edition of *The Araignment* argues that publishers kept printing Swetnam's work because it appealed to the popular masses and not necessarily to an educated audience. Swetnam "relies on assumptions about the nature of women which were the staple fare of attacks on women," thus he "does not raise any serious issues concerning the status of women."[68]

64. William Vaughan, *The Golden Grove*, as provided in Aughterson, ed., *Renaissance Woman*, 97.

65. F. W. Van Heertum, ed., *A Critical Edition of Joseph Swetnam's the Araignment of Lewd, Idle, Froward, and Unconstant Women (1615)* (Nijmegen: Cicero, 1989), 205.

66. For this and other responses written by women, see *The Early Modern Englishwoman: A Facsimile Library of Essential Works*. Part I, *Printed Writings, 1500–1640*. Vol. 4, *Defences of Women: Jane Anger, Rachel Speght, Ester Sowernam, Constantia Munda* (ed. Betty S. Travitsky and Patrick Cullen (Brookfield, Vt.: Ashgate, 1996).

67. Rachel Speght, "Certaine Quaeres to the Bayter of Women," in *The Polemics and Poems of Rachel Speght* (ed. Barbara Kiefer Lewalski; New York: Oxford University Press, 1996), 35.

68. Heertum, ed., *A Critical Edition of Joseph Swetnam's the Araignment of Lewd, Idle, Froward, and Unconstant Women (1615)*, 19.

Swetnam, nevertheless, reverberates popular ideas about the nature of Job's wife's words as urging Job to commit blasphemy. One of Milton's literary sources, "Job Militant" from 1624 by Francis Quarles, an English poet, upholds the suggested blasphemy of Job's wife's words.[69] Quarles paraphrases Job's wife's speech:

> Her passion waxt, made strong, with scorne and spleene; Like as the Winds, imprison'd in the earth, and barr'd the passage of their naturall birth, Grow fierce; and nilling to be longer pent, Breake in an Earthquake, shake the World, and vent; So brake she forth, so forth her Fury brake, Till now pent in with shame; and thus she spake. *Fond Saint, thine Innocence finds timely speed, A foolish Saint receives a Saintly meed; Is this the lust man's Recompence? Or hath Heaven no requital for thy painefull Faith Other than this? What, have thy zealous Qualmes, Abstemious Fastings, and thy hopefull Almes, Thy private Groanes, and often-bended knees, No other End, no other Thanks, but these? Fond man, submit thee to a kinder Fate, Cease to be righteous, at so deare a rate: 'Tis Heaven and Fortune, that thy Weale debarres; Curse Heaven then, and not thy wayward Starres: 'Tis God that plagues thee, God not knowing why; Curse then that God, revenge thy Wrongs, and Dye.* (V, 30–50)[70]

As mentioned above, the evil so prominently viewed through Satan in medieval sources of Job and his wife begin to dissipate especially by the seventeenth century. Henricus Cornelius Agrippa, in *Declamation on the Nobility and Preeminence of the Female Sex*, suggests that Job's wife acted in a far more superior way than the Devil in terms of being able to "dislodge him from his original simplicity and patience of spirit and provoke him to anger."[71] Rather than catalogue women of importance, Agrippa utilized the biblical sources commonly used to support the inferiority of women in order to subvert their standard meanings. The words of Job's wife held power; she was "more daring" than the Devil, being able to incite Job "to use abusive language." Agrippa, a German student of occult philosophy and theology, traveled throughout France and Italy, and originally wrote his treatise, *Declamatio de nobilitate et praecellentia foeminei sexus* in 1529 but it quickly became available in French, German, Italian, and English.

69. As argued by Barbara Kiefer Lewalski, *Milton's Brief Epic: The Genre, Meaning, and Art of Paradise Regained* (Providence, R.I.: Brown University Press, 1966), 129.

70. Alexander Grosart, ed., *The Complete Works in Prose and Verse of Francis Quarles*, vol. 2 (Edinburgh: Edinburgh University Press, 1880), 78.

71. Henricus Cornelius Agrippa, *Declamation on the Nobility and Preeminence of the Female Sex* (trans. Albert Rabil; Chicago: University of Chicago Press, 1996), 66.

Contrary to medieval interpretations that accord Satan's power as the primary mover of Job's wife's words, Agrippa assumes autonomy in her actions. It is similar to Vives's ideas in *Instruction of Christen Woman* (*De institutione feminae christianae*) from 1523. However, Agrippa writes of the power of women, because, "Aristotle may say that of all the animals the males are stronger and wiser than the females, but St. Paul writes that weak things have been chosen to confound the strong."[72] Agrippa lists biblical instances to prove his point, including the notion that "Job was patient" until a woman, not Satan, provoked him to anger, "therein proving herself stronger than the devil."[73] Agrippa implicitly holds a masculine expectation for Job in his writing; he expected Job to show rational self-control, but, his wife, more threatening than the Devil, caused him to lapse in his control. Men, fulfilling the role as husband, should exercise sound governance of the household, with mastery reflective of the governing powers of society. The concept of "master-hood" in all of one's roles meant that even an unmarried man experienced insecure masculinity. The married man was expected to function as the "household head."[74] Yet, contradictions and tensions existed in conduct literature because the authors prescribed husbands their autonomy, while at the same time implying their mutual dependence upon their wives.[75] R. W. Connell, for instance, notes gradient forms of masculine constructions in the world of the West, naming "complicity" as one of them. Complicit masculinity is crafted because "marriage, fatherhood and community life often involve extensive compromises with women rather than naked domination."[76] A paradoxical message exists in an ideal of marriage for achieving masculinity—a husband's domination over a wife, yet becoming a "yoke-fellow" to his wife. Marriage threatens manhood, yet remains part of how one achieves manhood.[77]

Sixteenth- and seventeenth-century paintings register Job's emotion with controlled Christian piety in the form of his Christ-like pose of clasped hands. For Agrippa, as for many others, demonstration of

72. Heinrich Cornelius Agrippa, *The Philosophy of Natural Magic* (Chicago: The deLaurence Company, 1913), 267.

73. Ibid.

74. Roper, *Oedipus and the Devil*, 46.

75. A topic discussed in Shepard, *Meanings of Manhood in Early Modern England*.

76. Connell, *Masculinities*, 79.

77. The discrepancy, for Alexandra Shepard, evidences a gap in what the conduct literature prescribed and how marriage was actually practiced. Of concern for this chapter, though, is the ideal presentation made by the authors. Shepard, *Meanings of Manhood in Early Modern England*, 84.

emotion belonged to the weak or effeminate.[78] In popular preaching, Job's wife becomes an example of the weakness of sensuality, a feminine characteristic found in women. John Donne, appointed Dean of St. Paul's Cathedral in London in 1621, not only preached but also wrote poetry and epigrams. In a sermon from 1620, Donne recalls Augustine's teachings on Job's story, only to make a point about temporal suffering and the relation of husband and wife as "one flesh," for good and bad:

> *Uxor relicta erat,* Job had not lost all, because his wife was left, *Misericordem putatis diabolum,* says that father, *qui ei reliquit Uxorem?* Do you think that Job lighted upon a merciful and good-natured devil, that the devil did this out of pity and compassion to Job, or that Job was beholden to the devil for this, that he left his wife? *Norerat per quam deceperat Adam,* says he, the devil knew by what instrument he had deceived the first man, and by the same instrument he practices upon Job; *Suam reliquit adjutricem, non mariti consolatricem,* He left Job a helper, but a helper for his own ends, but for her husband a miserable comforter. *Caro conjux,* says the same father in another place, this flesh, this sensual part of ours, is our wife: and when these temporal things by any occasion are taken from us, that wife, that flesh, that sensuality is left to murmur and repine at God's corrections, and that is all the benefit we have by that wife, and all the portion we have with that wife.[79]

Another preacher later than Donne, Thomas Watson, a well-known minister dismissed from his post at St. Stephen's, Walbrook, in London under the Act of Uniformity under the reign of King Charles II in 1662, covers the subtlety and underhandedness of the Devil. Satan uses those ones closest to people to tempt them, as "he tempted Job by a proxy,—he handed over a temptation to him, by his wife."[80] Watson explains: "Thus Satan made use of Job's wife to do his work; the woman was made of the rib, and Satan made a bow of this rib, out of which he shot the arrow of his temptation."[81] Matthew Poole, an English biblical scholar with Presbyterian and antipapal leanings, took up a large task of writing a biblical commentary. Poole's friends helped finish his *English Annotations on the Holy Bible* after his death in 1679. Though considered a

78. Anthony Fletcher, *Gender, Sex and Subordination in England 1500–1800* (New Haven: Yale University Press, 1995).

79. Sermon 74, Preached at Whitehall, April 30, 1620, on Ps 144.15, in John Donne, *The Works of John Donne* (ed. Henry Alford; 6 vols.; London: Parker, 1839), 3:332–33.

80. "Of the Sixth Petition in the Lord's Prayer," in Thomas Watson, *A Body of Practical Divinity: In a Series of Sermons on the Shorter Catechism* (Philadelphia: James Kay, Jun. & Co., 1833), 559.

81. Ibid.

religious non-conformist, he still echoes the old adage that the Devil spared Job's wife "with cruel intent to be the instrument of his temptations, and the aggravation of Job's misery."[82]

Some theologians, preachers, and exegetes seriously engage the topic, and some use the example of Job and his wife in cheaply printed sources that booksellers and printers produced to sell to the masses. The anonymous ironic response to the 1706 *The Fifteen Comforts of Matrimony* provides an example. The humorous response, "The Batchelors and Maids Answer to the Fifteen Comforts of Matrimony," refutes each comfort of marriage and in the sixth "mock comfort," the poet states, "but here I differ from the Poet's Thought,/Who says, A Schold as even good for nought,/For like Job's Wife she will Man's Patience try,/And bring Repentance too, before he die:/Then who'd live single, if a Scolding Wife/Works such great Wonders in a Husband's Life?"[83]

When it comes to humorous ballads and prose, Samuel Colville in 1643 composed a pasquil, a satirical lampoon, of Sir Alexander Gibson. Little is known of Colville's profession, although his brother taught theology and Hebrew at Edinburgh. Gibson was a Commissioner from Scotland who attended the English Parliament in 1642. He died in London in 1656. Colville pokes fun at the tense submission of Gibson to the powers-that-be: "Nor this no furder can thou flie./Bot with Job's wyffe curse God and die./Quhen thou shalt suffer all this evill,/Thou shalt be pitied of the devil."[84]

Even Shakespeare jokingly uses the example of Job's wife while dismissing Satan's powers at the same time. Scholars have compared Shakespeare's tragic characters of Hamlet and King Lear with Job in terms of suffering and the human condition,[85] yet Shakespeare's comedy, *The Merry Wives of Windsor*, published in 1602, references Job's wife. The connection with the Devil continues for Job's wife in a conversation between Ford and Page. The conversation takes place in a context of cuckolded husbands, in fashion of *fabliau*, when Sir John Falstaff's desire to sleep with Mrs. Page is revealed. The wives trick Falstaff in the

82. Matthew Poole, *A Commentary on the Holy Bible*, vol. 1 (London: Banner of Truth Trust, 1962), 925.

83. Christ Mounsey and Rictor Norton, eds., *Eighteenth-Century British Erotica*, vol. 1 (London: Pickering & Chatto, 2002), 62.

84. See Anonymous, *A Book of Scotish Pasquils, 1568–1715* (Edinburgh: Paterson, 1868), 142–44.

85. For Hamlet and Job, see William Burgess, *The Bible in Shakespeare* (New York: Haskell House, 1968), 64–66. See also Chapter 4, "'Within a Foot of the Extreme Verge': *The Book of Job* and King Lear," in Steven Marx, *Shakespeare and the Bible* (New York: Oxford University Press, 2000), 59–78.

play. Mrs. Page asks Falstaff if he ever really thought that "ever the devil could have made you our delight," after which the husbands Ford and Page chime in, adding to the list of Falstaff's faults:

> Ford. And one that is as slanderous as Sathan?
> Page. And as poor as Job?
> Ford. And as wicked as his wife?[86]

Falstaff, being compared to Job's wife, becomes a character of "comic wooing," a "broad target for women's jests."[87] Analogous sources for *Merry Wives* elude scholars; the biblical references in the play come directly from Shakespeare's cultural setting and purpose in writing, especially in comedies, to use the holy text for a brief joke.[88]

Richmond Noble suggests that Shakespeare mainly consulted two versions of the Bible, the Bishops' Bible (1568) and the Geneva Bible (1560). David Daniell traces Shakespeare's near one thousand biblical references to the Geneva Bible.[89] The Bishops' Bible was read in churches, whereas the Geneva Bible was a somewhat scholarly translation in Calvin tradition, not read in church,[90] but printed in popular formats. Both formats contained marginal notes. Interestingly, the marginal note for Job 2:9 in the Bishops' Bibles from 1568 and 1572 describes the situation as "a cruel temptation of an evil and ungodly wife." The Geneva Bible from 1585, however, does not contain the note.[91]

---

86. *Merry Wives of Windsor*, V, 5: 155–157. *The Riverside Shakespeare* (2d ed.; Boston: Houghton Mifflin, 1997), 355.

87. Pamela Allen Brown, *Better a Shrew Than a Sheep: Women, Drama, and the Culture of Jest in Early Modern England* (Ithaca, N.Y.: Cornell University Press, 2003), 47.

88. Beatrice Groves, *Texts and Traditions: Religion and Shakespeare 1592–1604* (Oxford: Clarendon, 2007), 22–25.

89. David Daniell, *The Bible in English: Its History and Influence* (New Haven: Yale University Press, 2003), 354.

90. A group of English exiles who left England for Geneva created the Geneva Bible in 1560. They fled England due to religious frustrations, especially during Queen Mary's attempt at restoring Catholic dogma. The Reformers who produced the Geneva Bible felt that study aids were needed and that an English translation should be available to every man. For more details, visit Donald L. Brake, *A Visual History of the English Bible: The Tumultuous Tale of the World's Bestselling Book* (Grand Rapids, Mich.: Baker, 2008), 143–70. For more on biblical translation in English, see Daniell, *The Bible in English*; David Lawton, "The Bible," in *The Oxford History of Literary Translation in English* (ed. Roger Ellis; Oxford: Oxford University Press, 2008), 193–233.

91. Richmond Noble, *Shakespeare's Biblical Knowledge* (New York: Octagon, 1970), 272.

For Shakespeare and many others, Job and his wife act as a biblical couple who exemplify the wiles of marriage. Robert Burton, an Oxford scholar of the Church of England, published *Anatomy of Melancholy* in 1621 under the pseudonym Democritius Junior. The work was very popular, demonstrating a theoretical dependency on Aristotelian humors, a variety of ironical statements about melancholy, and witty, humorous insights. In the section on Love-Melancholy, Burton draws from a vast collection of sources of the cultural history of melancholy.[92] Burton explains how Job's wife caused Job's melancholy. Job had a "wicked wife" whom the Devil left to "vex and gall him worse" than "all the fiends in hell, as knowing the conditions of a bad woman" (part III, sec. 2).[93]

In the same section, Burton quotes Jacobus de Voragine who "elegantly delivered...twelve motions to mitigate the miseries of marriage."[94] Jacobus de Voragine, the author of *The Golden Legend* from the thirteenth century, relates the life of St. Eustace (previously Placidus) and his sufferings to the sufferings of Job. At least Job had dung to sit on, suggests Eustace, and the company of his wife remained with him.[95] The connection between Job and Eustace seems widespread; the German mystic Hermann von Fritzlar refers to Job's wife in his poem on the Eustace legend as well.[96] In 1483, William Caxton compiled his version of *The Golden Legend* from the Latin, French, and English source known as the *Gilte Legende*.[97] Caxton added the life of Job but chose to

92. A fact that has led to Mark Breitenberg's discussion on cultural manifestations of masculinity in relation to melancholy in Burton's work in a chapter "Fearful Fluidity: Burton's *Anatomy of Melancholy*": Mark Breitenberg, *Anxious Masculinity in Early Modern England* (New York: Cambridge University Press, 1996), 35–68. For a context of the idea of melancholy in the Renaissance, see Angus Gowland, *The Worlds of Renaissance Melancholy: Robert Burton in Context* (New York: Cambridge University Press, 2006).

93. Robert Burton, *The Anatomy of Melancholy*, vol. 3 (London: Nimmo, 1886), 229.

94. Ibid., 272.

95. See, respectively, section 50, St. Eustace, 20 September, in Jacobus de Voragine, *The Golden Legend: Selections* (trans. Christopher Stace; New York: Penguin Putnam), 236–42.

96. Franz Pfeiffer, ed., *Deutsche Mystiker Des Vierzehnten Jahrhunderts*. Vol. 2, *Hermann Von Fritslar, Nicolaus Von Strassburg, David Von Augsburg* (Göttingen: Vandenhoeck & Ruprecht, 1907), 233. For more discussion on Fritzlar's work and the Eustace/Job connection, see Ulf Wielandt, "Hiob in der Alt- und Mittelhochdeutschen Literatur" (Ph.D. diss., Albert-Ludwigs-Universität zu Freiburg, 1970), 88–90, 96–100.

97. Daniell, *The Bible in English*, 107.

highlight the first three chapters of the book rather than the whole poetic sections.[98] This omission of Job's misfortunes comes as no surprise given Caxton's mission to compile lives of saints.[99]

The connection with Job and the Eustace legend, though, does not figure in Burton's discussion of marriage in *The Anatomy of Melancholy*. Burton attempts to persuade the reader, perhaps in an ironical sense, that marriage is both a cure and a cause of love-melancholy. He adds his response to Jacobus de Voragine's mitigations of the misery of marriage with a bit on Job's wife: "Art in adversity? Like Job's wife, she'll aggravate thy misery, vex thy soul, make thy burden intolerable."[100] Yet, Burton concludes that marriage is a viable alternative to the kinds of sexual lusts that lead to melancholy. Burton's support of marriage, Mark Breitenberg explains, comes from a Protestant "valorization of marriage and family as analogous to the patriarchal state and as primary means to contain and legitimate male and female sexual desire."[101]

Burton's work, influential among many nineteenth- and twentieth-century authors, represents the continued use of Job and his wife for those who wish to make a point about marriage. The nineteenth-century text *How to Be Happy Though Married* quotes this section from Burton, continuing with the allusion to Job's wife as an irritant to the marital state.[102] Also, Laurence Sterne takes long sections of Burton's *The Anatomy of Melancholy* and incorporates them in his nine-volume novel *Tristam Shandy*, the first volume published in 1759. After the success of the first two volumes, Laurence Sterne preached a series of sermons at York and published them in a collection in 1760—his "Job's Expostulation with His Wife" is the last sermon of the series.[103] For Sterne, Job is not necessarily a hero as much as he is representative of a suffering person who knows that only religion, particularly Christianity, can bring consolation to the sorrowful. Sterne allows for a possibility of multiple meanings behind Job's wife's words to her husband, which could offer a remedy for his sufferings or a harsh condemnation. He relates her words to wifely "natural" concern and affection toward her husband and her

98. N. F. Blake, *Caxton and His World* (London: Deutsch, 1969), 120.

99. At the University of Glasgow Library, special collections Hunterian Bg.1.1, one can find a manuscript of Caxton's *Golden Legend* which includes an illustration on folio 74v. of a grotesque Satan wielding a club at Job in typical medieval fashion.

100. Burton, *The Anatomy of Melancholy*, 273.

101. Breitenberg, *Anxious Masculinity in Early Modern England*, 41–42.

102. E. J. Hardy, *How to Be Happy Though Married* (London: Collins Clear-Type, ca. 1900), 15.

103. Laurence Sterne, *The Sermons of Mr. Yorick* (New York: Taylor & Co., 1904), 239–55.

"heart bled" for him and "her spirits sinking" under a "sea of troubles."[104] In doing so, according to Melvyn New, "Sterne shifts the moment of scriptural dialogue into a domestic scene, binding husband and wife together in mutual affection and desperation."[105] Making marriage an idealized context of mutual concern and affection, Sterne avoids placing the stereotype of shrew onto Job's wife.

As exemplified in Sterne's work, discourse on marriage does not end in the seventeenth century, and biblical precedents continue with varied approaches. In an example from 1722, Oswald Dkyes intercepted Prov 31 for his *The Royal Marriage: King Lemuel's Lesson... Practically Paraphrased, with Remarks, Moral and Religious, upon the Virtues and Vices of Wedlock*. Job's wife provides plenty of example for what a wife should not do; she should "never put him upon doing any dishonourable thing to better his condition, but willingly share in his sufferings, and help him to preserve his integrity: not like Job's wife."[106] However, in the early twentieth century, Helen Beecher Long humorously comments on the shared suffering of Job and his wife, having her character, Mrs. Day, scold her husband for not fixing the water pump: "no woman never had to put up with all I hafter put up with—not even Job's wife!"[107]

Summary

Art of the sixteenth and seventeenth centuries commonly portrays Job's wife as a problematic old woman, while at the same time, the popular literature of this period discusses her role as wife, mostly a "bad wife" who fails to live up to her wifely responsibilities to support her husband. This connection is not coincidental, for in giving Job's wife aged features and vulgar gestures, the artists communicate the gendered stereotype of Job's wife as an unfit wife.

Beginning in the seventeenth century, artistic images also begin to down-play Satan's company at the dungheap, with evil taking on generic or dramatic demonic forms. Baroque style in general influences many artists, with attention to light and the human condition. Humanist movements sparked individualized portraits of Job, and both Catholic and

104. "Job's Expostulation with His Wife." Ibid., 241–42.
105. Melvyn New, "Job's Wife and Sterne's Other Women," in *Out of Bounds: Male Writers and Gender(ed) Criticism* (ed. Laura Claridge and Elizabeth Langland; Amherst, Mass.: University of Massachusetts Press, 1990), 56–57.
106. Oswald Dykes, *The Royal Marriage, King Lemuel's Lesson* (London, 1722), 170.
107. Helen Beecher Long, *Janice Day at Poketown* (Cleveland: Goldsmith, 1914), Chapter 5.

Protestant Renaissance art was keen to emphasize Job's relationship to Christ. Job's sufferings signaled the possibility of ultimate restoration for the individual Christian, and, therefore, Job's once afflicted flesh radiates with a Christ-like glow, even as Job clasps his hands and looks toward heaven. Even Job's dungheap, which figured prominently in the many Books of Hours for instance, no longer offers a necessary symbol of the transience of life and the need for immediate salvation.

This notion of inwardness holds implications for Joban art. With a focus on inwardness comes a disappearance of clear Satanic forms at the dungheap in early sixteenth-century art. Furthermore, as noted above, the disappearance, or fading, of Satan in favor of generic forms of evil changes Job's wife's role as part of Satan's schemes to just another "bad wife." Or, on the flip side, one could argue that with Satan out of the picture, the evil of the scene transfers heavily to Job's wife.

Late sixteenth- and seventeenth-century art of Job's wife reflects how authors add Job's wife to their list of "bad wives" to make arguments about the nature of marriage. The artistic tradition echoes the "debate over women" in print in the sixteenth and seventeenth centuries. In her discussion of Elizabethan portraiture, Nanette Salomon observes a trend prevalent in this chapter as well, that of a wife and husband as "one flesh." As a result, real women's bodies became an "abstract site of good and evil," which categorized women as "essentially good and evil."[108] In other words, rather than conceive of female virtues in abstract terms, the transfer of ideals to *real* wives of the early modern Western world takes place. The marriage of Job and his wife becomes a *real* site of contention, getting caught up in social and economic transformations of early modern Europe.

Satan's grotesque image is prevalent in medieval art and a Gothic emphasis on Satan as a fleshed entity reminds viewers of the need for salvation. Baroque art subtly adjust the imagery; Job's Christ-like pose and his melancholic demeanor emphasize more of an inner struggle. The modern artist William Blake, the subject of the next chapter, carries the notion of Job's inner struggle to new Romantic and Christological heights. The place of Job's wife within the interior spaces of Job's miseries, and within Blake's system of gender and mythology, raises more questions than it answers. Though, as usual in Christian art, Job's wife stays by Job's side throughout the perilous journey (for better or for worse).

---

108.   Salomon, "Positioning Women in Visual Convention: The Case of Elizabeth I," in Travitsky and Seeff, eds., *Attending to Women in Early Modern England*, 71.

Chapter 5

WILLIAM BLAKE'S JOB

The previous chapter included an investigation of domestic conduct manuals of the sixteenth and seventeenth centuries. The conduct manuals and numerous treatises demonstrate a cultural concern for the overall status of women in education and marriage, most often using Job's wife as an example of a bad wife. Given the treatment of Job's wife by Baroque artists, intertextual relationships exist between art and literature, as shown in the previous chapters.

The previous chapters also considered how the concept of Satan as an external evil force capable of tempting humanity gives way to a more introspective kind of evil as the eighteenth century emerged. The development affects the way Baroque artists paint Job at the dungheap. Artists remove the grotesque medieval Satan from images of the dunghill in favor of more complex, individualistic, and even skeptical kinds of presentations of evil that reflect a change in ways of thinking about evil and Satan that took root by the 1700s. Satan still remains a key player in the Job story; theologians continue to point to Satan's presence in the book in the eighteenth century.

In a poetic rendition of the book of Job in five books, Daniel Baker maintains Miltonic representation of Satan, as he returns to hell after visiting God at the throne. Belial, one of the angels who rebelled against God in *Paradise Lost*, speaks up and reminds the council that they tempted the first man through his wife.[1] So, an agent of the Devil changes Job's wife's appearance to depict "hollow Cheeks, sunk Eyes, and Toothless Mouth," and whispers to her in her sleep to encourage Job to provoke his God. Then, the Devil promises that the gods that Job's wife worships will provide her with a better, second husband. Job's wife goes to Job, telling him that "with bold Curses I would satisfy/My just Revenge, and then with Pleasure die."[2] To recall Eve and Adam, Baker

---

1. Book 2, Daniel Baker, *The History of Job: A Sacred Poem* (London: Clavel, 1706), 33–34.

2. Ibid., 43.

adds the image of a serpent which curls around Job's feet after Job's wife makes her speech. Job responds, "From GOD come Good and Evil; Both design'd/By different Methods to improve Mankind:/And Both we ought to take with a contented Mind."[3] The sublime design of God, according to Baker's rendition of Job, is meant to capture and pacify the human mind.

James May has pointed out that as the 1700s unfold poets focused on the natural descriptions in Job in order to maintain God's beautiful and sublime design of nature.[4] Even though they considered the poem of Job among the oldest of the Hebrew Bible, they still turned to Job for its representation of Christian morality and God's just rule of the world. In other words, God's creation stirs humanity's faith in its sublimity.

Eighteenth-century writers tend to grapple with one main idea—whether Job's sufferings represent a historical situation in the past or an ongoing symbol of the suffering of the body politic. Laurence Sterne's sermon on Job mentioned in the previous chapter touches on an important eighteenth-century theme of the failings of Stoic philosophy to provide consolation to those who continue to suffer, like Job.[5] William Warburton's *The Divine Legation of Moses*, first written around 1738, represents Job as an allegory of the Jews after the Babylonian exile and Job's wife acts as a symbol of the exogamous marriages reproved by Nehemiah. Warburton served as Bishop of Gloucester in the mid-eighteenth century and opposed the Deists. Warburton's allegorical reading remained controversial, especially when it comes to Job and the idea that Job's sufferings can apply allegorically as a symbol of the suffering of a people.[6]

According to Warburton, Satan took possession of Job's wife so as to spiritually assault him; she is Satan's agent. More of a concern for Warburton is how Job could marry such an infidel. Warburton concludes that Moses, the "sacred writer," meant to teach his audience a lesson through Job's wife to deter marriages to heathens (Book VI, Section II).[7]

3. Ibid., 44.
4. See James E. May, "Early Eighteenth-Century Paraphrases of the Book of Job," in *Man, God, and Nature in the Enlightenment* (ed. Donald Charles Mell and Theodore E. D. Braun; East Lansing, Mich.: Colleagues Press, 1988), 151–61.
5. Sterne, *The Sermons of Mr. Yorick*, 239–55.
6. See, for example, William Worthington, *An Essay on the Scheme and Conduct, Procedure and Extent of Man's Redemption... To Which Is Annexed a Dissertation on the Design and Argumentation of the Book of Job* (London: Edward Cave at St. John's Gate, 1743).
7. William Warburton, *The Divine Legation of Moses Demonstrated* (2 vols.; London: Thomas Tegg & Son, 1837), 2:405–8. In this work, Warburton writes to establish Moses' divinely inspired authorship, against the deists.

Theologians contemporary to Warburton argued this point. For example, John Garnett critiques Warburton's assumption of the pagan descent of Job's wife, noting that even Jewish wives can "utter blasphemy upon occasion."[8] Regardless, Garnett suspects that since the Devil failed to get Job to curse God to his face, "he laid hold of" his wife, "the next instrument" in his experiment, engaging Job in a "domestic affliction."[9] In a similar way, Charles Peters suggests that Job's wife would have attempted to lead Job into idolatry if she were in fact a Pagan. Instead, Peters suggests that she is a wicked woman, wishing Job to blaspheme God, but that her presence with God remains sufficient in the end because God reproves Job's friends but does not mention Job's wife at the conclusion of the poem.[10]

One of Warburton's most serious opponents, Robert Lowth, who served as a Bishop of the Church of England, dates and locates Job in its historical setting, maintaining the historical details of the real Job, his personal affliction, and his innocence. Like many commentators of his time, Lowth believes that the debate between Job and his friends concerns Job's innocence rather than questions God's justice. Lowth contests Warburton's argument that Job's wife actually suggests that Job "curse" God because she expresses a Pagan impiety and practice, but opts for the alternative translation which suggests that Job's wife means for Job to "bless" God and go on living a pious life. She suggests this because she believes that Job will end up dying for his pains and for his piety. Job's answer to her represents the preservation of his "constancy and moderation," expressing "himself rightly and properly with regard to God's justice."[11] As a Hebrew scholar, Lowth demonstrates a harmonization of "discrete historical particulars" of Job "with figures of the sublime."[12] A major contribution of Lowth's Hebrew poetry scholarship comes from

8. John Garnett, *A Dissertation on the Book of Job: Its Nature, Argument, Age and Author* (London: Cooper, 1749), 123. After all, Garnett argues, Job's wife understood Israelite custom that to curse God would lead to suicide.

9. Ibid., 124–27.

10. Charles Peters, *A Critical Dissertation on the Book of Job, Wherein the Account Given by That Book by the Author of the Divine Legation of Moses Demonstrated* (London: W. Johnston, in St. Paul's Church-Yard, 1757), 51–58.

11. Robert Lowth, *A Letter to the Right Reverend Author of the the Divine Legation of Moses* (4th ed.; London: Millar & Dodsley, 1766), 59–60.

12. Jonathan Lamb, *The Rhetoric of Suffering: Reading the Book of Job in the Eighteenth Century* (Oxford: Clarendon, 1995), 119. For a discussion on the Warburton/Lowth debate on the nature of Job, see Lamb's Chapter 6, "The Job Controversy," 110–27.

his challenging the notion that "sublimity requires conformity to a single standard of diction, of imagery, and of subject."[13]

In general, eighteenth-century commentators on Job, like Lowth, debate the book's terrible sublimity of Job's character and his lack of vindication. Lowth maintains that Job, the true object of the poem, is irreverent of God's justice and irrationally blames God for moral suffering. God, the omnipotent judge, demonstrates the greatness of the role as Creator to Job and thus provides all of humanity a moral lesson of the beautiful, magnificent, and powerful view of nature. In this view, Job, not God, is the object of question in terms of behavior but God is the presenter of sublimity[14]

God can present magnificent terror. That terror transfers to the readers; their "delight" in reading Job comes when Job is vindicated and thus the readers experience a removal of pain and a moral message to find sublimity in God's magnificence.[15] This stems from Edmund Burke's notion that sublime "delight," or aesthetic pleasure, comes when one's pain is removed through an encounter with the "sublime object."[16] For Burke, the sublime arises from terror, which opens the mind to God's moralistic message.[17] As noted, God remains the sublime object.

A question remains about Job's afflicted body, surrounded by uncertain and incomprehensible affect, functioning as the sublime object. Richard Blackmore, in his *Paraphrase on Job* from 1700, presents Job's sufferings and ultimate restoration as a reflection of the body politic.[18]

13. David B. Morris, *The Religious Sublime: Christian Poetry and Critical Tradition in 18th-Century England* (Lexington: University Press of Kentucky, 1972), 163.

14. Thomas A. Vogler, "Eighteenth-century Logology and the Book of Job," *Religion & Literature* 20, no. 3 (1988): 28–29.

15. Lamb, *The Rhetoric of Suffering*, 123–24.

16. Edmund Burke, *A Philosophical Enquiry into the Origin of Our Ideas of the Sublime and Beautiful* (ed. J. T. Boulton; New York: Columbia University Press, 1958).

17. For more on the historical context of the sublime, consult Andrew Ashfield and Peter de Bolla, eds., *The Sublime: A Reader in British Eighteenth-century Aesthetic Theory* (New York: Cambridge University Press, 1996).

18. As argued in James Noggle, *The Skeptical Sublime: Aesthetic Ideology in Pope and the Tory Satirists* (New York: Oxford University Press, 2001), 105. Richard Blackmore first published his paraphrase in 1700, but his second edition in 1716 was used by Alexander Pope: Richard Blackmore, *A Paraphrase on the Book of Job* (2d ed.; London: Tonson, 1716). During the eighteenth century, the literary category of biblical paraphrase stems from sublimity and the desire to render biblical books in verse and poetry for aesthetical purposes: Morris, *The Religious Sublime*, 104–14.

Since Job, a wealthy man, experiences loss and torturous pain, then releases that in his expressions, only to receive God's justice in the end, the story provided the Whigs, like Blackmore, with a reason to support a peoples' common law during the late seventeenth and throughout the eighteenth centuries.[19] Alexander Pope, in Torian fashion, debates Blackmore and questions Job as a human form of the sublime object when that place should be reserved only for the divine; he was also suspect of the political use of Job.[20]

The controversy between Blackmore and Pope becomes part of the artist William Blake's life when a critic of his 1784 exhibition in the Royal Academy alludes to Pope's reaction to Blackmore's over-the-top and strange impressions as an example of the critics' response to Blake's work.[21] In 1816, during the middle part of Blake's career, bibliographer Thomas Frognall Didbin remarked that Blake sometimes "reached the sublime; but the sublime and the grotesque seemed, somehow or the other, to be ever amalgamated in his imagination."[22] Romanticism, a vague movement that emphasizes the emotional over the rational and a literary and artistic movement against neoclassicism, remains linked with the sublime because it stems from that which is terrifying and obscure. Romantics, such as William Blake, located the sublime within human inspiration and imagination rather than in God and the Devil alone.[23] Romanticism maintains ambivalence about good and evil and, therefore, as in the case of William Blake, expresses dissatisfaction with the established Church and bourgeois control.

19. Noggle, *The Skeptical Sublime*, 104–7. See also, Lamb, *The Rhetoric of Suffering*, 132–35.

20. Pope heavily quotes Blackmore in his attempt to de-sublime Job in Alexander Pope, *The Art of Sinking in Poetry: Martinus Scriblerus* (ed. Edna Leake Steeves; New York: King's Crown, 1952). For more detail see Chapter 10, "'Deformed he lay, disfigur'd': Pope Reads Blackmore's Job," in Lamb, *The Rhetoric of Suffering*, 205–25.

21. G. E. Bentley, *Blake Records* (2d ed.; New Haven: Published for the Paul Mellon Centre for Studies in British Art by Yale University Press, 2004), 32.

22. Ibid., 327. Although not referring to Blake's designs for Edward Young's *Night Thoughts*, the quote can refer to Blake's engravings for the work in 1797. Young's *Night Thoughts* is a modern theodicy, and Young's *Paraphrase of Job* recounts similar themes: Lamb, *The Rhetoric of Suffering*, 77–81. See also Stephen Cornford, ed., *Night-Thoughts* (Cambridge: Cambridge University Press, 1989); Edward Young, *Night Thoughts, and a Paraphrase on Part of the Book of Job* (London: Chiswick, 1812).

23. Russell, *Mephistopheles*, 174.

If, then, a Romantic could make Job out as one who questions God's established authority, the book could provide a Romantic model of the hero who encounters the terrifying object and stands as an assertive individual. In this light, Job provides a biblical counterpart to the classical Prometheus myth and its afterlife in the Romantic Era. In 1818, Mary Shelley produced *Frankenstein, or The Modern Prometheus* and shortly after her husband Percy Shelley composed *Prometheus Unbound*. Much like Zeus in *Prometheus Bound*, God in Job acts as an oppressive, authoritative opponent, and Satan's rebellion is therefore a formative moment for human liberation.[24] William Blake's work also stands in the midst of this often confusing reversal in which Satan represents a true form of selfhood and God sequesters human freedom in rigid judgment. In this complex model, Jesus represents the rebellious religious leader who embodies active energy and human freedom as the true God.

Romantics read John Milton's Satan character as a representative of the beginnings of liberation for humanity and a symbol of rebellion against religious authority.[25] In his poem, *Milton* (1804–1810), Blake casts John Milton as his main character, placing him on a spiritual journey that culminates in his confrontation with Satan. Milton realizes that he must both annihilate and embrace his own Satanic selfhood or meld both the physical world and the divine world into his being in order to achieve his full role as prophet. In other words, Blake suggests that Milton, especially in *Paradise Lost*, created a fragmented reality which kept a division between God and Satan, heaven and hell, and the divine and the human, and so Blake attempts to redeem Milton's prophetic vision in light of utopian reunification.[26]

As an example of a response to the popularity of Milton's Satan in terms of radical political dissonance and Romantic sublimity, Daniel Defoe wrote a treatise on the *Political History of the Devil* in 1726, in which he criticizes Milton's *Paradise Lost*, which reached staggering heights of popularity in the early eighteenth century. Defoe thought Milton engaged in fanciful mythography, portraying the Devil in ways that violate scripture and common sense. Defoe's debt to reason, biblical history, and the experience of the natural world leads him to maintain logical argumentation that the Devil exists and continues to work as a

24. Gilbert Murray, "Prometheus and Job," in *Twentieth Century Interpretations of the Book of Job* (ed. Paul Sanders; Englewood Cliffs, N.J.: Prentice–Hall, 1968), 56–65.

25. Russell, *Mephistopheles*, 175.

26. For a critical version of this work, see William Blake, *Milton* (ed. Kay Parkhurst Easson and Roger R. Easson; New York: Random House, 1978).

dynamic evil force within human affairs. Defoe consulted Matthew Poole's commentary on the Bible, used satire to convey his message, and attempted, in the words of R. Michael Bowerman, "to achieve the impossible: to write an interesting, instructive, humorous, yet corrective, orthodox work on the devil which would sell in the marketplace."[27]

Defoe criticizes Milton's poetical liberties on hell, making a poetical, yet satirical, account of his own, in which he uses Milton's style to describe the time in hell between Lucifer's fall from heaven and the creation of human beings. The frightful, shamed, little devils are horrified at their defeated pride and lament the misery of their damned state. Defoe notes that devils cannot die, because then hell would end. Humans at least have the option to die whereas Satan does not; according to the devils: "The Wretch, whose crimes had shut him out on high,/Could be reveng'd on God himself and die;/Job's Wife was in the right, and always we/Might end by death all human misery,/Might have it in our choice, to be or not to be."[28]

Defoe turns the words of Job's wife into powerful symbols of human responsibility to God by having devils claim that she was in the right in terms of human will. In a Romantic context, her words could connote rebellion against God, who, for William Blake, represented the evil tyrant under whose name traditional Christians established "a tyrannical system of reason and external morality."[29] Blake's view of God was not one of mainstream Protestant Christianity. For instance, John Warton, a rural pastor who writes of his eighteenth-century pastoral care situations in *Death-bed Scenes and Pastoral Conversations*, tells of a young woman named Martha who fell under the unfortunate ruse of a man who wedded her, took her money, told her he was married to another, and abandoned her pregnant. The case of Job naturally comes up. Warton responds to Martha's situation with acknowledgment of her trials and with assurance that she must thank God for all that makes her stronger in faith. Warton uses Job's wife as an example of what not to do: "if Job's wife could have persuaded herself of this certain truth, that all which comes from God is good, she would have acted otherwise, and her name would not have been so detested throughout all ages as it has been."[30]

27. R. Michael Bowerman, "Headnote," in *The Political History of the Devil* (ed. Irving N. Rothman and R. Michael Bowerman; New York: AMS, 2003), lxiii.

28. Chapter 3 in Daniel Defoe, *The Political History of the Devil* (New York: AMS, 2003), 32.

29. Russell, *Mephistopheles*, 179.

30. John Warton, *Death-Bed Scenes and Pastoral Conversations* (4th ed.; 3 vols.; London: Murray, 1860), 2:51–52.

What happens when Job's wife actually speaks the truth in terms of the assumption that God might not have good intentions? Unfortunately, William Blake did not directly answer the question. However, as the quintessential Romantic artist and poet, Blake's work on Job brings new questions to the role of Job's wife.[31]

In 1826, William Blake published *Illustrations for the Book of Job*.[32] Blake's 21-plate series on the book of Job features Job's wife in almost every scene. When Anna Jameson (1794–1860), a London author in the late nineteenth century, died, her successor Lady Eastlake took over her art history project, *The History of Our Lord As Exemplified in Works of Art*. She observes a history of "calumnious treatment" of Job's wife by "older Art," and conjectures that Blake knew of this history and sought to vindicate it by "tenderly" depicting the "gentle sympathizing" woman.[33] Clearly, Blake departs from traditional iconography of Job and his wife evident in the chiaroscuro style of Baroque artists. In fact, one of his earliest biographers, Allan Cunningham (1830), noted how Blake spoke against the "Chiaro-Scuro demons, 'like the "Venetian and Flemish demons" whose 'laboring destroy imaginative power,' blocking it with 'brown shadows; they put the artist in fear and doubt of his own original conception.'"[34] Blake's departure from Baroque art, though, does not necessarily grant Job's wife a sympathetic role as much as it represents Blake's nonconformity and his focus on imagination and vision.

First, this chapter will present a general overview of Blake's engravings of Job. For Blake, Job must cast off a rigid system, a habitual and rational religion, and open his eyes to the kind of liberative Christianity, a perspective through vision and imagination. Through Christ's immanent presence, Job experiences communion with God.[35]

After the overview, the complexities of Blake's views on gender will be introduced as a way of analyzing reasons for Blake's depictions of Job's wife. For Blake, Job's wife functions as a tool to represent the

31. Audrey Schindler, "One Who Has Bourne Most: The Cri De Coeur of Job's Wife," *Australian Biblical Review* 54 (2006): 24–36.

32. William Blake, *Blake's Illustrations for the Book of Job* (New York: Dover, 1995).

33. Anna Jameson, *History of Our Lord as Exemplified in Works of Art* (London: Longmans, Green & Co., 1892), 229–31.

34. Cunningham takes this statement of Blake's as proof that Blake felt insecure about his artistic abilities in light of the Masters. As quoted in Bentley, *Blake Records*, 647.

35. This section is indebted to Christopher Rowland, *Blake and the Bible* (New Haven: Yale University Press, 2010), 15–19.

possibility of utopian reunification of the sexes, a vision more fully developed in Blake's other works. The fact that Blake depicts Job's wife in non-traditional ways in terms of iconography brings with it uncertain conclusions because it remains unclear whether Blake means to empower the role of Job's wife or suggest that she provides a simple support for Job's journey.

Overview of Blake's Job Engravings

Blake began engraving a 21-plate series on the book of Job in 1825 and published the series in 1826 with very little financial success. He only sold a few copies of the series to his friends.[36] William Blake's large mythical works, such as *The Marriage of Heaven and Hell* (1790s), *America* (1793), and *Jerusalem* (1804, finished in 1818) hardly attracted any purchasers. His final copy of *Jerusalem: The Emanation of the Giant Albion*, a series of poetry and engravings of 25 pages in four separate books, 100 plates, and Blake's culminating epic poem, was not published during Blake's lifetime.[37] Blake's popularity in twentieth-century Western culture, however, has catapulted his images of Job into popular culture. In a 2002 BBC public vote on the 100 Greatest Britons, Blake made it to number 38.[38] *The Hutchinson Dictionary of Symbols in Art* lists Blake's illustrations of the book of Job as the only example under its "Job" heading.[39] A scholar of Blake's cultural popularity, Jason Whittaker, contends that Blake's ability to capture something of the mystical nature of good and evil in esoteric language, without absolute objectivity, continues to engage postmodern imaginations.[40] Indeed, Blake scholars have not reached any consensus on the exact meanings of his work. Despite the high level of scholarship surrounding William Blake today, Blake's own lifetime brought him little success or attention as an artist.

William Blake was born in London in 1757. Blake's parents, who participated in the "Dissenting tradition," maintained devotional Bible

36. Publishers note, Blake, *Blake's Illustrations for the Book of Job*.

37. William Hughes, introduction to William Blake, *Jerusalem* (New York: Barnes & Noble, 1964).

38. BBC News, "100 Great British Heroes," BBC News, World Edition. Online: http://news.bbc.co.uk/2/hi/entertainment/2208532.stm.

39. Sarah Carr-Gomm, ed., *The Hutchinson Dictionary of Symbols in Art* (Oxford: Oxford University Press, 1995).

40. Jason Whittaker, "From Hell: Blake and Evil in Popular Culture," in *Blake, Modernity and Popular Culture* (ed. Steve Clark and Jason Whittaker; New York: Palgrave Macmillan, 2007), 192–204.

reading and private worship in the home.[41] His parents engaged in a synthesized religious life (Blake was soon to follow this synthesis), attending meetings of the New Jerusalem Church or possibly engaging in Muggletonian gatherings in private homes or ale houses. Not much is known about Blake's childhood religious life, except that Blake learned to reject the state Church and public displays of pomp and circumstance and personally read the Bible with devotion, expecting to participate in prophecy and vision in his own time.[42]

Blake himself only experienced three major Church of England rituals—baptism, marriage, and burial—no other evidence of his participation within the established Church exists.[43] Blake was not theologically trained; he participated in nontraditional forms of Christianity. Blake historians of the nineteenth and twentieth centuries have attempted to uncover various influences on Blake: Plato, Neoplatonism, Emanuel Swedenborg, the "Dissenters," Kabbalism, and the Muggletonians.[44]

With emphasis on prophecy and vision in everyday life, Blake felt comfortable speaking about his religious visions as a child and as an adult. At age four, he saw God at his window; a few years later he experienced a vision of a tree filled with angels while he and his father traveled through the countryside.[45] Such visions carried on throughout his life, and he drew many pictures of spirits who came to speak to him (called "Visionary Heads"), including Voltaire and the Scottish patriot William Wallace.[46]

Blake held a steady, contemplative, life-long relationship with the book of Job, as evidenced throughout Blake's whole portfolio. Blake entered the Royal Academy in 1779 where he exhibited historical works in the 1780s. He even listed his "historical engraving" of Job in the Academy's list of works for sale in 1793.[47] Thomas Butts, a steady commissioner of Blake, offered enough work to support Blake and his wife Catherine from 1799–1810. Blake included *Job and His Daughters* in a Butts commission of 50 bible paintings from 1799–1800. *Job Confessing His Presumption to God Who Answers Him from the Whirlwind* came a

41. Bentley, *Blake Records*, 7–9. Bentley suggests the Dissenting tradition comes from eighteenth-century Enthusiasm. He also suggests that it might be a form of the Baptist tradition.

42. Ibid.

43. J. G. Davies, *The Theology of William Blake* (London: Archon, 1966), 8.

44. Williams, *Ideology and Utopia in the Poetry of William Blake*, 1.

45. G. E. Bentley, *The Stranger from Paradise: A Biography of William Blake* (New Haven: Yale University Press, 2001), 7–21.

46. Bentley, *Blake Records*, 368–71.

47. Peter Ackroyd, *Blake: A Biography* (New York: Knopf, 1996), 96.

few years later (1803–5). Butts then went on to commission a series of 19 designs of Job in 1805–1806, which Blake and Catherine colored together with water colors.[48]

After a failed exhibition in 1809, Blake nearly sunk into "total obscurity, neglect and indigency."[49] For ten years afterward, Blake withdrew from the public eye. Then, in 1818, Blake met John Linnell, a prosperous engraver, fellow Dissenter, and successful dealer with patrons, who became his good friend. Linnell offered Blake some work by commissioning engravings of Job in 1818. The Linnell watercolor set of illustrations for the book of Job are a result, 21 full color page designs, similar to Thomas Butts's earlier commission.[50]

Both the Butts and Linnell watercolor sets provided the designs for what was to become Blake's engravings for the book of Job. By 1821, Blake still experienced financial hardships, so Linnell petitioned the Royal Academy for a donation in recognition of Blake's work. The donation was the only expression or recognition Blake received from the Academy. The monetary gift was not enough for Blake to live on, so Linnell also suggested that Blake engrave and publish his designs of the book of Job.[51]

Throughout his time in the Academy, Blake sketched Ezekiel and Job, who he saw as two "biblical and mythical figures from a sublime past who have the power of revelation and who generally stand alone against the world."[52] In his Dissenting conceptualization, the prophetic tradition also spoke against the rationalism of his day.[53] Therefore, the theological background of William Blake remains crucial to determining the meanings of his engravings of the book of Job.

Blake brings Job through a Christological journey from stultified piety within an old rigid religion to creative engagement of the world as revealed through Jesus Christ. Job engages in an inner struggle with an Old Testament God, which results in Job's transformation from a complacent follower to an imaginative worshiper of the true God found in

48. Bentley, *Blake Records*, 185–95, 287–89. For more discussion, see Chapter 23, "The History of the Job Designs," in Geoffrey Keynes, *Blake Studies: Essays on His Life and Work* (2d ed.; Oxford: Clarendon, 1971), 176–86.

49. Publisher's note in Blake, *Blake's Illustrations for the Book of Job*, iii.

50. Ibid.

51. Bentley, *Blake Records*, 395.

52. Ibid., 167. See Christopher Rowland, *"Wheels Within Wheels": William Blake and the Ezekiel's Markabah in Text and Image* (The Père Marquette Lecture in Theology; Milwaukee, Wisc.: Marquette University Press, 2007).

53. Kathleen Raine, *The Human Face of God: William Blake and the Book of Job* (London: Thames & Hudson, 1982), 23.

Jesus Christ. A political message also comes through in Blake's Job; Job moves "from belief in the divinely transcendent monarch to a religion of divine immanence," suggests Christopher Rowland, and the move "corresponds with one of Blake's major political pre-occupations: a challenge to the way in which theology becomes an ideological under-girding for political monarchy."[54]

Blake's Christology remains part of his own Christian mythology, as rendered in his pivotal and most telling work, *Jerusalem*. Also in *Jerusalem*, Blake offers his most expansive view of gender as it functions in his poetry. In *Jerusalem*, Blake depicts the fall of Albion. Albion represents the human race (sometimes just England) that will eventually be united with Christ. In his systematic treatment of Blake's entire work, Northrop Frye states, "Albion includes, presumably, all the humanity that we know in the world of time and space, though visualized as a single Titan or giant."[55] Albion's "fall" happens in Blake's understanding of Eden, known as "Beulah." The reason Albion falls remains obscure, but he relapses "from active creative energy to passivity."[56]

Due to the fall, Albion is divided into four personas, known as the Zoas, who attempt to awaken Albion. Blake's symbolism becomes even more complicated because he does not explicitly define the four Zoas, even in his unengraved prophetic work called *The Four Zoas*. Further-more, the four Zoas each contain a female counterpart, also called an emanation. One of the Zoas is Los, a hero of Imagination; his counterpart is Enitharmon. The other Zoa is Urizen, the epitome of Reason, with his counterpart, Ahania. Another Zoa, Luvah, personifies Emotion, and is accompanied by Vala. Lastly, Tharmas symbolizes Perception and Enion is his counterpart.

Jerusalem, a life-long project for Blake, creates an epic conflict between Los and Urizen, namely, between imagination and reason. Urizen hopes to reach "Self-hood," a state Satan had wanted to reach, and a state he achieved. Satan, an androgynous "fusion of subject and object into an indivisible abstract or spectral world," is also called Spectre.[57] Los, imagination, fights for restoration, not "Self-hood." In other words, only human imagination, when embraced by the human race, will bring wholeness. After the death and resurrection of Jesus

    54. Rowland, *"Wheels Within Wheels"*, 37.
    55. Northrop Frye, *Fearful Symmetry: A Study of William Blake* (Princeton, N.J.: Princeton University Press, 1969), 125.
    56. Ibid., 126.
    57. Ibid., 135.

Christ, Albion is reunited with the various personifications of personality to create a whole entity.[58]

With Blake's basic emphasis on imagination and vision, what follows is a brief overview of each plate in Blake's Job series. The main focus here is how Blake situates Job and his wife in the broader context of the series and, therefore, other key aspects and further developments of Blake's interpretations are left to the noted experts.

Plate 1: Job and His Family

Figure 5.1. William Blake, *Illustrations of the Book of Job*, plate 1, B2005.16.2. Yale Center for British Art, Gift of J. T. Johnston Coe in memory of Henry E. Coe, BA 1878, Henry E. Coe, Jr., BA 1917, and Henry E. Coe III, BA 1946.

58. Hughes, ed., *William Blake, Jerusalem* (1964), 33–37.

According to Blake's mythology, the "fallen" nature of humanity is evident in endless battles, wars, human sufferings, and bloodshed of any
kind. Such is the case when the four Zoas do not work together for
harmony. In the first plate of the Job series (Fig. 5.1), the gothic cathedral
behind Job and his family, the books on the laps of the parents, and the
musical instruments hanging in the trees, offer clues to Blake's understanding of the seemingly serene pastoral portrait of pious devotion. The
sleeping sheep seem at peace, but the altar at the bottom, with the phrase
"thus Job did continually" symbolizes otherwise. Job is engaged in a
kind of habitual religion.

Plate 2: Satan Before the Throne of God
In plate 2, Blake quotes 2 Cor 3:6 and 1 Cor 2:14, thereby presenting a
Christian perspective of Job's spiritual life resting in Emanuel Swedenborg's understanding of the development of humanity from the "Ancient
Church." One of Blake's greatest influences was the philosopher and
spiritualist Emanuel Swedenborg (1688–1772). Swedenborg's father, a
bishop of the Swedish Church, raised Emanuel in a devout Christian
context. Swedenborg also experienced visions; one such powerful vision
came in 1745 which influenced Swedenborg's decision to stop studying
physical science and instead focus on theology.[59] From this point onward,
the Bible, the Protestant canon anyway, became central to Swedenborg's
study and analysis. Over 30 theological volumes from him followed.
Swedenborg visited England around seven times, where he published
*Heaven and Hell, Earths in the Universe, Last Judgment, New Jerusalem
and Its Heavenly Doctrine*, and *White Horse of the Apocalypse* in 1758.
His spiritualization of scripture was met with criticism and claims that
his method was nothing more than allegorical. This holds true especially
for Germany, where Immanuel Kant published his critical work against
Swedenborg, *Dreams of a Spirit-Seer*, in 1766.[60]
      Around 1788, Blake bought Swedenborg's writings, *A Treatise
Concerning Heaven and Hell* (after which Blake names his artistic work
The Marriage of Heaven and Hell) and *The Wisdom of Angels* and,
subsequently, Blake and his wife Catherine joined a meeting of over 60
Swedenborg readers and followers in London in 1789.[61] The meeting,

---

      59. Harvey F. Bellin and Darrell Ruhl, eds., *Blake and Swedenborg: Opposition
Is True Friendship* (New York: Swedenborg Foundation, 1985), 5–6.
      60. Robert H. Kirven and Robin Larsen, "Emanuel Swedenborg: A Pictorial
Biography," in *Emanuel Swedenborg: A Continuing Vision* (ed. Robin Larse et al.;
New York: Swedenborg Foundation, 1988), 3–50.
      61. Bentley, *The Stranger from Paradise*, 127.

calling themselves the New Jerusalem Church, adopted 32 Swedenborg spiritual propositions, including the following resolutions: "The Old Church, which means all other churches, is dead"; "The Old Church faith should be abolished"; and "The Second Coming, which has begun, involves the destruction of the Old Church and the formation of the New."[62]

Figure 5.2. William Blake, *Illustrations of the Book of Job*, plate 2, B2005.16.3. Yale Center for British Art, Gift of J. T. Johnston Coe in memory of Henry E. Coe, BA 1878, Henry E. Coe, Jr., BA 1917, and Henry E. Coe III, BA 1946.

62. The entire list can be found in Bentley, *Blake Records*, 51–53. See also Robert Hindmarsh, "An Account of the First General Conference of the Members of the New Jerusalem Church," in Bellin and Ruhl, eds., *Blake and Swedenborg*, 121–31.

Blake's *The Marriage of Heaven and Hell* (1790s) directly stems from Swedenborgian thought. *The Marriage of Heaven and Hell* exists as "a kind of fictional autobiography" in which Blake both embraces Swedenborg elements and struggles with Swedenborg thought.[63] Given Blake's history with Swedenborg's thought, the idea of "Old Church" is most likely symbolized in the books on the laps of Job and his wife. The same stiff book appears on God's lap in plate 2 because Blake understood Jesus Christ as the fulfillment of human imagination. God the Father, giver of Law, without Jesus Christ, represents an oppressive force.[64]

Another clear image of imbalance rests in the instruments hanging in the tree in plate 1 (Fig. 5.1). Blake means to make a connection between Job and Ps 137; similar sentiments in Blake's water-color drawing of Ps 137, *By the Waters of Babylon*, exist because the exiles hang their harps on the willow trees refusing to sing their songs for their captives.[65] The cross-reference notes alienation and exile—"Job and his family were, so to speak, in exile, alienated from their true good, as symbolized by the unused instruments of their art."[66] Blake's illustration of *The Hymn of Christ and His Apostles*, the New Testament counterpart to his *By the Waters of Babylon*, depicts Jesus' disciples singing praises with the accompaniment of musical instruments. The stiffly bound books on the laps of Job and his wife in plate 1 remain in tension with the unused instruments in the tree. This tension resolves itself full-circle in the final illustration, plate 21 (Fig. 5.22), when the instruments come down from the tree into the hands of Job's family.

When God appears for the first time in plate 2, God's face holds a striking similarity to Job's face. Job and God share similar, if not identical, features. Numerous accounts exist for why God's face echoes Job's face. Andrew Wright states that "it is God created by Job in his own image."[67] Jungian psychoanalytical theorists point out that Blake

63. Everett C. Frost, "The Education of the Prophetic Character: Blake's the Marriage of Heaven and Hell as a Primer in Visionary Autography," in *Prophetic Character: Essays on William Blake in Honor of John E. Grant* (ed. Alexander S. Gourlay; West Cornwall, Conn.: Locust Hill, 2002), 71.

64. As will become apparent in plate 11. Mary Lynn Johnson, "David's Recognition of the Human Face of God in Blake's Designs for the Book of Psalms," in *Blake and His Bibles* (ed. David V. Erdman; West Cornwall, Conn.: Locust Hill, 1990), 117–56.

65. Lindberg, *William Blake's Illustrations to the Book of Job*, 196.

66. Harold Fisch, *The Biblical Presence in Shakespeare, Milton, and Blake: A Comparative Study* (Oxford: Clarendon, 1999), 292–95.

67. Andrew Wright, *Blake's Job: A Commentary* (Oxford: Clarendon, 1972), 9.

depicts the archetype of the Self in the face of God. According to Jung in his *Archetypes and the Collective Unconscious*, the human psyche contains a deep unconscious level that holds elements common to all humans.[68] Those elements, archetypes, manifest differently for different people and become projected outwardly in art, narrative, myth, folklore, and other creative endeavors of humankind. Edward Edinger carries the Jungian archetype of the Self throughout all the plates of Job, claiming that the Job narrative itself is an archetypal story, depicting the ego's encounter with the Great Personality (God) that results in the persever-ance of the ego, its defeat, and its reward with insight into the trans-personal psyche. Edinger maintains that Blake unconsciously meant to communicate the nature of the unconscious human.[69] June Singer also reads Blake from a psychological point-of-view, noting that Blake, as he is concerned with the inner spiritual journey of Job, visually depicts God as an archetype of Job's Self. Accordingly, Blake has an ability to "illuminate the dark and murky regions of the unconscious."[70]

Raine describes Blake's view of Job as "Jungian" in terms of his art anticipating Jungian thought.[71] Jung, of course, did not establish his work in psychoanalysis until the early 1900s. When Jung deals with Job in his work entitled *Answer to Job*, he does so in the form of a sweeping theological treatise rather than an exegetical treatment of the book of Job and Job's wife holds no primary role in Jung's analysis.[72]

Though Jungian theory provides commentators with a wealth of possibilities, the limits of this study cannot entertain them all. At any rate, it is more likely that Blake adopts Swedenborg's concept of "correspondences," which provide an earlier and separate set of ideas that interestingly has overtones in Jung's *Archetypes of the Collective Unconscious*. Both Swedenborg and Jung seek an "innerworld" of the biblical text. Swedenborg argues that "each and all things in nature

68. C. G. Jung, *The Archetypes and the Collective Unconscious*, vol. 9 (ed. Herbert Read, Michael Fordham, and Gerhard Adler; The Collected Works of C. G. Jung; New York: Pantheon, 1953).

69. Edward F. Edinger, *Encounter with the Self: A Jungian Commentary on William Blake's Illustrations of the Book of Job* (Toronto: Inner City, 1986).

70. June Singer, *The Unholy Bible: Blake, Jung and the Collective Unconscious* (Boston: Sigo, 1986), 9.

71. Raine, *The Human Face of God*, 24.

72. C. G. Jung, *Answer to Job* (trans. R. F. C. Hull; 15th Anniversary ed.; Princeton, N.J.: Princeton University Press, Bollingen Series, 2002). Jung does not mention William Blake's artistic interpretation of Job in this work. Ironically, the Princeton University Press 50th anniversary edition of Jung's *Anwer to Job* features a water-color painting of plate 14, "the morning stars."

correspond to spiritual things,"[73] so both Satan and God would function for Blake as spiritual correspondences with earthly humanity. It is important to note here how Jung's legacy with commentators of Blake's Job series comes in the form of many works with psycho-allegorical interpretations, including that of Joseph Wicksteed, who suggests that Blake wanted to portray the inward life of Job because, according to Blake, one's inmost being is a reflection of God.[74]

Whether or not one commits to Jungian analysis, Blake, in general, illustrates inner struggle and deep angst over God's enigmatic nature, loving and gentle *and* fierce and frightful, in his poetry. His poem "The Tyger" asks, "When the stars threw down their spears,/And water'd heaven with their tears,/Did he smile his work to see?/Did he who made the Lamb make thee?" (SIE 42:17–20; E 24–25).[75] In this poem, God remains both beautiful and terrible. Crabb Robinson, a friend of Blake's, notes in his diary in 1826 that Blake's philosophy elevates this struggle:

> His philosophy he repeated—Denying Causation asserting everything to be the work of God or the Devil, That there is a constant falling off from God—Angels becoming Devils Every man has a Devil in him and the conflict is eternal between a man's Self and God.[76]

The sleeping sheep-dog at Job's feet in plates 1 and 2 (Figs. 5.1 and 5.2) recalls that Job is still "asleep" to any inner struggle. At the top of the page in plate 2, Blake anticipates Job's awakening to the full capacity of his human imagination, for when that occurs, Job will understand God's true purpose for living as noted on the plate: "We shall awake up in thy Likeness."

Plate 3: Job's Sons and Daughters Destroyed

Blake's Satan arrives in plate 3, delighting in the scene of the destruction of Job's children. Rather than engage wind as in the book of Job, Blake's Satan uses fire. Particularly, he engages the "fire of God."[77] He sits on Roman pillars and extends his bat-wings. The bat-wings, as part of Blake's visual vocabulary, appear in plate 10 of *Marriage*.

---

73. Samuel M. Warren, ed., *A Compendium of the Theological Writings of Emanuel Swedenborg* (New York: Swedenborg Foundation, 1974), 98–99.

74. Joseph H. Wicksteed, *Blake's Vision of the Book of Job* (New York: Haskell House, 1971), 51–52.

75. *Songs of Experience*, Plate 42.

76. Bentley, *Blake Records*, 435.

77. Lindberg, *William Blake's Illustrations to the Book of Job*, 210.

Figure 5.3. William Blake, *Illustrations of the Book of Job*, plate 3, B2005.16.4. Yale Center for British Art, Gift of J. T. Johnston Coe in memory of Henry E. Coe, BA 1878, Henry E. Coe, Jr., BA 1917, and Henry E. Coe III, BA 1946.

In *Marriage*, the Devil instructs two others on either side of him with the Proverbs of Hell. His proverbs function as a critical commentary, not only of Swedenborg, but also on a popular book in England during his time, Johann Kasper Lavater's *Aphorisms on Man* (1741–1801).[78]

---

78. Blake engraved a design by his friend Henry Fuseli for the J. C. Lavater. *Aphorisms on Man: Translated from the Original Manuscript of the Rev. John Casper Lavater, Citizen of Zuric* (London: printed for J. Johnson, 1789). See Bentley, *Blake Records*, 54.

Lavater, a Swiss minister and physiognomist who suggested that a person's physical characteristics reflected moral character, melded theology with psychological maxims in *Aphorisms*. Blake made annotations in his personal copy of *Aphorisms*.[79] Lavater attempted to classify humankind into moral categories—aphorism 533 says, "This discovery of momentary folly, symptoms of which assail the wisest and the best, has thrown a great consolatory light on my inquiries into man's moral nature; by this the theorist is enable to assign to each class and each individual its own peculiar fit of vice or folly."[80]

Blake responds in the margin of his copy of *Aphorisms* that "man is the ark of God... If thou seekest by human policy to guide this ark remember Uzzah[,] II Sam VI."[81] Upon transporting the ark from the hands of the Philistines to Jerusalem, the oxen stumbled and Uzzah touched the ark to steady it, which rendered him dead, according to law (Num 4:15). Blake denies any system Lavater might set out before him; through his rendition of proverbs, Blake denies any set of morals, but instead insists that humankind has forgotten that "all deities reside in the human breast."[82]

The archetypal bat-winged Satan also appears in a watercolor of biblical subjects commissioned by Butts around 1795, *Satan Exulting Over Eve*.[83] A tradition of the Dissenters speaks of Satan entering Eve's womb at his outcast from heaven and impregnating her with Cain. Cain, a child of Reason, resulted, whereas Adam fathered Abel, a spiritual man.[84] A woman lies in a similar position in plate 3 of the Job illustrations as Eve does in the watercolor. One of the young women lies with a tambourine at her feet and her left hand rests on a lyre in plate 3 as well. Jean Hagstrum suggests that the woman signifies Job's neglect of art; Job instead is living in "bookish piety."[85] The image relates to both the bat-winged Satan in the Proverbs of Hell in *Marriage* and the Satan with Eve. As with Eve, Satan, the epitome of Reason, has taken over, and spiritual imagination collapses under the weight.

---

79. Bentley, *Blake Records*, 473, 447.

80. As quoted in Jason Allen Snart, *The Torn Book: Unreading William Blake's Marginalia* (Selinsgrove: Susquehanna University Press, 2006), 164.

81. As quoted in ibid., 163.

82. Blake, *Marriage*, Plate 11. See also Anthony Blunt, *The Art of William Blake* (New York: Columbia University Press, 1959), 51.

83. William Blake, 1795. The J. Paul Getty Museum, Los Angeles, Calif.

84. Bentley, *The Stranger from Paradise*, 10–11.

85. Jean H. Hagstrum, *William Blake: Poet and Painter* (Chicago: University of Chicago Press, 1964), 132.

Plate 4: The Messengers Tell Job and His Wife of Their Misfortunes
Blake reverses the narrative order in plates 3 and 4; the destruction of
goods and property, plate 3 (Job 1:13–17) comes before the destruction
of Job and his wife's children, plate 4 (1:18–19). In plate 4, three messengers run to tell Job and his wife the news. The sheep still serenely graze,
but Druid-like columns take the place of the tree that was in plate 1.[86]

Figure 5.4. William Blake, *Illustrations of the Book of Job*, plate 4,
B2005.16.5. Yale Center for British Art, Gift of J. T. Johnston Coe in
memory of Henry E. Coe, BA 1878, Henry E. Coe, Jr., BA 1917, and
Henry E. Coe III, BA 1946.

86. Wright, *Blake's Job*, 17; Wicksteed, *Blake's Vision of the Book of Job*, 65.

During Blake's time, a cultural religious reawakening took place, and the Druids, as ancient people occupying Britain before Christians, became part of the popular religious imagination. Popular Druidian literature circulated around London during this time. "The Ancient Order of the Druids" established themselves in an ale house near Blake's Poland Street London home.[87]

Plate 5: Satan Going Forth from the Presence of the Lord

Figure 5.5. William Blake, *Illustrations of the Book of Job*, plate 5, B2005.16.6. Yale Center for British Art, Gift of J. T. Johnston Coe in memory of Henry E. Coe, BA 1878, Henry E. Coe, Jr., BA 1917, and Henry E. Coe III, BA 1946.

87. Ackroyd, *Blake: A Biography*, 99–100.

Plate 5 brings the viewer back to an enthronement scene. The Gothic Church and the tree of God's protection disappear after this scene, replaced with Druid temple structures in plate 5. The pastoral trellis framing the engraving of the throne scene in plate 2 now becomes infested with a slithery serpent as angelic figures look down in sorrow and dismay. God's body position has changed from plate 2 as well; the book does not rest on God's lap but flops to God's left side. Blake quotes Gen 6:6 and Ps 104:4, as if to suggest that God grieves the decision, as the repulsed angels also communicate. Now the cloud seems to weep in time with Job. According to Blake's assumption that "We are all coexistent with God—Members of the Divine Body—And partakers of the divine nature,"[88] what happens to Job is reflected in heaven. Also in plate 5, Satan is seen leaving God's enthroned presence while below, Job's wife sympathetically rests her head on Job's shoulder as he gives out bread to a poor man and his dog with a sad sense of "external obligation."[89]

Plate 6: Satan Smiting Job with Boils
Bat-winged angels dangle spiders in the outskirts of the picture on plate 6 (Fig. 5.6 [overleaf]). The pastoral objects, the shepherd's crook and pottery, lie in shambles. The broken pottery anticipates Job scraping himself with a shard (Job 2:8). Four arrows come out from Satan's hand, which recall Job's words in Job 6:4, "For the arrows of the Almighty are in me; my spirit drinks their poison; the terrors of God are arrayed against me" (NRSV).

Job's wife leaves his right side for the first time in plate 6. She kneels at his feet with her head in her hands, and this garners much attention from scholars with mixed interpretations. In regard to her position in plate 6, Wright suggests that "she is beyond being able to bring comfort to her husband."[90] Emily Hamblen calls her a "symbolic seer" who "sinks into black deeps at his feet."[91] Damon notes that the separation only emphasizes her ability to minister to Job's lowest needs at his feet.[92] Wicksteed compares Job's wife to "a figure of ideal womanly fidelity."[93]

88. Bentley, *Blake Records*, 696.
89. Christopher Rowland, *Blake and the Bible* (New Haven: Yale University Press, 2010), 33.
90. Wright, *Blake's Job*, 21.
91. Emily Hamblen, *Interpretation of William Blake's Job* (New York: Occult Research Press, 1930), 14.
92. Damon, *Blake's Job*, 22.
93. Wicksteed, *Blake's Vision of the Book of Job*, 72.

Rowland notes the visual elements: "Job's wife is much darker and appears to be suffering terribly, helpless in the face of her partner's solitary agony."[94]

Figure 5.6. William Blake, *Illustrations of the Book of Job*, plate 6, B2005.16.7. Yale Center for British Art, Gift of J. T. Johnston Coe in memory of Henry E. Coe, BA 1878, Henry E. Coe, Jr., BA 1917, and Henry E. Coe III, BA 1946.

94. Rowland, *Blake and the Bible*, 35.

Plate 7: Job's Comforters

Figure 5.7. William Blake, *Illustrations of the Book of Job*, plate 7, B2005.16.8. Yale Center for British Art, Gift of J. T. Johnston Coe in memory of Henry E. Coe, BA 1878, Henry E. Coe, Jr., BA 1917, and Henry E. Coe III, BA 1946.

The closest Blake gets to traditional iconography of Job on the dung-heap comes in plate 7 (Fig. 5.7), in which Blake includes Job's words in response to his wife: "What! Shall we receive Good at the hand of God & shall we not also receive Evil" (2:10). He does not, however, indicate that Job's wife speaks to him. Rather, she stands behind Job and exhibits a traditional mourning or distress gesture as the friends enter the scene.

Visually in this plate, Blake connects Jerusalem to Job's wife. Jerusalem, the female counterpart of Albion, raises her hands in plate 92 of *Jerusalem* in a similar fashion to that of Job's wife in plate 7, with elbows to their sides and both palms facing up (see Fig. 5.8).[95]

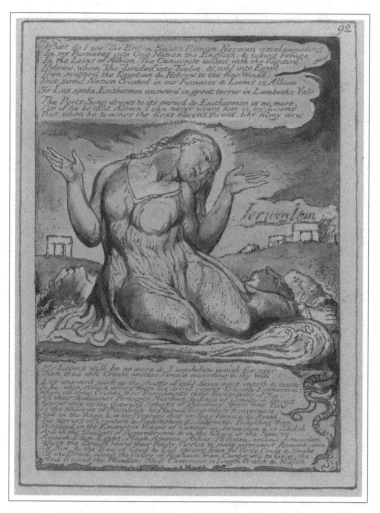

Figure 5.8. William Blake, Plate 92 of *Jerusalem: The Emanation of the Giant Albion*, Bentley Copy E. B1992.81 (92). Yale Center for British Art, Paul Mellon Collection.

95. David V. Erdman, *The Illuminated Blake* (New York: Anchor, 1974), 371.

Jerusalem laments over the heads of the fallen four Zoas with raised hands and a cocked head. Isaiah 3:25–26 is a possible influence for Blake: "Thy men shall fall by the sword, and thy mighty in the war. And her [Jerusalem's] gates shall lament and mourn; and she being desolate shall sit upon the ground."[96] The connection insinuates the mourning status of Job's wife. In plate 7, Blake does not clearly vindicate nor repudiate Job's wife's words to her husband but omits them altogether.

While the exact meaning behind Job's wife's gesture remains unknown, the connection with Job to traditional Christian understandings comes through more clearly in plate 7. Malcolm Cormack relates Job's reclining on his wife in plate 7 to Michelangelo's *Pietà*.[97] Job's head rests on her right side, like Jesus' head rests on his mother Mary's right side. In this light, Blake holds to the tradition of Job as a type of Christ, or a *Prefiguratio Christi*, or at least Blake notes Job's example of the endurance of the human spirit through his incorporation of James. James 5:11 says, "Indeed we call blessed those who showed endurance. You have heard of the endurance of Job, and you have seen the purpose of the Lord, how the Lord is compassionate and merciful" (NRSV). Thus, a hint exists that even for Blake's Job remains an example of patient suffering.

Plate 8: Job Laments the Day of His Birth
In plate 8 (Fig. 5.9 [overleaf]), Job's wife moves to Job's right side and his friends move to his left, a more standard position for his wife throughout the series. Job laments the day of his birth (Job 3) with his hands raised above his head. His friends and wife hide their faces in mournful sorrow, in what Jean Hagstrum calls "Urizenic grief."[98] The thistles found at the bottom right of plate 6 (Fig. 5.6) have now overgrown on the ground in plate 8. The thistles provide a semiotic connection between Albion's brokenness and Job's despair. When Albion falls in *Jerusalem*, his children lament around him similar in position to Job's friends. As stated, "His Giant beauty and perfection fallen into dust: Till from within his witherd breast grown narrow with his woes: The corn is turn'd to thistles & the apples into poison" (J 19; E 164).[99]

96. Ibid.
97. Malcolm Cormack, *William Blake, Illustrations of the Book of Job* (Richmond: Virginia Museum of Fine Arts, 1997), 39.
98. Hagstrum, *William Blake: Poet and Painter*, 133.
99. Erdman, *The Illuminated Blake*, 298.

Figure 5.9. William Blake, *Illustrations of the Book of Job*, plate 8, B2005.16.9. Yale Center for British Art, Gift of J. T. Johnston Coe in memory of Henry E. Coe, BA 1878, Henry E. Coe, Jr., BA 1917, and Henry E. Coe III, BA 1946.

Plate 9: The Vision of Eliphaz

For Blake, Eliphaz's vision held important implications for his understanding of the power of vision (see plate 9, Fig. 5.10). Robinson noted that at times Blake considered "all things as alike the work of God," and that even error exists in heaven. When Crabb Robinson asked Blake about the existence of evil, Blake quotes Eliphaz and answers, "Do you think there is any purity in Gods eyes—the angels in heaven are no more so than we. 'He chargeth his Angels with folly.'"[100]

100.   Bentley, *Blake Records*, 422. Blake also quotes this in *Jerusalem*, Plate 49.

Figure 5.10. William Blake, *Illustrations of the Book of Job*, plate 9, B2005.16.10. Yale Center for British Art, Gift of J. T. Johnston Coe in memory of Henry E. Coe, BA 1878, Henry E. Coe, Jr., BA 1917, and Henry E. Coe III, BA 1946.

Blake understood God's personality as incorporating Satan, that "Satan acts both as a contrary voice within God's personality" and as God's agent on earth.[101]

Plate 10: Job Rebuked By His Friends
In the image on plate 10 (Fig. 5.11), Job pleads his case against the accusatory pointing of his friends: "Have pity upon me! Have pity upon me! O ye my friends for the hand of God hath touched me... Though he

101. Connolly, *William Blake and the Body*, 164.

slay me yet will I trust in him." By combining two different sections (Job 19:21 and 12:4), Blake drives the message home that God remains the cause of Job's suffering. The three-fold finger pointing of Job's friends relates to plate 93 of *Jerusalem*.[102]

Figure 5.11. William Blake, *Illustrations of the Book of Job*, plate 10, B2005.16.11. Yale Center for British Art, Gift of J. T. Johnston Coe in memory of Henry E. Coe, BA 1878, Henry E. Coe, Jr., BA 1917, and Henry E. Coe III, BA 1946.

102. As noted by both Raine, *The Human Face of God*, 93, and Paley, *Jerusalem*, 288.

Again, multiple interpretations come from the wife's position given that Blake continues to place Job's wife in places non-traditional for Joban iconography. Job's wife stays on Job's right side, despite Wright's observation that "She is in a state of despair less remediable because her faith is more superficial than Job's. Her tears are those of self-pity, for she thinks the friends may be right."[103] Wright suggests this because Job's wife sits on the ground instead of kneeling. Similarly, James Smetham comments, "Then, again, Job kneels, and the six scornful hands of his friends are leveled against his expanded Neptunian breast like spears, as he proclaims his integrity; and worse than this, the fearful hissing whisper of the over-tempted wife of his bosom rises to his ear, bidding him to curse God and die."[104] No visual sign indicates, however, that Job's wife accepts the words of Job's friends, for Job's wife's right hand gestures that of confusion and her gaze at Job's friends holds questionable certainty. And, if Job's wife corresponds even slightly with Jerusalem, one could hear the words of Jerusalem coming from Job's wife in light of the moralization and accusation of human nature and sin: "Jerusalem then stretch'd her hand toward the Moon and spoke: Why should Punishment Weave the Veil with Iron Wheels of War When Forgiveness might it Weave with Wings of Cherubim?" (J 22:34–35; E 168).

Plate 11: Job's Evil Dreams
Devils reach up from the fire and grasp Job's body in plate 11 (Fig. 5.12 [overleaf]) to indicate Job's words from the KJV, "My bones are pierced in me in the night season: and my sinews take no rest" (Job 30:17) and "My skin is black upon me, and my bones are burned with heat" (Job 30:30). Separated from his wife, Job remains in total isolation. Job's isolation bolsters his terror. Plate 11 represents the nadir of Job's inflictions.[105]

The terror Blake finds in "Jehovah," the name Blake gives to the God of the Old Testament and the Father of Jesus Christ, culminates in plate 11. The cloven-hoofed, snake-wrapped being with the face of Job points to law with his right hand and points down to the fire that licks Job's body. Is he Satan or God? The creature is both.[106]

103. Wright, *Blake's Job*, 29.
104. James Smetham, reprinted from *London Quarterly Review*, January 1869, in Alexander Gilchrist, *Life of William Blake*, vol. 2 (London: Macmillan & Co., 1880), 348.
105. Morton D. Paley, *The Traveller in the Evening: The Last Works of William Blake* (Oxford: Oxford University Press, 2003), 244.
106. Connolly, *William Blake and the Body*, 165.

Figure 5.12. William Blake, *Illustrations of the Book of Job*, plate 11, B2005.16.12. Yale Center for British Art, Gift of J. T. Johnston Coe in memory of Henry E. Coe, BA 1878, Henry E. Coe, Jr., BA 1917, and Henry E. Coe III, BA 1946.

Blake quotes 2 Cor 11:14–15 above the image: "Satan himself is transformed into an Angel of Light & his Ministers into Ministers of Righteousness." Yet, Blake also quotes 2 Thess 2:4 at the very base of the plate: "Who opposeth & exalteth himself above all that is called God, or is worshipped." Cormack suggests the afflicter is Satan disguised as God.[107]

107.   Cormack, *William Blake, Illustrations of the Book of Job,* 49. Damon says something similar, in that "the God of Justice is only Satan, masquerading as an angel of light" (*Blake's Job*, 32).

When one reads from top to bottom on the plate, one sees that Job discovers that Satan and God as Blake understands him engage in the same work. Job accuses God for his affliction: "Then thou scarest me with dreams, and terrifiest me through visions" (Job 7:14). A. D. Nuttall writes, "Blake hated rationalist theologians of the eighteenth century who liked to point out that God could be inferred from the reasonable"; Blake thought of God in Job as "the source of all that is frighteningly, magnificently unintelligible."[108] The words on the plate read:

> Why do you persecute me as God & are not satisfied with my flesh. Oh that my words were printed in a Book that they were graven with an iron pen & lead in the rock for ever For I know that my Redeemer liveth & that he shall stand in the latter days upon the Earth & after my skin destroy thou This body yet in my flesh shall I see God whom I shall see for Myself and mine Eyes shall behold & not Another tho consumed be my wrought Image. (from Job 19:22–27)

Blake holds to the traditional Christian understanding of this passage. Around 1741, Handel composed his *Messiah* in London, which includes the soprano aria, "I Know That My Redeemer Liveth."[109] For Blake, the redeemer comes in the form of Jesus Christ, who appears to Job and his wife in plate 17 (Fig. 5.18).

Plate 12: Elihu
In plate 12 (Fig. 5.13 [overleaf]), Blake quotes the beginning of Elihu's speech (Job 33–37), "I am Young & ye are very Old wherefore I was afraid" (Job 32:6) and thus emphasizes Elihu's youth and vision. Elihu exhibits youthful energy and as emotional nature, aspects Blake appreciates.[110] God speaks to humans through dreams, "For God speaketh once yea twice/& Man percieveth it not/In a Dream in a Vision of the Night/in deep Slumberings upon the bed/Then he openeth the ears of Men & sealeth their instruction" (Job 33:14–15). The rising figures in the margin symbolize a reawakening: "To bring back his soul from the pit, to be enlightened with the light of the living" (Job 33:29–30, NRSV).

---

108.   A. D. Nuttall, *The Alternative Trinity: Gnostic Heresy in Marlowe, Milton, and Blake* (Oxford: Clarendon, 1998), 236.

109.   John Tobin, *Handel's "Messiah": A Critical Account of the Manuscript Sources and Printed Editions* (London: Cassell, 1969).

110.   Paley, *The Traveller in the Evening*, 246.

Figure 5.13. William Blake, *Illustrations of the Book of Job*, plate 12, B2005.16.13. Yale Center for British Art, Gift of J. T. Johnston Coe in memory of Henry E. Coe, BA 1878, Henry E. Coe, Jr., BA 1917, and Henry E. Coe III, BA 1946.

Plate 13: God in the Whirlwind

In plate 13 (Fig. 5.14), Blake quotes Ps 104:3: "Who maketh the Clouds his Chariot & walketh on the Wings of the Wind." The wind in this engraving becomes so strong it bends over the trees at the base of the engraving. Here, Blake interprets a traditional rendition of God for Christianity: Blake's God in the whirlwind recalls Michelangelo's creation of Adam on the ceiling of the Sistine chapel from several decades earlier. Blake, in his affinity to incorporate Michelangelo's themes in this work, utterly transforms Michelangelo's themes to comment on Christian orthodoxies (see also the discussion of plate 7 above).[111]

Figure 5.14. William Blake, *Illustrations of the Book of Job*, plate 13, B2005.16.14. Yale Center for British Art, Gift of J. T. Johnston Coe in memory of Henry E. Coe, BA 1878, Henry E. Coe, Jr., BA 1917, and Henry E. Coe III, BA 1946.

111. As in Blake's rendition of Cain and Abel, as discussed by Jenijoy La Belle, "Blake's Visions and Re-Visions of Michelangelo," in *Blake in His Time* (ed. Robert N. Essick and Donald Pearce; Bloomington: Indiana University Press, 1978), 31.

In comparing Michelangelo's creation of Adam with Blake's creation of Adam, insinuations of the complexities of human relations with the divine emerge. For one thing, Blake's rendition of the creation of Adam, as opposed to Michelangelo's, maintains physical proximity, radiating darker shades of divine mystery. Also, a symbol of mortality, a worm, wraps around Adam. As Connolly states about Blake's adaptation of Michelangelo's bodily forms, Blake exaggerates Michelangelo "to the point of physical impossibility, the limitations and pain of existence in a mortal body."[112]

Job's friends hide their faces from the presence of God, who appears in a whirlwind (Job 38:1) and asks, "Who is this that darkeneth counsel by words without knowledge?" (Job 38:2). But Job and his wife look at God face-to-face. Job's wife shares in her husband's divine epiphany and continues to do so throughout the rest of the series. However, God's hand extends over Job's head and Job's wife is placed at the back of the experience.

Blake assumes here that the friends hold on to a traditional understanding that one must avoid gazing directly upon God's face. Using Paul's letters to the Corinthians elsewhere in the series, Blake has Job do what Paul states, "Since, then, we have such a hope, we act with great boldness, not like Moses, who put a veil over his face to keep the people of Israel from gazing at the end of the glory that was being set aside" (2 Cor 3:12–13, NRSV).

In Blake's Christian interpretation, the Law of Moses as the "old covenant" continues to veil the spiritual nature of humanity in moral law-codes. Paul continues: "Now the Lord is the Spirit, and where the Spirit of the Lord is, there is freedom. And all of us, with unveiled faces, seeing the glory of the Lord as though reflected in a mirror, are being transformed into the same image…" (2 Cor 3:17–18). Job needs to cast off his connection to any divinity that does not inspire imagination and vision and Job learns this through visions of the created world in the next plate, plate 14 (Fig. 5.15), which depicts God's display of creation.

Plate 14: "When the Morning Stars Sang Together" (Job 38:7)
During his apprenticeship with the engraver James Basire (1772–79), Blake was sent to sketch Westminster Abbey tombs. Samuel Palmer remembers: "In Westminster Abbey were his earliest and most sacred recollections. I asked him how he would like to paint on glass, for the great west window, his 'Sons of God shouting for Joy,' from his designs

112. Connolly, *William Blake and the Body*, 60.

in the *Job*. He said, after a pause, 'I could do it!' kindling at the thought."[113] In his Linnell and Butts watercolors, Blake only painted four "sons." The "sons of God" relay Blake's "four Zoas"—Tharmas, the flesh; Urizen, the intellect; Luvah, the emotions; and Los, the creative spirit.[114] In plate 14 (Fig. 5.15), however, Blake adds more arms, to communicate an infinite chorus line.

Figure 5.15. William Blake, *Illustrations of the Book of Job*, plate 14, B2005.16.15. Yale Center for British Art, Gift of J. T. Johnston Coe in memory of Henry E. Coe, BA 1878, Henry E. Coe, Jr., BA 1917, and Henry E. Coe III, BA 1946.

113.　Bentley, *Blake Records*, 17.
114.　As denoted in Damon, *Blake's Job*, 38.

The six days of creation that rest on each side of the engraving and contain their appropriate quotes from Gen 1 also speak to this infinite world. Again, the seventh day of creation can be found in the infinities of the human imagination. The leviathan in the sea and the worm at the bottom relate to the essence of the universe marked with light and dark, good and evil, mortality and immortality. The same form of worm wraps around Adam in *God (Elohim) Creating Adam*. The earthly body, created from the dust of the ground, juxtaposes with the spiritual heavenly realm and the "sweet influences" of Plaides and Orion (Job 38:31).

The figures under God's left and right arms represent Apollo, the sun-god, riding his chariot of four horses to "widen the realm of light," and the moon goddess Diana, riding the dragon of emotion.[115] In this picture, Blake brings complementary elements together. Apollo represents intellect that drives the horses of instruction; Diana, the heart, guides the dragon of passion. The picture of the universe depicts a balance between wisdom and experience, between knowledge and emotion.[116] The figures represent two aspects of an "incomprehensible whole," as "two aspects of life are shown in their right relationship one with another; it is the moment of harmony and unitive vision."[117]

Plate 15: Behemoth and Leviathan (Job 40:15–41:1)
The image in plate 15 (Fig. 5.16) once again reveals Blake's struggle with spiritualism and materialism, reason and imagination. God (Elohim), like Urizen (reason/intellect/law), points down as creator of the material world. Blake's gesture for God in plate 15 echoes his Urizen pose from his 1794 watercolor *Ancient of Days*, now located in the British Museum, London.

The observers—Job, his wife, and his friends—now sit above the image. They still remain covered with divine cloud but they elevate to the level of the stars. As quoted from Job 40:15, "Behold now Behemoth which I made with thee." God shows the observers that as long as Leviathan and Behemoth wage war in the world, spiritual peace remains unlikely. In *Jerusalem*, for instance, Blake describes Behemoth and Leviathan as products of the Spectre (Satan) who "reads the Voids Between Stars; among the arches of Albions Tomb sublime Rolling the Sea in rocky paths! Forming Leviathan And Behemoth; the War by Sea

115.   Milton Klonsky, *William Blake: The Seer and His Visions* (New York: Harmony, 1977), 137.

116.   Damon, *Blake's Job*, 38.

117.   George Wingfield Digby, *Symbol and Image in William Blake* (Oxford: Clarendon, 1957), 71–72.

enormous & the War By Land astounding: erecting pillars in the deepest Hell" (J 91). In plate 15, Blake quotes Job 40:15, 19; 41:34, to make this point. "Of Behemoth he saith, He is the chief of the ways of God/Of Leviathan he saith, He is King over all the Children of Pride." Los (imagination and creativity) breaks those pyramids and pillars of Spectre with his hammer in *Jerusalem,* "driving down the pyramids of pride." In a similar way, Satan falls in the next plate of the series.

Figure 5.16. William Blake, *Illustrations of the Book of Job,* plate 15, B2005.16. Yale Center for British Art, Gift of J. T. Johnston Coe in memory of Henry E. Coe, BA 1878, Henry E. Coe, Jr., BA 1917, and Henry E. Coe III, BA 1946.

Plate 16: The Fall of Satan

Figure 5.17. William Blake, *Illustrations of the Book of Job*, plate 16, B2005.16.17. Yale Center for British Art, Gift of J. T. Johnston Coe in memory of Henry E. Coe, BA 1878, Henry E. Coe, Jr., BA 1917, and Henry E. Coe III, BA 1946.

The two angels on each side of the throne appear in plates 2, 5, and 16. In plate 16 (Fig. 5.17), their countenances change. The one on the left smiles and its halo brightly glows. The one on the right watches the descent of Satan along with two other figures. Given Blake's affinity with Swedenborg, it is possible to connect the two figures with Swedenborg's idea that two angels from heaven accompany every person and yet, two spirits from hell also exist with every human. Both pairs become necessary, for humans cannot live without one hand communicating with hell and "the other with heaven."[118] When one chooses good "the two

118. Warren, ed., *A Compendium of the Theological Writings of Emanuel Swedenborg*, 284.

angels from heaven draw near, and the two spirits from hell are removed."[119] The two figures that fall with Satan, figures of Job and his wife, could represent Job's two accompanying spirits from hell. The casting out of the two spirits from hell becomes a final and necessary step, a Last Judgment for Job and his female emanation, so that the two angels of heaven can fully take over. In similar fashion, Albion throws himself into the flames of affliction in order that humanity becomes united and Jesus can appear (J 96:35–43). An important distinction to make between Albion and his emanation Jerusalem and Job and his wife is that plate 16 portrays one of many possible judgments of Job and his wife because, as Rowland explains, Job and his wife end up where they started in the series, which suggests "that they may, as opportunity arises, have to go through the whole experiential process again (and again)."[120]

Plate 17: The Vision of Christ

Blake originally titled plate 17 (Fig. 5.18 [overleaf]) "I have heard thee with the hearing of the Ear but now my Eyes seeth thee" (Job 42:5) but later publishers called it "The Vision of Christ."[121] The friends once again hide their faces, although the middle one comically attempts a peek. Blake depicts Christ's blessing upon Job and his wife. Job's wife looks up and smiles. The main point of this culminating picture of blessing remains the unity of Father and Son and Spirit and Human (John 10: "I & my Father are One"). Blake quotes extensively from John 14 as the angel at the bottom looks upon the words: "He that seen me hath seen my Father" and "Believe me that I am in the Father & the Father in me," in order to drive this point home.

According to Crabb Robinson, Blake reported, "He [Christ] is the only God... And so am I and so are you."[122] This is why Blake quotes 1 John 3:2, "we know that when he shall appear, we shall be like him for we shall see him as He Is." Regarding Blake, W. B. Yeats poetically observes, "He cried again and again that every thing that lives is holy, and that nothing is unholy except things that do not live—lethargies, and cruelties, and timidities, and that denial of imagination which is the root they grew from in old times."[123]

---

119. Ibid.
120. Rowland, *Blake and the Bible*, 57.
121. Paley, *The Traveller in the Evening*, 251.
122. Bentley, *Blake Records*, 696.
123. W. B. Yeats, "William Blake and the Imagination," in *The Collected Works of W. B. Yeats* (ed. George Bornstein and Richard J. Finneran; New York: Scribner, 2007), 85.

Figure 5.18. William Blake, *Illustrations of the Book of Job*, plate 17, B2005.16.18. Yale Center for British Art, Gift of J. T. Johnston Coe in memory of Henry E. Coe, BA 1878, Henry E. Coe, Jr., BA 1917, and Henry E. Coe III, BA 1946.

Christ's body is illuminated in this plate to represent heightened senses and transformed vision.[124] The vision changes Job's perception of reality. In his *Laocoön* engraving, Blake writes "God himself The Divine Body" and "Jesus we are his Members" because Blake means to communicate a Christian concept that "all are like the Saviour, the imagination, the divine body."[125]

124.   Connelly, *William Blake and the Body*, 205.
125.   Ibid., 206.

Plate 18: And My Servant Job Shall Pray for You
For the first time, the artist's palette and brushes appear along with
scrolls at the base of the engraving on plate 18 (Fig. 5.19). Job stands
before an altar made of hewn stones. His wife kneels on one side, while
his friends kneel on Job's other side. The burnt offering rises to heaven
in a flame; the arc of sun-like glory reaches from the top into the picture,
as if to connect heaven with earth.

Figure 5.19. William Blake, *Illustrations of the Book of Job*, plate 18,
B2005.16.19. Yale Center for British Art, Gift of J. T. Johnston Coe in
memory of Henry E. Coe, BA 1878, Henry E. Coe, Jr., BA 1917, and
Henry E. Coe III, BA 1946.

Blake moves back to the biblical book in the design of plate 18, Job praying for his friends. From Job 40: "Also the Lord accepted Job; And my Servant Job shall pray for you; And the Lord turned the captivity of Job when he prayed for his Friends." As Luke 6:28 states, "pray for them that despitefully use you." Blake offers a Christian interpretation here; as David Bindman notes, "Job offers them the Christian mercy of forgiveness. Christ is no longer separate from Job."[126]

The image also relates to Blake's *Noah and the Rainbow* watercolor painting.[127] The likeness between Noah and Job comes from Blake's understanding of the Old Testament Patriarchs and their relation to the Christian Church. In the plate "To the Jews" in *Jerusalem*, Blake writes,

> Ye are united O ye Inhabitants of Earth in One Religion. The Religion of Jesus: the most Ancient, the Eternal: & the Everlasting Gospel... Your Ancestors derived their origin from Abraham, Heber, Shem, and Noah who were Druids: as the Druid Temples (which are the Patriarchal Pillars & Oak Groves) over the whole Earth witness to this day. (J 27; E 171)

Blake associates both Job and Noah with the Druids of the Old Testament, those who worshiped a pre-existent Christ as part of the Ancient Church.[128] Therefore, in the next plate, plate 19, the tall Druidic structure that was behind Job's wife and Job in plate 4 now lies in ruins. Job and his wife sit upon the tree root instead of the Druid seat.

Plate 19: Every One also Gave Him a Piece of Money

The tall Druidic structure behind Job's wife and Job in plate 4 now lies in ruins in plate 19 (Fig. 5.20). Job sits upon the tree root instead of the Druid seat. Instead of a bat-winged figure hovering in the clouds above the picture, numerous angels cover the margins. Clear skies behind the people offering money replace the shadowy sky behind the messengers in plate 4. Furthermore, in contrast to plate 5, in which Job gives bread to a begger, both Job and his wife receive charity. Rowland remarks: "Blake, like Job, was rescued by his two patrons, Butts and Linnell, just as he was by the beauty of the dedication and solidarity of Catherine."[129] Here, as in many cases, it remains natural for authors to relate Job's wife to Blake's wife, Catherine, as will be noted later in this chapter.

126. David Bindman, *Blake as an Artist* (New York: Dutton, 1977), 212.
127. As noted by Archibald G. B. Russell, *The Engravings of William Blake* (New York: Blom, 1968). Also known as "The Covenant," watercolor painting, ca. 1803–5, in Houghton Library, Harvard University, Cambridge, Mass.
128. Lindberg, *William Blake's Illustrations to the Book of Job*, 221.
129. Rowland, *Blake and the Bible*, 66.

Figure 5.20. William Blake, *Illustrations of the Book of Job*, plate 19, B2005.16.20. Yale Center for British Art, Gift of J. T. Johnston Coe in memory of Henry E. Coe, BA 1878, Henry E. Coe, Jr., BA 1917, and Henry E. Coe III, BA 1946.

Plate 20: There Were Not Found Women Fair as the Daughters of Job in All the Land
In plate 20 (Fig. 5.21 [overleaf]), Job's daughters surround him in a structure that resembles a church or sanctuary. Job refers to works of art to tell his story instead of text; "Blake has made Job an artist."[130]

---

130.   Lindberg, *William Blake's Illustrations to the Book of Job*, 342.

Figure 5.21. William Blake, *Illustrations of the Book of Job*, plate 20, B2005.16.21. Yale Center for British Art, Gift of J. T. Johnston Coe in memory of Henry E. Coe, BA 1878, Henry E. Coe, Jr., BA 1917, and Henry E. Coe III, BA 1946.

Harold Fisch calls this plate "the strangest of the illustrations," the one that "stands at the greatest possible distance from the text of the biblical book."[131] In the lower margin rests a harp and a lyre. Bo Lindberg argues that Blake knew of the first-century text, the *Testament of Job*, but no

131.   Fisch, *The Biblical Presence in Shakespeare, Milton, and Blake*, 315. One could argue, however, that the vision of Christ in plate 17 acts as the most distant from the text of the biblical book of Job, especially in its Christological content.

record exists to support Blake's exposure to such traditions. And, Blake could not have read the T. Job, since it was published in 1833.[132] Since Job, in T. Job, gives his daughters musical instruments at the hour of his death in order that they might sing hymns (T. Job 52), a vague connection between Blake and Joban textual traditions exists. However, Blake's concern for musical instruments here stems from his overall message for Job.

The notes from Ps 139 on plate 20 suggest a unity of heaven and hell: "If I ascend up into Heaven thou art there/If I make my bed in hell behold Thou art there." Job's values have changed from material to spiritual, as indicated in the quotation, "How precious are thy thoughts unto me O God/how great is the sum of them." Though the biblical text accounts for Job's restored fortune, Blake chooses to portray his own version of the daughters' inheritance (Job 42:15)—his art and his vision of God.[133]

In the biblical account, Job's named daughters, Jemimah, Keziah, and Keren-happuch, contrast with his unnamed sons (Job 42:13–17). Job gives his daughters their inheritance alongside their brothers. An ambiguous reversal of norms takes place in the epilogue.[134] As an avid Bible reader, Blake could have noted such a unique aspect of the book. And, as a Dissenter, Blake would recognize societal deviance. Blake's rational for depicting Job's daughters, according to Raine, comes from Blake's sense of imagination: "Societies that give too high a place to rational thought necessarily undervalue woman, who is man's initiator into the world of Beulah [utopian Eden], a world of feeling and gateway to the world of the Imagination."[135] Yet, if Blake meant to demonstrate a concern to value females, one wonders why Job's wife is not present in the scene. It is more possible that Blake relates Job's beautiful daughters who come after Job's restoration as the products of Job's renewed artistic vision. In other words, their beauty reflects more of Job's journey than that of Blake's personal concerns to empower real women.

132.   In A. Mai's ten-volume *Scriptorum veterum nova collection a Vaticanis codicibus edita* published in 1833. See Russell P. Spittler, "The Testament of Job: A History of Research and Interpretation," in Knibb and van der Horst, eds., *Studies on the Testament of Job*, 7–32.

133.   La Belle, *Words Graven with an Iron Pen*, 546. The instruments at the bottom of the engraving also indicate a connection with T. Job. In ch. 52, Job gives his daughters musical instruments at the moment of his death so that they might sign hymns upon his death. A clear connection between Blake and T. Job remains unsubstantiated, due to T. Job's publishing date.

134.   See Morrow, "Toxic Religion and the Daughters of Job."

135.   Raine, *The Human Face of God*, 255.

In his drawing of *Laocoön*,[136] Blake exclaims, "Art is the Tree of Life" and "Christianity is Art."[137] His *Laocoön* functions as a comment on Blake's distaste for neoclassicism, as he renames the sculpture and thus interprets it as God, along with God's sons Adam and Satan, wrestling with two serpents.[138] The words scattered about the image, however, present Blake's unique style of "testing the boundary," as Irene Chayes states, of rational viewing.[139] Blake also inscribes around *Laocoön* that "morality is the weapon of empire"; a real Christian exercises artistic abilities: "A Poet a Painter a Musician an Architect: The Man Or Woman who is not one of these is not a Christian."[140] Job imparts his "inheritance" to his daughters, the appreciation of art as a Christian family. The final plate provides a culmination of the artistic abilities of Job's family.

Plate 21: So the Lord Blessed the Latter End of Job More Than the Beginning
As noted earlier, plate 21 (Fig. 5.22) serves as a counterpart to plate 1 (Fig. 5.1). Job and his wife stand surrounded by their seven sons and three daughters. The instruments no longer hang in the tree. The sun and the moon have switched places. The altar is inscribed with a quote from Heb 10:6, "In burnt Offerings for Sin thou hast had no Pleasure." The spiritual pleasure comes in artistic expression, to sing the apocalyptic song from Rev 15:3, "Great & Marvellous are thy Works Lord God Almighty/Just & True are they Ways O thou King of Saints." Job plays the harp, a symbol of the ancient British and Celtic Bardic traditions. Blake understood the ancient Bardic system to contain ancient truths,

---

136.   Blake sketched Laocoön during his time in the Royal Academy in 1815 but later reinterpreted and engraved it by surrounding it with marginalia. It seems a personal enterprise for Blake to do so, as only two copies survive and it seems none were sold during his lifetime. Bentley, *The Stranger from Paradise*, 427.

137.   As pointed out by Wright (*Blake's Job*, 49), who states, "That the story of Job has been made into art is cardinally important in view of Blake's often iterated view of the primacy of art as a theological fact." The first part of this phrase includes the words "Science is the Tree of Death," because Blake opposed materialistic science. See Frederick Burwick, "Blake's Laocoön and Job; or, on the Boundaries of Painting and Poetry," in *The Romantic Imagination: Literature and Art in England and Germany* (ed. Frederick Burwick and Jürgen Klein; Atlanta, Ga.: Rodopi, 1996), 125–55.

138.   Richard Brilliant, *My Laocoön: Alternative Claims in the Interpretation of Artworks* (Discovery Series; Berkeley: University of California Press, 2000), 36.

139.   Irene H. Chayes, "Words in Pictures: Testing the Boundary: Inscriptions by William Blake," *Word & Image* 7, no. 2 (1991): 85–97.

140.   As quoted in Bentley, *The Stranger from Paradise*, 426–27.

long forgotten and re-revealed.[141] The Bard calls to the "Youth of delight," to "come hither, and see the opening morn, image of truth new born" (SIE 54 2–3; E 31). Blake sees Job's responsibility to impart his revealed truths to his children, as visually demonstrated in the previous plate. This is not unlike Blake towards the end of his life, when a group of young men, calling themselves "The Ancients," gathered around Blake, whom they deemed "The Interpreter."

Figure 5.22. William Blake, *Illustrations of the Book of Job*, plate 21, B2005.16.22. Yale Center for British Art, Gift of J. T. Johnston Coe in memory of Henry E. Coe, BA 1878, Henry E. Coe, Jr., BA 1917, and Henry E. Coe III, BA 1946.

141.   Bentley, *The Stranger from Paradise*, 327.

Blake passed on his wisdom of visions to the young men. He spent the last years of his life (1818–27) boasting in the presence of energetic youth eager to learn of his spiritual, ideological, mythological, and artistic genius. They talked about Christian art and "the divine gift of Art and Letters, and of spiritual vision and inspiration," the same content Job and his family celebrate in plate 21.[142]

One of the Ancients recalls his first meeting with Blake: "The copper of the first plate—'Thus did Job continually'—was lying on the table where he had been working at it. How lovely it looked by the lamplight, strained through the tissue paper."[143] Blake's 35-year relationship with the book of Job thus ends with an autobiographical comment on Blake's specific Christianity. Inscriptions Blake made on the first and last plates of Job, which he later erased, sum up his intended message:

Prayer to God is the Study of Imaginative Art
Praise to God is the Exercise of Imaginative Art[144]

Job and His Wife in Blake's Job Series

Lodowick Muggleton (1609–1698), a London tailor, began a Protestant movement in 1651; the group known as the Muggletonians gathered with Muggleton and his fellow prophet John Reeve to discuss their theology, which was extremely opposed to philosophical reason. Some biographers have lightly associated Blake's parents with the Muggletonians, at least claiming they attended a meeting.[145] E. P. Thompson goes further than most Blake scholars to associate the ideas of Muggleton with Blake, at least in terms of the London antinomianistic scene of the 1690s. The Muggletonians believed in oppositions, such as God/Nature, Faith/Reason, and good seed/bad seed. After the Fall, Satan implanted himself into Eve's womb when she gave birth to Cain. But, Seth was the son of Adam who was the son of God. In other words, this Two Seeds doctrine made humanity into the bearers of both evil reason and good faith.[146] For example, to demonstrate that no other spirit than the Devil gives witches their powers, and the evil of the seed of reason, which comes from Satan,

142. Ibid., 407.
143. Bentley, *Blake Records*, 391.
144. G. E. Bentley, ed., *Blake Books Supplement* (Oxford: Clarendon, 1995), 195.
145. Bentley refutes this claim in *Blake Records*, xxxii n., and David Erdman dismisses it as well: David V. Erdman, *Blake: Prophet Against Empire* (rev. ed.; Princeton, N.J.: Princeton University Press, 1969), 142 n. 57.
146. E. P. Thompson, *Witness Against the Beast: William Blake and the Moral Law* (New York: New Press, 1993), 70–76.

as opposed to the seed of faith that comes from God as manifested in Jesus Christ, Muggleton suggests that Job's wife embodied "the spirit of unclean reason" because through her Satan "tempted Job to curse God and die."[147] Thompson does not set out to prove any direct Muggletonian influence on Blake, but he does point out that "at certain points Blake's vocabulary has a markedly Muggletonian accent."[148] Blake shares a vocabulary with many different Christian movements besides the Church of England that surfaced in London during his time.

Given that Blake himself pits reason against imaginative faith in his Job series, it would follow that Blake could maintain an adversarial position for Job's wife. No written indication exists in the Job series that Blake means to focus on Job's wife beyond her role as a wife to her husband. Therefore, this section argues that Blake depicts Job's wife as Job's companion along Job's journey and loosely relates her as a sign, visually anyway, of the emanations of humanity, that is, the division of the sexes in the present world. Job's wife undergoes the imaginative transformation with Job, but still remains part of the division of the sexes. Given that Job and his wife finally embrace a visionary form of religious expression in the final plate of the series, Blake provides Job and his wife some connection, but only in Blake's utopian vision does man ever reunify with his emanation.

The previous section about Blake's overall message for Job has already revealed some of Blake's ideas about the marriage of Job and his wife. First, a consistent visual separation exists between Job's friends and his wife, with his friends often cut off from seeing or experiencing things that Job and his wife experience. For instance, in the whirlwind illustration on plate 13 (Fig. 5.14), Job and his wife look at God with prayerful hands while his friends prostrate with their heads to the ground. In plate 16 (Fig. 5.17), Job and his wife sit together on one side of the flame of judgment while his friends sit on the other side. In plate 17, the Christ figure appears only to bless Job and his wife while the friends cower in fear (Fig. 5.18). Visually, his wife shares some of Job's journey.

Some commentators suggest that Job and his wife reflect the real marriage of William and Catherine Blake. An early biographer of Blake, Alexander Gilchrist, notes parallels with Job and his wife and Blake and his wife Catherine: "To friends who remember Blake in Fountain Court [1821–27], those calm, patriarchal figures of Job and his Wife in the

147. Lodowick Muggleton, "A True Interpretation of the Witch of Endor," in *The Works of John Reeve and Lodowicke Muggleton* (London: Joseph & Isaac Frost, 1831), Chapter XVI, 69.
148. Thompson, *Witness Against the Beast*, 86.

artist's own designs, still recall the two, as they used to sit together in that humble room."[149] Blake taught Catherine how to read, write, and help him in his trade. Gilchrist also adds, "Not only was she wont to echo what he said, to talk as he talked, on religion and other matters— this may be accounted for by the fact that he had educated her; but she, too, learned to have visions."[150] Catherine remained the one person privy to Blake's artistic process and she even produced her own artwork alongside Blake.[151]

Catherine's support seems harmonious in this view, and one that Job's wife seems to mirror in the illustrations, but feminist Blake scholars point out the possibility of masochistic "pious snippets" from authors propagating patriarchal marital assumptions of the passive wife and active husband.[152] Anne Mellor sees the Blake marriage in terms of a "subservient wife in a patriarchal marriage."[153] She goes on to suggest that a mutual interdependence of the sexes in Blake's work "should not obscure the fact that, in Blake's metaphoric system, the masculine is both logically and physically prior to the feminine."[154]

Increasing Enlightenment notions among the urban middle classes during Blake's time include an expected "emotional compatibility within marriage and cherished domesticity as an ideal that was fundamental to social order."[155] Thus, when Henry Crabb Robinson describes Mrs. Blake in 1852, he does so as the woman "to make him happy," as if "she had been formed by him Indeed" with "an implicit reverence of her husband...like the first Wife Eve worshipped God in her Husband."[156] Thus assigning Catherine Blake to the domestic role of making her

149. Bentley, *Blake Records*, 322.
150. Ibid., 321.
151. Catherine Blake produced *Verso: A Man's Head and Other Drawings*, ca. 1805, found at the Tate Gallery (Britain), including Agnes and a head of William Blake as a young man. While it is true that Catherine knew of Blake's artistic process, Robert Essick also notes the wives of Blake's major commissioners and the impact they may have had on Blake's view of gender, especially when one of his commissioners chose Catherine Watson's engravings over those of Blake. See Robert N. Essick, "William Blake's 'Female Will' and Its Biographical Context," *Studies in English Literature, 1500–1900* 31, no. 4 (1991): 615–30.
152. Shirley Dent and Jason Whittaker, *Radical Blake: Influence and Afterlife from 1827* (New York: Palgrave Macmillan, 2002), 124.
153. Anne K. Mellor, "Blake's Portrayal of Women," *Blake: An Illustrated Quarterly* (Winter 1982–83): 154.
154. Ibid., 153.
155. Douglas Hay and Nicholas Rogers, *Eighteenth-century English Society* (Oxford: Oxford University Press, 1997), 40.
156. Bentley, *Blake Records*, 699.

husband happy, Robinson offers an example of such domestic ideology. Yet, such an ideology does not exist in its purest form, especially since Blake worked from within his home. Industrial production as a mode of creation began to develop in his society during the 1790s. Blake himself critiqued industrial forms of organization that squelch the imagination of its subservient.[157]

For Blake, Jesus, the "Poetic Genius," inspires humans to use their imaginations to transcend the fallen world.[158] Blake did not set out to create his own system of gender, but in creating his own point of view about the world, his gendered viewpoint emerges as a consequence. In Blake's "Circle of Destiny," which Job exemplifies, God intended coexistence in liberty of the human imagination. The Fall, however, destroyed that unity and Albion becomes part of the material world, a shadow of the whole self. Rigid systems over-simplified parts of the everyday world in which male and female opposition become reinforced by social codes. Through Jesus, humans find forgiveness of others and a realization of one's infinite capacities of the eternal self. Jesus saves not the world, but saves *from* the world.[159] Above all, Blake plays with contraries.[160] As Albert Roe notes, Blake uses aspects of feminine and masculine in both traditional and non-traditional ways. In a non-traditional sense, "every person in this world has both masculine and feminine aspects of personality, not peculiar to the two sexes as we think of them, but mingled in each," but "man may fall by turning away from the active imaginative life, so may woman through denying her dependence upon man and seeking to dominate him."[161] Feminine need for domination is the dreaded "Female Will." But, Roe goes on to say that Blake does not

157. Saree Makdisi, *William Blake and the Impossible History of the 1790s* (Chicago: Chicago University Press, 2003), 120.

158. Jesus also acts as an agent in the creation of women because Jesus needs women in order to exist: David Fallon, "'She Cuts His Heart Out at His Side': Blake, Christianity and Political Virtue," in *Blake and Conflict* (ed. Sarah Haggarty and Jon Mee; New York: Palgrave Macmillan, 2009), 84–104.

159. Kathleen Raine, *Blake and the New Age* (London: George Allen & Unwin, 1979).

160. For a psycho-social investigation into Blake's sexual contradictions that argues for Blake's denial of female sexuality in *Jerusalem*, see Brenda Webster, "Blake, Women, and Sexuality," in *New Casebooks: William Blake* (ed. David Punter; New York: St. Martin's, 1996), 188–206; Brenda Webster, "Blake, Sex and Women Revisited," in *Women Reading William Blake* (ed. Helen P. Bruder; New York: Palgrave Macmillan, 2007), 254–60.

161. Albert Roe, "Blake's Symbolism," in *Sparks of Fire: Blake in a New Age* (ed. James Bogan and Fred Gross; Richmond, Calif.: North Atlantic, 1982), 79–80.

imply that there are no jealous and materialistic men and no magnanimous and imaginative women. The dominance of Female Will, which is the besetting sin of life in our world, is the pursuit of vain ends and the disregarding of visionary life.[162]

Through exploring the challenging concepts of Female Will and Emanation, this final section will give further insight into Blake's system of gender as found in his art and poetry and how that system applies to Job and his wife.

Turning toward Blake's mythology rather than his marriage or personal acquaintances, Kathleen Raine suggests that Blake means to signify Job's wife as Job's "emanation" or "feminine counterpart." She does not elaborate further on Job's wife's exact function as emanation, although she compares Job with Albion and Job's wife with Jerusalem, Albion's emanation.[163] Such visual connections have been discussed above, especially in terms of Jerusalem's body gesture in relation to Job's wife's gesture in plate 7 (Figs. 5.7 and 5.8).

Yet, for Blake, emanations reunite in Utopia and the Job series is not set in a utopian vision. As seen in the above overall discussion of Blake's Job, it is not Job's journey to reach Utopia. Rather, Job provides an example of a religious re-awakening. Furthermore, Ankarsjö maintains that the sexes must work together to bring about Blake's utopian sense of reunion of male and female. Eden, as a state of spiritual utopia for Blake, takes place when humanity embraces its unifying divine nature.[164] In the meantime, Blake's *Four Zoas* and *Jerusalem* take place within the world of fallen existence. Therefore, the sexes are not equal. The sexualized image makes sense in a utopian, apocalyptic concept, as wholeness restored means harmony between the sexes.[165]

Though emanations can identify with both genders, Blake considered emanations in terms of wives for husbands. Like his wife Catherine, they inspire the creative capacities of their husbands.[166] Damon goes the furthest in uplifting a marital ideal and suggesting that Job's wife "is part of him, his inspiration, his feminine aspect (which Blake elsewhere

---

162. Ibid., 80.

163. Raine, *The Human Face of God*, 78.

164. Ankarsjö, *William Blake and Gender*, 158–90.

165. See Magnus Ankarsjö, who states that "Jerusalem being equally strong, the two characters at the end of the poem are thus reunited in togetherness, making them the most successful representation of gender equality in the whole Blake canon" (*William Blake and Gender*, 162).

166. Tristanne J. Connolly, *William Blake and the Body* (New York: Palgrave Macmillan, 2002), 175–80.

called an Emanation), who shares his errors."[167] Damon's assessment remains involved in a romantic tone, one that simplifies the matter greatly. For instance, in Mellor's assessment of Blake's poetry, the female characters remain dependent on the male characters. If they do not depend on their male characters, then their autonomy ends in disaster. The notion of "Female Will," which she defines as "egoistic selfhood," rests at the heart of Mellor's claim. Male characters have real, intelligent bodies, but "emanations," as Mellor suggests, are "divided from and intended to be finally reabsorbed into the male."[168] Yet, sexual division does not exist when an emanation is absorbed into the male; neither does she have a separate will after that point: "In Eternity they neither marry nor are given in marriage" (J 30 [34]:15; E 176).

For Blake, a problem exists with a separate "Female Will." The "Female Will" naturally turns against her consort in selfishness and jealousy, as part of the fallen world: "The Feminine separates from the Masculine & both from Man, Ceasing to be His Emanations, Life to Themselves assuming! And while they circumscribe his Brain, & while they circumscribe His Heart, & while they circumscribe his Loins!" (J 90:1–4; E 249). Meanwhile, the male remains a rational being in need of imaginative and artistic vision. To reunite with Jerusalem, Albion annihilates his selfhood, and like Jesus Christ, sacrifices his selfhood (J 96; E 375). In other words, "When the Individual appropriates Universality He divides into Male & Female: & when the Male & Female, Appropriate Individuality, they become an Eternal Death" (J 90:52–54; E 250). Both the "Selfhood of the Male and the Female Will wage 'war' on humanity" and, according to Rachel Billigheimer, Blake's "sublime vision is achieved by self-sacrifice through love and forgiveness."[169]

In *Jerusalem*, Los, Blake's character of Imagination, states that humanity cannot fully become itself without a unification of both male and female: "For Man cannot unite with Man but by their Emanations Which stand both Male & Female at the Gates of each Humanity" (J 88:10–11; E 246). Common for his time, Blake uses the term "Man" and "Brotherhood" in the generic sense and it hasn't escaped scholars to note the limits of Blake's genderless utopia in the midst of gendered language.[170] At any rate, Enitharmon, Los's emanation, laments in plate 87

167. Damon, *Blake's Job*, 3.
168. Mellor, "Blake's Portrayal of Women," 148, 151.
169. Rachel V. Billigheimer, "Conflict and Conquests: Creation, Emanation and the Female in William Blake's Mythology," *Modern Language Studies* 30, no. 1 (2000): 116.
170. Nicolas M. Williams, *Ideology and Utopia in the Poetry of William Blake* (Cambridge: Cambridge University Press, 1998).

that "in Eden our loves were the same/here they are opposite"(J 87:16; E 246). The Spectre, the reasoning power of man that frames moral law and causes human division, knows that "the Man who respects Woman shall be despised by Woman" (J 88:37). Ankarsjö maintains that utopia, reaching another Eden, remains central to Blake's portrayal of gender: "Blake tries to show the exigency of movement and active male–female cooperation through the symbolic interaction of his male and female characters."[171] The key to Ankarsjö's understanding of gender in Blake's work is that Blake insisted that the sexes cooperate and work together to reach pure harmony among the sexes. Discord and gender conjunction exist in a fallen world.

A popular yet apocryphal story from Blake's life offers a sense of Blake's own utopian Eden vision. Mr. Butts called upon Blake and Catherine in the garden of their summer home in Lambeth one afternoon. He found them sitting naked in the garden reciting words from Milton's *Paradise Lost*. "Come in!" cries Blake, "it's only Adam and Eve, you know!"[172]

Although the story of Blake and Catherine nude in the garden hoping to regain a form of Eden-like innocence did not take place, the story helps illustrate the gendered issues involved in utopian visions, which, in the very least, associate with pleasure and passion rather than with denial of the flesh, order, and discipline. Blake maintains a hierarchal binary of male/female in his poetry because that binary reflects the reality of his historical location; whether he succeeds in deconstructing or subverting the binary remains debatable.[173] In the same way, whether Blake succeeds in presenting a more empowered idea of Job's wife in the Job series is arguable.

The feminine aspects of the main characters remain central to Blake's creation of the pleasurable and desirable utopian vision beyond the world of reality. Blake states himself that in his vision, "Humanity is far above/sexual organization" (J 79:73–4; E 236). In *Ideology and Utopia in the Poetry of William Blake*, Nicholas Williams argues that Blake not only seeks mentally or imaginatively to depict change in some ideological sense, but also that his use of utopia meant to face a "notion of the

171.   Ankarsjö, *William Blake and Gender*, 36.
172.   Bentley, *Blake Records*, xxvi–xxvii. For a feminist discussion of this story, see Tracy Chevalier, "Peeking Over the Garden Wall," in Bruder, ed., *Women Reading William Blake* (New York: Palgrave Macmillan, 2007), 12–15.
173.   Some critics claim that Blake's "Female Will" reflects misogynist stereotypes, while others claim that Blake means to transcend gendered hierarchy through his vision of utopian liberation.

social determination of reality with a desire for meaningful liberational change."[174] Williams cautions the reader against reducing Blake's utopia to mere ideology rather than grounding it in real-world consequences of power dynamics and genuine interest in transformation. Blake, then, observes the inequality of gender relations in the eighteenth century, and, like Wollstonecraft, means to take part in the liberation of women through his portrayal of a utopian liberation of the body.[175] A contrary point to Williams is that the androgynous body of liberation in Blake's poetry always has the female body absorb into the male body, which seems to cancel the female independence while sustaining the male identity.[176] Furthermore, as part of his culture, Blake uses sexually differentiated language that cannot sustain an androgynous ideal.[177]

Gender in utopia is complex. In order for one to create a utopian vision of what is good, an implicit comparison must be made with what is bad. In other words, Blake's utopia of gender reveals a tension between desire and absence, between imaginary conceptualization of the sexes and actual societal standards. The entire idea of utopia in Blake's poetry holds together opposing viewpoints in the same way that, implicitly, his utopian fiction playfully negotiates gender difference.[178] In the very least, gender is unstable: Los asks, "When Souls mingle & join thro all the Fibres of Brotherhood/Can there be any secret joy on Earth greater than this?" (J 88:14–15; E 246), after which Enitharmon responds, "This is Womans World... A triple Female Tabernacle for Moral Law I weave/ That he who loves Jesus may loathe terrified Female love/Till God himself become a Male subservient to the Female" (J 88:16–21; E 247). Enitharmon sits at her loom and sings while Los, aware of both Female love and jealousy, wields his hammer, until Jesus appears to Albion as the Good Shepherd demonstrating that humanity cannot exist without

174.   Williams, *Ideology and Utopia in the Poetry of William Blake*.
175.   Ibid., 70–71.
176.   Essick, "William Blake's 'Female Will' and Its Biographical Context," 616–17.
177.   Kathleen Middleton Murphy, "'All the Lovely Sex': Blake and the Woman Question," in Bogan and Goss, eds., *Sparks of Fire*, 272–75. Middleton Murphy distinguishes between "what the concepts imply and what (or how) the language says" (p. 275).
178.   The concept of playful negotiations, though not applied to Blake's work, can be found in Lee Cullen Khanna, "Utopian Exchanges: Negotiating Difference in Utopia," in *Gender and Utopia in the Eighteenth Century: Essays in English and French Utopian Writing* (ed. Nicole Pohl and Brenda Tooley; Burlington, Vt.: Ashgate, 2007), 17.

Albion's denying his selfhood.[179] Albion throws himself in the furnaces of affliction, and then Albion unites with all, male and female, as he stands before Jesus (J 96:27–43; E 256).

It remains possible that Albion represents Everyman as does Job.[180] As noted earlier, the four Zoas each have their own feminine counterparts. Albion becomes whole once again when England, otherwise called Britannia, another female personification like Jerusalem (Blake has Britannia function differently in various different plates but she often coincides with Jerusalem), enters Albion's bosom (J 93).[181] But the question remains for Job and his wife, who never enters her husband's bosom, how their relationship reflects that of man and his emanation. Job's wife and Job do not embrace to become one again because Job and his wife are left to the world to express their visionary faith; Blake's message for Job is more for Job's conversion from rational dependent to imaginative visionary.

Blake's concern remains not for a reunification of Job and his wife, but for depicting Job's journey and transformation, during which his wife stands as witness. The tree under which Job and his family stand in the final plate (plate 21) is not, for Blake, a new Eden for Job because Job and his wife still remain in the world. Blake remains true to the text of Job in this regard. Rather, as Rowland argues, "the eyes of Job and his wife are opened to the panorama of creation through which the divine life is made manifest."[182] Job's wife remains a companion, an echo of Job's emanation but never fully revealed as such. For such a revelation takes place in the kind of utopian visions Blake did not mean to set out for his renditions of the book of Job.

Nevertheless, Blake's deviation from an artistic norm for Job and his wife at the dungheap becomes even more defined in comparison to Herbert Granville Fell's illustration of Job and his wife from 1896 (Fig. 5.23), 70 years after the creation of Blake's Job illustrations. With the art nouveau tradition sweeping the country at the turn of the twentieth century, British book illustrator H. Granville Fell offers his version of a common theme—the reproval of a wife who turns her arm away from

179.   The gendered image of the furnace and the loom provides Essick with another example of a male/primary and female/secondary association in Blake; Blake cannot be separated from his cultural constructs, especially in terms of the gender divisions in the household: Essick, "William Blake's 'Female Will' and Its Biographical Context," 619.

180.   Raine, *The Human Face of God*, 78.

181.   Morton D. Paley, ed., *William Blake's Jerusalem* (Princeton, N.J.: Princeton University Press, 1991), 290–93.

182.   Rowland, *Blake and the Bible*, 71.

Job, similar in form to Job's wife's retreating right arm on the sculpture at Notre Dame Cathedral in Paris (Fig. 2.2). Fell decorates Job's wife in a highly ornate Oriental fashion. Makdisi suggests that Blake remains radically different in his refusal to "dabble in recognizably Orientalist themes or motifs" which were common in his time, considering Britain's imperial project and colonial rule.[183]

Figure 5.23. Herbert Granville Fell, in *The Book of Job With Designs by Herbert Granville Fell and an Introduction by Joseph Jacobs* (London: J. M. Dent; New York: Dodd/Mead, 1896). Photo: Katherine Low.

183.   Makdisi, *William Blake and the Impossible History of the 1790s*, 209. One of the best definitions of Orientalism comes from Chung Hyun Kyung: "Orientalism is a form of cultural imperialism, manufactured inside the minds of Westerners" (Kyung, "Your Comfort vs. My Death," 136).

However, Blake's view of gender does not exist outside of his Christian conceptualizations. In Blake's view, becoming a true Christian takes place when an individual embarks on a journey of the denial of the individual which ultimately leads to the open embracing of liberation. In the Job series, this meant that Job and his wife trade in the books of pious law for the instruments of true Christian expression in art, vision, and imagination.

CONCLUSION

This study has emphasized the valuable places of meanings that reside within readers and their communities, especially in the realm of cultural constructs of gender and biblical interpretation. Cultural ideologies of gender shape the way people have read Job and his wife. This is why cultural studies advances reception history of the Bible; cultural artifacts, including, but not limited to, literature all serve to represent the Bible in culturally defined ways. Biblical interpreters can learn a great deal about how their own cultural ideas about gender shape their exegetical work of biblical texts by understanding how gender has shaped cultural traditions and biblical interpretations of the past. Furthermore, those engaged in cultural and gender studies benefit from turning their attention to biblical studies because religion and the interpretation of sacred texts consistently inform culture and politics.

Textual ruptures in the biblical text cause waves of conjectures and expansions. Another broader implication of this study allows for analysis of other biblical couples in terms of gender. Readers take seriously the fissures of a wife's unnamedness, as evident in early receptions of Job and his wife. Continued analysis of the biblical afterlives of unnamed wives in terms of how readers understand gender roles within marriage remains necessary. For instance, when gender theorists and biblical scholars investigate why biblical unnamed women receive names in post-biblical traditions, and the cultural significance of those names, they gain both insight into the functions of the biblical character and the cultures that engage them.

In turn, those conjectures and expansions inspire one to revisit the biblical text to explore the richness therein. T. Job expands on Job's wife, Sitidos, just as early Latin Church Fathers elaborate on a wife's tempting speech to her husband, symbolic of unorthodox transmissions throughout their society. When the SHS depicts Job's wife whipping him with words, the symbolic nature of deviant speech brings forth a cultural ideology of the complexity of women and words. In Job 2:9, as part of a male-oriented society, Job's wife speaks to her husband, and that fact alone requires one to assess seriously the power of gendered speech, not only in Job, but in the entire biblical corpus.

Heather McKay has already pointed out that interruptive speech of women in biblical narratives disrupts normal operations of power.[1] Taking her assessment a step further, a reception history study of Job and his wife reveals the ways readers use biblical married couples to broker their power claims. And, in turn, one might reassess some of the religious meanings of marriage and society in biblical times and beyond.

The ways authors differentiate between spiritual and material when it comes to Job and his wife also provide evidence for how the body figures prominently in religio-political discourses. One overall observation about the impact of the marriage of Job and his wife is that authors and artists connect marriage, religion, and politics. Although alternative forms of relationships existed within early Christian society, such virtues for biblical predecessors remained important to the establishment of Christianity as an institution. Early modern authors engage biblical marriage as a way to uphold political virtues. In other words, gender order reflects political order in a way that reinforces established social hierarchies through prescribed masculine and feminine behaviors. Those who uphold hegemonic masculinity in favor of heterosexual hierarchal marriage suppresses not only the single woman or "bad" wife, but the cuckold husband as well. The authors of such marital instruction engage masculine norms and practices most valuable for maintaining political dominance; during a time of political and religious reformation, they use marriage as a way to maintain authority in their society. Therefore, when William Blake engages his system of gender for his interpretation of Job, his alternative form of Christian theology holds no sway in his contemporary society. His non-traditional view of Christianity and deviance from the established Church of England demonstrates how engrained some ideals of marriage remain in society.

When it comes to marriage, religion, and politics, this study also informs contemporary debates on marriage in current American culture. As evident in a reception history of Job and his wife, societies of the West have consistently negotiated what gendered performances remain important for them in marital relationships. Marriage, then, becomes more about power relations than heterosexual desire. This becomes evident when Christians make claims about how marriage should function in the

---

1. Heather A. McKay, "She Said to Him, He Said to Her: Power Talk in the Bible or Foucault Listens at the Keyhole," *BTB* 28, no. 2 (1998): 45–51.

political realm. Examples come from the early modern domestic manuals that exemplify the marriage of Job and his wife as incorrect reflections of political structures, or, from medieval concerns that a biblical wife's speech reflects the oral traditions of "pagans." Marital ideals, for biblical couples and beyond, remain intricately linked to the fluctuating cultural negotiations of power, class, religion, and gender.

BIBLIOGRAPHY

Abelard, Peter. *The Letters of Abelard and Heloise*. Translated by Betty Radice. Harmondsworth: Penguin, 1974.

Ackroyd, Peter. *Blake: A Biography*. New York: Knopf, 1996.

Ælfric. *Sermones Catholici; or, Homilies of Aelfric*. Translated by Benjamin Thorpe. 2 vols. London: Taylor, 1844–46.

Agrippa, Heinrich Cornelius. *The Philosophy of Natural Magic*. Chicago: The deLaurence Co., 1913.

———. *Declamation on the Nobility and Preeminence of the Female Sex*. Translated by Albert Rabil. Chicago: University of Chicago Press, 1996.

Allen, Prudence. *The Concept of Woman: The Early Humanist Reformation, 1250–1500*, vol. 2. Grand Rapids: Eerdmans, 2002.

Alsop, Rachel, Annette Fitzsimons, and Kathleen Lennon. *Theorizing Gender*. Cambridge: Polity, 2002.

Ambrose. *Saint Ambrose: Letters*. Translated by Sister Mary Melchior Beyenka. The Fathers of the Church: A New Translation. New York: Fathers of the Church, Inc., 1954.

Anonymous. *A Book of Scotish Pasquils, 1568–1715*. Edinburgh: Paterson, 1868.

Apostolos-Cappadona, Diane. *Dictionary of Christian Art*. New York: Continuum, 1994.

Aquinas, Thomas. *The Literal Exposition on Job: A Scriptural Commentary Concerning Providence*. Edited by Carl A. Raschke. Translated by Anthony Damico. Classics in Religious Studies. Atlanta: Scholars Press, 1989.

Ariès, Philippe. *Centuries of Childhood: A Social History of Family Life*. Translated by Robert Baldick. New York: Knopf, 1962.

Ashfield, Andrew, and Peter de Bolla, eds. *The Sublime: A Reader in British Eighteenth-Century Aesthetic Theory*. New York: Cambridge University Press, 1996.

Astell, Ann. *Job, Boethius, and Epic Truth*. Ithaca, N.Y.: Cornell University Press, 1994.

———. "Job's Wife, Walter's Wife, and the Wife of Bath." Pages 92–107 in *Old Testament Women in Western Literature*. Edited by Raymond-Jean Frontain. Conway, AR: UCA, 1991.

Auerbach, Erich. *Scenes from the Drama of European Literature*. New York: Meridian, 1959.

Aughterson, Kate, ed. *The English Renaissance: An Anthology of Sources and Documents*. New York: Routledge, 1998.

———, ed. *Renaissance Woman: A Sourcebook*. New York: Routledge, 1995.

Augustine. *Treatises on Various Subjects*. Edited by Roy Joseph Deferrari. Translated by Mary Sarah Muldowney. The Fathers of the Church: A New Translation. New York: Fathers of the Church, Inc., 1952.

Bacon, Paul M. "Mirror of a Christian Prince: Frederick the Wise and Art Patronage in Electoral Saxony, 1486–1525." Ph.D. dissertation. University of Wisconsin-Madison, 2004.

Baker, Daniel. *The History of Job: A Sacred Poem*. London: Clavel, 1706.

Bal, Mieke. "Introduction." Pages 1–14 in *The Practice of Cultural Analysis: Exposing Interdisciplinary Interpretation*. Edited by Mieke Bal. Stanford, Calif.: Stanford University Press, 1999.

———. "Reading Art?" Pages 25–41 in *Generations and Geographies in the Visual Arts: Feminist Readings*. Edited by Griselda Pollock. New York: Routledge, 1996.

Ball, Philip. *Universe of Stone: A Biography of Chartres Cathedral*. New York: Harper-Collins, 2008.

Barasch, Moshe. *Gestures of Despair in Medieval and Early Renaissance Art*. New York: New York University Press, 1976.

Bardsley, Sandy. "Men's Voices in Late Medieval England." Pages 163–83 in Craun, ed., *The Hands of the Tongue*.

———. *Venomous Tongues: Speech and Gender in Late Medieval England*. Philadelphia: University of Pennsylvania Press, 2006.

Barnhouse, Rebecca. *The Book of the Knight of the Tower: Manners for Young Medieval Women*. New York: Palgrave Macmillan, 2006.

Baskin, Judith R. *Pharaoh's Counsellors: Job, Jethro, and Balaam in Rabbinic and Patristic Tradition*. Brown Judaic Studies. Chico, Calif.: Scholars Press, 1983.

———. "Rabbinic Interpretations of Job." Pages 101–10 in Perdue and Gilpin, eds., *Voice from the Whirlwind*.

Baxter, Richard. *The Practical Works of Richard Baxter*. 4 vols. Morgan, Pa.: Soli Deo Gloria, 1673.

Belle, Jenijoy La. "Blake's Visions and Re-Visions of Michelangelo." Pages 13–22 in *Blake in His Time*. Edited by Robert N. Essick and Donald Pearce. Bloomington: Indiana University Press, 1978.

Bellin, Harvey F., and Darrell Ruhl, eds. *Blake and Swedenborg: Opposition Is True Friendship*. New York: Swedenborg Foundation, 1985.

Ben-Barak, Zafrira. "The Daughters of Job." *Eretz-Israel* 24, Avraham Malamat Volume (1993): 41–48.

———. "Inheritance by Daughters in the Ancient near East." *Journal of Semitic Studies* 25 (1980): 22–33.

Benesch, Otto. *The Drawings of Rembrandt*. 6 vols. London: Phaidon, 1973.

Bentley, G. E., ed. *Blake Books Supplement*. Oxford: Clarendon, 1995.

———. *Blake Records*. 2d ed. New Haven: Published for the Paul Mellon Centre for Studies in British Art by Yale University Press, 2004.

———. *The Stranger from Paradise: A Biography of William Blake*. New Haven: Yale University Press, 2001.

Besserman, Lawrence. "Biblical Exegesis, Typology, and the Imagination of Chaucer." Pages 183–205 in Keenan, ed., *Typology and English Medieval Literature*.

———. *The Legend of Job in the Middle Ages*. Cambridge, Mass.: Harvard University Press, 1979.

Bever, Edward. "Old Age and Witchcraft in Early Modern Europe." Pages 150–90 in *Old Age in Preindustrial Society*. Edited by Peter N. Stearns. New York: Holmes & Meier, 1982.

Billigheimer, Rachel V. "Conflict and Conquests: Creation, Emanation and the Female in William Blake's Mythology." *Modern Language Studies* 30, no. 1 (2000): 93–120.

Bindman, David. *Blake as an Artist.* New York: Dutton, 1977.

Blackmore, Richard. *A Paraphrase on the Book of Job.* 2d ed. London: Tonson, 1716.

Blake, N. F. *Caxton and His World.* London: Deutsch, 1969.

Blake, William. *Blake's Illustrations for the Book of Job.* New York: Dover, 1995.

———. *Jerusalem.* New York: Barnes & Noble, 1964.

———. *Milton.* Edited by Kay Parkhurst Easson and Roger R. Easson. New York: Random House, 1978.

Blamires, Alcuin. *The Case for Women in Medieval Culture.* Oxford: Clarendon, 1997.

———. "Paradox in the Medieval Gender Doctrine of Head and Body." Pages 13–29 in *Medieval Theology and the Natural Body.* Edited by Peter Biller and A. J. Minnis. Rochester, N.Y.: York Medieval, 1997.

Blass-Simmen, Brigit. "*Studi Dal Vivo E Dal Non Più Vivo*: Carpaccio's Passion Paintings with Saint Job." *Metropolitan Museum Journal* 41 (2006): 75–90.

Bleyerveld, Yvonne. "Chaste, Obedient and Devout: Biblical Women as Patterns of Female Virtue in Netherlandish and German Graphic Art, Ca. 1500–1750." *Simiolus: Netherlands Quarterly for the History of Art* 28, no. 4 (2000–2001): 219–50.

Bloom, Harold. *Ruin the Sacred Truths: Poetry and Belief from the Bible to the Present.* Cambridge, Mass.: Harvard University Press, 1989.

Blunt, Anthony. *The Art of William Blake.* New York: Columbia University Press, 1959.

Bogan, James, and Fred Goss, eds. *Sparks of Fire: Blake in a New Age.* Richmond, Calif.: North Atlantic, 1982.

Bornstein, Diane. *The Lady in the Tower: Medieval Courtesy Literature for Women.* Hamden, Conn.: Archon, 1983.

Bothelho, Lynn A. "The 17th Century." Pages 113–73 in Thane, ed., *A History of Old Age.*

Bowerman, R. Michael. "Headnote." Pages lxxv–xciii in *The Political History of the Devil.* Edited by Irving N. Rothman and R. Michael Bowerman. New York: AMS, 2003.

Bradley, Ritamary. "Backgrounds of the Title *Speculum* in Mediaeval Literature." *Speculum* 29 (1954): 100–115.

Brake, Donald L. *A Visual History of the English Bible: The Tumultuous Tale of the World's Bestselling Book.* Grand Rapids, Mich.: Baker, 2008.

Branner, Robert, ed. *Chartres Cathedral.* Norton Critical Study in Art History. New York: W. W. Norton & Co., 1969.

Brauner, Sigrid. *Fearless Wives and Frightened Shrews: The Construction of the Witch in Early Modern Germany.* Amherst: University of Massachusetts Press, 1995.

Breitenbach, Edgar. *Speculum Humanae Salvationis: Eine Typengeschichtliche Untersuchung.* Strassburg: Heitz, 1930.

Breitenberg, Mark. *Anxious Masculinity in Early Modern England.* New York: Cambridge University Press, 1996.

Brenner, Athalya. "On Female Figurations in Biblical Wisdom Literature." Pages 192–208 in *Of Prophets' Visions and the Wisdom of Sages: Essays in Honour of R. Norman Whybray on His Seventieth Birthday.* Edited by Heather A. McKay and David J. A. Clines. Sheffield: JSOT, 1993.

Brilliant, Richard. *My Laocoön: Alternative Claims in the Interpretation of Artworks.* Discovery Series. Berkeley: University of California Press, 2000.

Britton, Piers. "'Mio Malinchonico, O Vero…Mio Pazzo': Michelangelo, Vasari, and the Problem of Artists' Melancholy in Sixteenth-Century Italy." *Sixteenth Century Journal* 34, no. 3 (2003): 653–75.

Brown, Pamela Allen. *Better a Shrew Than a Sheep: Women, Drama, and the Culture of Jest in Early Modern England.* Ithaca, N.Y.: Cornell University Press, 2003.

Brubaker, Leslie. *Vision and Meaning in Ninth-century Byzantium: Images as Exegesis in the Homilies of Gregory of Nazianzus.* Cambridge: Cambridge University Press, 1999.

Bruder, Helen P., ed. *Women Reading William Blake.* New York: Palgrave Macmillan, 2007.

Bullinger, Heinrich. *The Christen State of Matrimonye.* Translated by Miles Coverdale. The English Experience Facsimile ed. Norwood, N.J.: Johnson, 1974.

Burgess, William. *The Bible in Shakespeare.* New York: Haskell House, 1968.

Burke, Edmund. *A Philosophical Enquiry into the Origin of Our Ideas of the Sublime and Beautiful.* Edited by J. T. Boulton. New York: Columbia University Press, 1958.

Burrow, J. A. *Gestures and Looks in Medieval Narrative.* New York: Cambridge University Press, 2002.

Burton, Robert. *The Anatomy of Melancholy,* vol. 3. London: Nimmo, 1886.

Burwick, Frederick. "Blake's Laocoön and Job; or, on the Boundaries of Painting and Poetry." Pages 125–55 in *The Romantic Imagination: Literature and Art in England and Germany.* Edited by Frederick Burwick and Jürgen Klein. Atlanta, Ga.: Rodopi, 1996.

Bussagli, Marco, and Mattia Reiche. *Baroque and Rococo.* Translated by Patrick McKeown. New York: Sterling, 2009.

Butler, Judith. *Antigone's Claim: Kinship Between Life and Death.* Wellek Library Lectures. New York: Columbia University Press, 2000.

———. "Capacity." Pages 109–19 in *Regarding Sedgwick: Essays on Queer Culture and Critical Theory.* Edited by Stephen M. Barber and David L. Clark. New York: Routledge, 2002.

———. *Gender Trouble: Feminism and the Subversion of Identity.* 10th Anniversary ed. New York: Routledge, 1999.

———. "Is Kinship Always Already Heterosexual?" Pages 123–50 in *Going Public: Feminism and the Shifting Boundaries of the Private Sphere.* Edited by Joan W. Scott and Debra Keates. Urbana: University of Illinois Press, 2004.

———. *Undoing Gender.* New York: Routledge, 2004.

Bynum, Caroline Walker. *The Resurrection of the Body in Western Christianity, 200–1336.* New York: Columbia University Press, 1995.

———. "Why All the Fuss About the Body? A Medievalist's Perspective." *Critical Inquiry* 22 (1995): 1–33.

Cabantous, Alain. *Blasphemy: Impious Speech in the West from the Seventeenth to the Nineteenth Century.* Translated by Eric Rauth. New York: Columbia University Press, 2002.

Calvin, John. *Sermons on Job.* Translated by Arthur Golding. 16th–17th Century Facsimile ed. Carlisle, Pa.: The Banner of Truth Trust, 1993.

Camille, Michael. "Seeing and Reading: Some Visual Implications of Medieval Literacy and Illiteracy." *Art History* 8 (1985): 26–49.

Cardon, Bert. *Manuscripts of the Speculum Humanae Salvationis in the Southern Netherlands (C. 1410–C. 1470)*. Corpus of Illuminated Manuscripts. Leuven: Uitgeverij Peeters, 1996.

Carrette, Jeremy R. "Prologue to a Confession of the Flesh." Pages 1–47 in *Religion and Culture: Michel Foucault*. Edited by Jeremy R. Carrette. New York: Routledge, 1999.

Carr-Gomm, Sarah, ed. *The Hutchinson Dictionary of Symbols in Art*. Oxford: Oxford University Press, 1995.

Caspi, Mishael, and Sara Milstein. *Why Hidest Thy Face: Job in Traditions and Literature*. Bibal Monograph Series. North Richland Hills: BIBAL, 2004.

Cassian, John. *The Conferences*. Translated by Boniface Ramsey. Ancient Christian Writers. New York: Paulist, 1997.

Castro, Ginette. *American Feminism: A Contemporary History*. Translated by Elizabeth Loverde-Bagwell. New York: New York University Press, 1990.

Chadwick, Henry. *Studies on Ancient Christianity*. Variorum Collected Studies. Burlington, Vt.: Ashgate, 2006.

Chaucer, Geoffrey. *The Canterbury Tales*. Translated by David Wright. Oxford: Oxford University Press, 1985.

Chayes, Irene H. "Words in Pictures: Testing the Boundary: Inscriptions by William Blake." *Word & Image* 7, no. 2 (1991): 85–97.

Cherniss, Michael D. "The 'Clerk's Tale' and 'Envoy,' the Wife of Bath's Purgatory, and the 'Merchant's Tale'." *The Chaucer Review* 6, no. 4 (1972): 235–54.

Chevalier, Tracy. "Peeking Over the Garden Wall." Pages 12–15 in Bruder, ed., *Women Reading William Blake*.

Chrysostom, John. *Commentaire sur Job*, vol. 1. Paris: Cerf, 1988.

———. *St. Chrysostom: On the Priesthood; Ascetic Treatises; Select Homilies and Letters; Homilies on the Statues*. Translated by Philip Schaff. New York: Christian Literature Publishing, 1886.

Clair, William St., and Irmgard Maassen, eds. *Conduct Literature for Women, 1500–1640*. 6 vols. Brookfield, Vt.: Pickering & Chatto, 2000.

Clanchy, M. T. *From Memory to Written Record: England 1066–1307*. 2d ed. Malden, Mass.: Blackwell, 1993.

Clark, Sandra. "'Hic Mulier,' 'Haec Vir,' and the Controversy Over Masculine Women." *Studies in Philology* 82, no. 2 (1985): 157–83.

Classen, Albrecht, ed. *Old Age in the Middle Ages and the Renaissance: Interdisciplinary Approaches to a Neglected Topic*. New York: de Gruyter, 2007.

Clemoes, Peter, ed. *Ælfric's Catholic Homilies: The First Series*. Oxford: Oxford University Press for the Early English Text Society, 1997.

Clines, David. *Job 1–20*. Word Biblical Commentary 17. Waco: Word, 1989.

Colbert, Stephen, Paul Dinello, and Amy Sedaris. *Strangers with Candy*. New York: THINKFilm, 2005.

Collins, John J. "The Testament of Job." Pages 349–55 in *Jewish Writings of the Second Temple Period*. Edited by Michael Stone. Philadelphia: Fortress, 1984.

———. "Testaments." Pages 325–55 in *Jewish Writings of the Second Temple Period. Apocrypha, Pseudepigrapha, Qumran Sectarian Writings, Philo, Josephus*. Edited by Michael E. Stone. Assen: Van Gorcum, 1984.

Connell, R. W. *Masculinities*. 2d ed. Berkeley: University of California Press, 2005.

Connell, R. W., and James W. Messerschmidt. "Hegemonic Masculinity: Rethinking the Concept." *Gender & Society* 19, no. 6 (2005): 829–59.

Connolly, Tristanne J. *William Blake and the Body*. New York: Palgrave Macmillan, 2002.

Cormack, Malcolm. *William Blake, Illustrations of the Book of Job*. Richmond: Virginia Museum of Fine Arts, 1997.

Cornford, Stephen, ed. *Night-Thoughts*. Cambridge: Cambridge University Press, 1989.

Covington, Sarah. *Wounds, Flesh, and Metaphor in Seventeenth-century England*. New York: Palgrave Macmillan, 2009.

Crane, Thomas Frederick, ed. *The Exempla or Illustrative Stories from the Sermones Vulgares of Jacques de Vitry*. Nendeln, Liechtenstein: Kraus Reprint, 1967.

Craun, Edwin D., ed. *The Hands of the Tongue: Essays on Deviant Speech*. Kalamazoo, Mich.: Medieval Institute Publications, Western Michigan University, 2007.

———. *Lies, Slander, and Obscenity in Medieval English Literature: Pastoral Rhetoric and the Deviant Speaker*. Cambridge: Cambridge University Press, 1997.

D'Avray, D. L. *Medieval Marriage Sermons*. New York: Oxford University Press, 2001.

Dalhoff, Meinolf. "Trouble at the Hermitage: A Note on Giovanni Bellini's 'Sacred Allegory'." *The Burlington Magazine* 144, no. 14 (2002): 22–23.

Damon, John Edward. *Soldier Saints and Holy Warriors: Warfare and Sanctity in the Literature of Early England*. Burlington, Vt.: Ashgate, 2003.

Daniell, David. *The Bible in English: Its History and Influence*. New Haven: Yale University Press, 2003.

Datema, C., ed. *Asterius of Amasea: Homilies I–Xiv*. Leiden: Brill, 1970.

Davies, J. G. *The Theology of William Blake*. London: Archon, 1966.

Davis, Isabel. *Writing Masculinity in the Later Middle Ages*. Cambridge: Cambridge University Press, 2007.

Davis, Lloyd, ed. *Sexuality and Gender in the English Renaissance: An Annotated Edition of Contemporary Documents*. New York: Garland, 1998.

Davlin, Mary Clemente. "William Langland." Pages 116–33 in *The Blackwell Companion to the Bible in English Literature*. Edited by Rebecca Lemon, Emma Mason, Jonathan Roberts and Christopher Rowland. Malden, Mass.: Wiley-Blackwell, 2009.

Day, Peggy L. *An Adversary in Heaven: Satan in the Hebrew Bible*. Harvard Semitic Monographs. Atlanta, Ga.: Scholars Press, 1988.

Debby, Nirit Ben-Aryeh. "The Preacher as Goldsmith: The Italian Preachers' Use of the Visual Arts." Pages 127–53 in Muessig, ed., *Preacher, Sermon and Audience in the Middle Ages*.

Defoe, Daniel. *The Political History of the Devil*. New York: AMS, 2003.

Delbanco, Andrew. *The Death of Satan: How Americans Have Lost the Sense of Evil*. New York: Farrar, Straus & Giroux, 1995.

Dell, Katharine J. *The Book of Job as Sceptical Literature*. Edited by Otto Kaiser. Beihefte zur Zeitschrift für die Alttestamentliche Wissenschaft. New York: de Gruyter, 1991.

Dendle, Peter. *Satan Unbound: The Devil in Old English Narrative Literature*. Toronto: University of Toronto Press, 2001.

Dent, Shirley, and Jason Whittaker. *Radical Blake: Influence and Afterlife from 1827*. New York: Palgrave Macmillan, 2002.

Deschamps, Eustache. *Le Miroir de Mariage*, vol. 9. Oeuvres Complètes De Eustache
     Deschamps. New York: Johnson Reprint Corporation, 1966.
Digby, George Wingfield. *Symbol and Image in William Blake*. Oxford: Clarendon, 1957.
Dimmick, Jeremy, James Simpson, and Nicolette Zeeman, eds. *Images, Idolatry, and
     Iconoclasm in Late Medieval England: Textuality and the Visual Image*. New York:
     Oxford University Press, 2002.
Ditz, Toby L. "The New Men's History and the Peculiar Absence of Gendered Power:
     Some Remedies from Early American Gender History." *Gender & History* 16, no. 1
     (2004): 1–35.
Dodwell, C. R. *Anglo-Saxon Gestures and the Roman Stage*. Cambridge: Cambridge
     University Press, 2000.
Dolan, Frances E., ed. *The Taming of the Shrew: Texts and Contexts*. Boston: Bedford
     Books of St. Martin's Press, 1996.
Donne, John. *The Works of John Donne*. Edited by Henry Alford. 6 vols. London: Parker,
     1839.
Doorly, Patrick. "Dürer's 'Melencolia I': Plato's Abandoned Search for the Beautiful."
     The Art Bulletin 86, no. 2 (2004): 255–76.
Douglas, Aileen. *Uneasy Sensations: Smollett and the Body*. Chicago: University of
     Chicago Press, 1995.
Douglas, Mary. *Natural Symbols: Explorations in Cosmology*. New York: Pantheon,
     1970.
Duby, Georges. "Affidavits and Confessions." Pages 483–91 in *A* Klapisch-Zuber, ed.,
     History of Women in the West.
———. *Medieval Marriage: Two Models from Twelfth-century France*. Baltimore: The
     Johns Hopkins University Press, 1978.
Duffy, Eamon. *The Stripping of the Altars: Traditional Religion in England 1400–1580*.
     2d ed. New Haven: Yale University Press, 2005.
Dykes, Oswald. *The Royal Marriage, King Lemuel's Lesson*. London, 1722.
Dziewicki, Michael Henry, ed. *Iohannis Wyclif: Tractus De Blasphemia*. London; New
     York: Trübner & Co.; Johnson Reprint Corporation, 1893. Repr. 1966.
The Early Modern Englishwoman: A Facsimile Library of Essential Works. Part I, *Printed
     Writings, 1500–1640*. Vol. 4, *Defences of Women: Jane Anger, Rachel Speght, Ester
     Sowernam, Constantia Munda*. Edited by Betty S. Travitsky and Patrick Cullen.
     Brookfield, Vt.: Ashgate, 1996.
Eco, Umberto. *The Search for the Perfect Language*. Translated by James Fentress.
     Malden, Mass.: Blackwell, 1997.
Edinger, Edward F. *Encounter with the Self: A Jungian Commentary on William Blake's
     Illustrations of the Book of Job*. Toronto: Inner City, 1986.
Ehresmann, Donald L. "Some Observations on the Role of Liturgy in the Early Winged
     Altarpiece." *The Art Bulletin* 64, no. 3 (1982): 359–69.
Emmerson, Richard K. "*Figura* and the Medieval Typological Imagination." Pages 7–42
     in Keenen, ed., *Typology and English Medieval Literature*.
Erdman, David V. *Blake: Prophet Against Empire*. Rev. ed. Princeton, N.J.: Princeton
     University Press, 1969.
———. *The Illuminated Blake*. New York: Anchor, 1974.
Erlande-Brandenburg, Alain. *Notre-Dame de Paris*. New York: Abrams, 1998.
Essick, Robert N. "William Blake's 'Female Will' and Its Biographical Context." *Studies
     in English Literature, 1500–1900* 31, no. 4 (1991): 615–30.

Evans, Ernest, ed. *Tertullian's Treatise on the Incarnation*. London: SPCK, 1956.

Evans, Joan. *Dress in Mediaeval France*. Oxford: Clarendon, 1952.

Exum, Cheryl. "Second Thoughts About Secondary Characters: Women in Exodus 1.8–2.10." Pages 75–87 in *A Feminist Companion to Exodus to Deuteronomy*. Edited by Athalya Brenner. Sheffield: Sheffield Academic, 1994.

Exum, J. Cheryl, and Ela Nutu. *Between the Text and the Canvas: The Bible and Art in Dialogue*. Sheffield: Sheffield Phoenix, 2007.

Fabiny, Tibor. *The Lion and the Lamb: Figuralism and Fulfilment in the Bible, Art and Literature*. New York: St. Martin's, 1992.

Fallon, David. "'She Cuts His Heart Out at His Side': Blake, Christianity and Political Virtue." Pages 84–104 in *Blake and Conflict*. Edited by Sarah Haggarty and Jon Mee. New York: Palgrave Macmillan, 2009.

Farmer, Sharon. "Persuasive Voices: Clerical Images of Medieval Wives." *Speculum* 61, no. 3 (1986): 517–43.

Fisch, Harold. *The Biblical Presence in Shakespeare, Milton, and Blake: A Comparative Study*. Oxford: Clarendon, 1999.

Fisher, John H., and Mark Allen, eds. *The Complete Canterbury Tales of Geoffrey Chaucer*. Boston: Thomson Wadsworth, 2006.

Fletcher, Anthony. *Gender, Sex and Subordination in England 1500–1800*. New Haven: Yale University Press, 1995.

Florio, John. "Fica." Page 186 in *Queen Anna's New World of Words, or Dictionarie of the Italian and English Tongues*. London: Blount & Barret, 1611.

Fontaine, Carole R. *With Eyes of Flesh: The Bible, Gender and Human Rights*. Sheffield: Sheffield Phoenix, 2008.

Forsyth, Neil. *The Old Enemy: Satan and the Combat Myth*. Princeton, N.J.: Princeton University Press, 1987.

Foucault, Michel. *The History of Sexuality*, vol. 1. Translated by Robert Hurley. New York: Vintage, 1990.

Fowler, David C. *The Life and Times of John Trevisa, Medieval Scholar*. Seattle: University of Washington Press, 1995.

Frank, Robert Worth. "The Art of Reading Medieval Personification-Allegory." Pages 217–31 in *Interpretations of Piers Plowman*. Edited by Edward Vasta. Notre Dame: University of Notre Dame Press, 1968.

Frost, Everett C. "The Education of the Prophetic Character: Blake's the Marriage of Heaven and Hell as a Primer in Visionary Autography." Pages 67–96 in *Prophetic Character: Essays on William Blake in Honor of John E. Grant*. Edited by Alexander S. Gourlay. West Cornwall, Conn.: Locust Hill, 2002.

Frye, Northrop. *Fearful Symmetry: A Study of William Blake*. Princeton, N.J.: Princeton University Press, 1969.

Furnivall, Frederick J., ed. *The Babees' Book, Etc.* Early English Text Society. London: Trübner, 1868.

Gard, Donald. *The Exegetical Method of the Greek Translator of the Book of Job*. Philadelphia, Pa.: Society of Biblical Literature, 1952.

Gardner, Arthur. "The Sculptures of Rheims Cathedral." *The Burlington Magazine* 26, no. 140 (1914): 53–64.

Garmonsway, G. N., and R. M. Raymo. "A Middle English Metrical Life of Job." Pages 77–98 in *Early English and Norse Studies*. Edited by Arthur Brown and Peter Foote. London: Methuen & Co, 1963.

Garnett, John. *A Dissertation on the Book of Job: Its Nature, Argument, Age and Author.* London: Cooper, 1749.

Garrett, Susan R. "The 'Weaker Sex' in the *Testament of Job.*" *Journal of Biblical Literature* 112 (1993): 55–70.

Gatch, Milton McC. *Preaching and Theology in Anglo-Saxon England: Ælfric and Wulfstan.* Toronto: University of Toronto Press, 1977.

Gilchrist, Alexander. *Life of William Blake,* vol. 2. London: Macmillan & Co., 1880.

Gill, Mirian. "Female Piety and Impiety: Selected Images of Women in Wall Paintings in England After 1300." Pages 101–20 in *Gender and Holiness: Men, Women and Saints in Late Medieval Europe.* Edited by Samantha J. E. Riches and Sarah Salih. New York: Routledge, 2002.

———. "From Urban Myth to Didactic Image: The Warning to Swearers." Pages 137–60 in Craun, ed., *The Hands of the Tongue.*

Gitay, Zefira. "The Portrayal of Job's Wife and Her Representation in the Visual Arts." Pages 516–26 in *Fortunate the Eyes That See: Essays in Honor of David Noel Freedman in Celebration of His Seventieth Birthday.* Edited by Astrid Beck et al. Grand Rapids: Eerdmans, 1995.

Godden, Malcolm, ed. *Ælfric's Catholic Homilies: The Second Series.* London: Oxford University Press for The Early English Text Society, 1979.

Goffen, Rona. "Bellini, S. Giobbe and Altar Egos." *Artibus et Historiae* 7, no. 14 (1986): 57–70.

González, Justo L. *The Story of Christianity.* Vol. 1, *The Early Church to the Dawn of the Reformation.* New York: HarperCollins, 1984.

The Good Wife's Guide: Le Ménagier de Paris, a Medieval Household Book. Translated by Gina L. Greco and Christine M. Rose. Ithaca, N.Y.: Cornell University Press, 2009.

Goring, Paul. *The Rhetoric of Sensibility in Eighteenth-century Culture.* Cambridge: Cambridge University Press, 2005.

Gouge, William. *Of Domestical Duties.* Edited by Greg Fox. Lulu.com, 2006.

Gowing, Laura. *Domestic Dangers: Women, Words, and Sex in Early Modern London.* Oxford: Clarendon, 1996.

Gowland, Angus. *The Worlds of Renaissance Melancholy: Robert Burton in Context.* New York: Cambridge University Press, 2006.

Grabar, André. *Byzantium: Byzantine Art in the Middle Ages.* Translated by Betty Forster. London: Methuen, 1966.

Gregg, Joan Young. *Devils, Women, and Jews: Reflections of the Other in Medieval Sermon Stories.* Suny Series in Medieval Studies. Albany, N.Y.: State University of New York Press, 1997.

Gregory I, Pope. *S. Gregorii Magni Moralia in Job.* Corpus Christianorum Series Latina 143. Turnholti: Brepols, 1979.

Grosart, Alexander, ed. *The Complete Works in Prose and Verse of Francis Quarles,* vol. 2. Edinburgh: Edinburgh University Press, 1880.

Groves, Beatrice. *Texts and Traditions: Religion and Shakespeare 1592–1604.* Oxford: Clarendon, 2007.

Gruber, Mayer. "The Rhetoric of Familiarity and Contempt in Job 2:9–10." *Scriptura* 87 (2004): 261–66.

Guillaume, Philippe. "Job le Nudiste ou la Genèse de la Sagesse." *Biblische Notizen* 88 (1997): 19–26.

Gunn, David M. "Bathsheba Goes Bathing in Hollywood: Words, Images, and Social Locations." Pages 75–101 in *Semeia 74: Biblical Glamour and Hollywood Glitz.* Edited by Alice Bach. Atlanta: Scholars Press, 1996.

———. "Cultural Criticism: Viewing the Sacrifice of Jephthah's Daughter." Pages 202–36 in *Judges and Method: New Approaches in Biblical Studies.* Edited by Gale A. Yee. Minneapolis: Fortress, 2007.

———. *Judges.* Edited by John Sawyer, Christopher Rowland and Judith Kovacs, Blackwell Bible Commentaries. Malden, Mass.: Blackwell, 2005.

Habel, N. C. *The Book of Job: A Commentary.* Philadelphia: Westminster, 1985.

Hagstrum, Jean H. *William Blake: Poet and Painter.* Chicago: University of Chicago Press, 1964.

Hall, James. *The Sinister Side: How Left–Right Symbolism Shaped Western Art.* Oxford: Oxford University Press, 2008.

Hall, Stuart. "Encoding, Decoding." Pages 90–103 in *The Cultural Studies Reader.* Edited by Simon During. London: Routledge, 1993.

Halvorson-Taylor, Martien A. "The Strange Case of the Disappearing Woman: Biblical Resonances in Kafka's Fräulein Bürstner." Pages 1:159–73 in Hawkins and Stahlberg, eds., *From the Margins.*

Hamblen, Emily. *Interpretation of William Blake's Job.* New York: Occult Research Press, 1930.

Hamel, Christopher De. *A History of Illuminated Manuscripts.* 2d ed. London: Phaidon, 1994.

Haralambakis, Maria. "'I Am Not Afraid of Anybody, I Am the Ruler of This Land': The Portrayal of Job in the *Testament of Job.*" Pages 127–44 in *Men and Masculinity in the Hebrew Bible and Beyond.* Edited by Ovidiu Creangă. Sheffield: Sheffield Phoenix, 2010.

Hardy, E. J. *How to Be Happy Though Married.* London: Collins Clear-Type, ca. 1900.

Hartt, Frederick. "Carpaccio's Meditation on the Passion." *The Art Bulletin* 22, no. 1 (1940): 25–35.

Hawkins, Peter S., and Lesleigh Cushing Stahlberg, eds. *From the Margins.* Vol. 1, *Women of the Hebrew Bible and Their Afterlives.* Sheffield: Sheffield Phoenix, 2009.

Hay, Douglas, and Nicholas Rogers. *Eighteenth-century English Society.* Oxford: Oxford University Press, 1997.

Healy, Margaret. "'Seeing' Contagious Bodies in Early Modern London." Pages 157–67 in *The Body in Late Medieval and Early Modern Culture.* Edited by Darryll Grantley and Nina Taunton. Burlington, Vt.: Ashgate, 2000.

Heertum, F. W. Van, ed. *A Critical Edition of Joseph Swetnam's the Araignment of Lewd, Idle, Froward, and Unconstant Women (1615).* Nijmegen: Cicero, 1989.

Henderson, Katherine Usher, and Barbara F. McManus. *Half Humankind: Contexts and Texts of the Controversy About Women in England, 1540–1640.* Chicago: University of Illinois Press, 1985.

Henry, Avril, ed. *Biblia Pauperum: A Facsimile and Edition.* Ithaca, N.Y.: Cornell University Press, 1987.

———. *The Mirour of Mans Saluacioun: A Middle English Translation of Speculum Humanae Salvationis.* Philadelphia: University of Pennsylvania Press, 1987.

———. "The Woodcuts of Der Spiegel Menschlicher Behältnis in the Editions Printed by Drach and Richel." *Oud Holland* 99 (1985): 1–15.

Henry, Holly. "Job's Wife's Name." *College Literature* 18, no. 1 (1991): 25–37.

Herlihy, David. *The Black Death and the Transformation of the West*. Cambridge, Mass.: Harvard University Press, 1997.

Heurtley, Charles A., ed. *On Faith and the Creed: Dogmatic Teaching of the Church of the Fourth and Fifth Centuries*. London: Parker & Co., 1886.

Hindman, Sandra. "Fifteenth-century Dutch Bible Illustration and the Historia Scholastica." *Journal of the Warburg and Courtauld Institutes* 37 (1974): 131–44.

Hindmarsh, Robert. "An Account of the First General Conference of the Members of the New Jerusalem Church." Pages 121–31 in Bellin and Ruhl, eds., *Blake and Swedenborg*.

Holsinger-Friesen, Thomas. *Irenaeus and Genesis: A Study of Competition in Early Christian Hermeneutics*. Winona Lake, Ind.: Eisenbrauns, 2009.

Horst, Pieter W. van der, and Michael A. Knibb, ed. *Studies on the Testament of Job*. Society for New Testament Studies. New York: Cambridge University Press, 1989.

Hoyt, Anna C. "The Mirror of Man's Salvation." *Bulletin of the Museum of Fine Arts* 54, no. 298 (1956): 88–92.

Hughes, William, ed. *William Blake, Jerusalem*, 1964.

Hull, Suzanne W. *Chaste, Silent and Obedient: English Books for Women, 1475–1640*. San Marino: Huntington Library, 1982.

Hunt, Lynn, Margaret C. Jacob, and Wijnand Mijnhardt. *The Book That Changed Europe: Picart and Bernard's Religious Ceremonies of the World*. Cambridge, Mass.: Belknap, 2010.

Infantes, Víctor. "Las Lecciones de Job en Caso de Amores, Trobadas por Garcí Sánchez de Badajoz." Pages 176–204 in *Un Volumen Facticio de Raros Post-Incunables Españoles*. Madrid: Antonio Pareja Editor, 1999.

Isherwood, Lisa. "Sex and Body Politics: Issues for Feminist Theology." Pages 20–34 in *The Good News of the Body: Sexual Theology and Feminism*. Edited by Lisa Isherwood. New York: New York University Press, 2000.

Jager, Eric. *The Tempter's Voice: Language and the Fall in Medieval Literature*. Ithaca, N.Y.: Cornell University Press, 1993.

Jameson, Anna. *History of Our Lord as Exemplified in Works of Art*. London: Longmans, Green & Co., 1892.

Janssen, Anouk. "The Good, the Bad, and the Elderly: The Representation of Old Age in Netherlandish Prints (Ca. 1550–1650)." Pages 437–83 in Classen, ed., *Old Age in the Middle Ages and the Renaissance*.

Jardine, Lisa. "Unpicking the Tapestry: The Scholar of Women's History as Penelope among Her Suitors." Pages 123–44 in Travitsky and Seeff, eds., *Attending to Women in Early Modern England*.

Johnson, Mary Lynn. "David's Recognition of the Human Face of God in Blake's Designs for the Book of Psalms." Pages 117–56 in *Blake and His Bibles*. Edited by David V. Erdman. West Cornwall, Conn.: Locust Hill, 1990.

Jongeling, B., C. J. Labuschagne, and A. S. Van Der Woude. *Aramaic Texts from Qumran*. Leiden: Brill, 1976.

Jung, C. G. *Answer to Job*. Translated by R. F. C. Hull. Fiftieth Anniversary ed. Bollingen Series. Princeton, N.J.: Princeton University Press, 2002.

———. *The Archetypes and the Collective Unconscious*. Edited by Herbert Read, Michael Fordham and Gerhard Adler. The Collected Works of C. G. Jung 9. New York: Pantheon, 1953.

Kauffmann, C. M. *Biblical Imagery in Medieval England, 700–1550.* London: Miller, 2003.

———. "The Bury Bible (Cambridge, Corpus Christi College, Ms. 2)." *Journal of the Warburg and Courtauld Institutes* 29 (1966): 60–81.

Kee, H. C. "Satan, Magic, and Salvation in the Testament of Job." Pages 53–76 in *Society of Biblical Literature 1974 Seminar Papers.* Edited by George MacRae. Atlanta: SBL, 1974.

Keenan, Hugh T., ed. *Typology and English Medieval Literature.* New York: AMS, 1992.

Kelly, Joan. *Women, History and Theory: The Essays of Joan Kelly.* Chicago: University of Chicago Press, 1984.

Kessler, Herbert L. "The Chantily *Miroir de l'humaine Salvation* and Its Models." Pages 274–82 in *Studies in Late Medieval and Renaissance Painting in Honor of Millard Meiss.* New York: New York University Press, 1977.

Keynes, Geoffrey. *Blake Studies: Essays on His Life and Work.* 2d ed. Oxford: Clarendon, 1971.

Khanna, Lee Cullen. "Utopian Exchanges: Negotiating Difference in Utopia." Pages 17–38 in *Gender and Utopia in the Eighteenth Century: Essays in English and French Utopian Writing.* Edited by Nicole Pohl and Brenda Tooley. Burlington, Vt.: Ashgate, 2007.

Kienzle, Beverly Mayne. "Medieval Sermons and Their Performance: Theory and Record." Pages 89–124 in Muessig, ed., *Preacher, Sermon and Audience in the Middle Ages.*

King, Margaret L. *Women of the Renaissance.* Chicago: University of Chicago Press, 1991.

Kirkegaard, Bradford A. "Satan in the *Testament of Job*: A Literary Analysis." Pages 4–19 in *Of Scribes and Sages: Early Jewish Interpretation and Transmission of Scripture.* Edited by Craig A. Evans. New York: T&T Clark, 2004.

Kirven, Robert H., and Robin Larsen. "Emanuel Swedenborg: A Pictorial Biography." Pages 3–50 in *Emanuel Swedenborg: A Continuing Vision.* Edited by Robin Larse, Stephen Larsen, James Lawrence and William Ross Woofenden. New York: Swedenborg Foundation, 1988.

Klancher, Nancy. "The Male Soul in Drag: Women-as-Job in the *Testament of Job.*" *Journal for the Study of the Pseudepigrapha* 19 (2010): 225–45.

Klapisch-Zuber, Christiane, ed. *A History of Women in the West: Silences of the Middle Ages.* Cambridge, Mass.: Belknap Press of Harvard University Press, 1992.

Klein, Lillian R. *From Deborah to Esther: Sexual Politics in the Hebrew Bible.* Minneapolis: Fortress, 2003.

Klibengajtis, Tomarsz. "Hiobs Weib in der Exegese der Lateinischen Kirchenväter: Ein Beitrag zur Patristischen Frauenforschung." *Analecta Cracoviensia* 38–39 (2006–7): 195–229.

Klonsky, Milton. *William Blake: The Seer and His Visions.* New York: Harmony, 1977.

Koldeweij, Jos. "Hieronymus Bosch and His City." Pages 20–83 in Koldeweij, Vanden-broeck and Vermet, eds., *Hieronymus Bosch.*

Koldeweij, Jos, Paul Vandenbroeck, and Bernard Vermet, eds. *Hieronymus Bosch: The Complete Paintings and Drawings.* New York: Abrams, 2001.

Kraft, Robert A., ed. *The Testament of Job: According to the Sv Text.* Texts and Transla-tions: Pseudepigrapha Series. Missoula, Mont.: Scholars' Press, 1974.

Krén, Emil. "Web Gallery of Art." No pages. Online: http://www.wga.hu/frames-e.html?/html/b/blommend/xantippe.html.

Kugler, Robert A. "Testaments." Pages 188–213 in *Justification and Variegated Nomism*. Edited by D. A. Carson, Peter T. O'Brien and Mark A. Seifrid. Grand Rapids: Baker Academic, 2001.

Kyung, Chung Hyun. "Your Comfort vs. My Death." Pages 129–40 in *Women Resisting Violence: Spirituality for Life*. Edited by Mary John Mananzan, Mercy Amba Oduyoye, Elsa Tamez, J. Shannon Clarkson, Mary C. Grey and Letty M. Russell. Maryknoll, N.Y.: Orbis, 1996.

Labriola, Albert C., and John W. Smeltz, eds. *The Bible of the Poor [Biblia Pauperum]: A Facsimile Edition of the British Library Blockbook C.9.D.2*. Pittsburgh, Pa.: Duquesne University Press, 1990.

———, eds. *The Mirror of Salvation [Speculum Humanae Salvationis]: An Edition of British Library Blockbook G. 11784*. Pittsburgh, Pa.: Duquesne University Press, 2002.

Lamb, Jonathan. *The Rhetoric of Suffering: Reading the Book of Job in the Eighteenth Century*. Oxford: Clarendon, 1995.

Landry, Geoffrey de La Tour. *The Book of the Knight of the Tower*. Translated by William Caxton. Early English Text Society. New York: Oxford University Press, 1971.

Langland, William. *Piers Plowman: The C Version*. Translated by George Economou. Philadelphia: University of Pennsylvania Press, 1996.

Latimer, Hugh. *Sermons, by Hugh Latimer, Sometime Bishop of Worcester*. London: Dent & Co., 1926.

Lawton, David. "The Bible." Pages 193–233 in *The Oxford History of Literary Translation in English*. Edited by Roger Ellis. Oxford: Oxford University Press, 2008.

———. *Blasphemy*. Philadelphia: University of Pennsylvania Press, 1993.

Legaspi, Michael C. "Job's Wives in the *Testament of Job:* A Note on the Synthesis of Two Traditions." *Journal of Biblical Literature* 127 (2008): 71–79.

Leontius. *Fourteen Homilies*. Translated by Pauline Allen and Cornelis Datema. Brisbane: Australian Association for Byzantine Studies, 1991.

Lesses, Rebecca. "The Daughters of Job." Pages 139–49 in *Searching the Scriptures*. Edited by Elisabeth Schüssler Fiorenza. New York: Crossroad, 1994.

Levack, Brian P. *The Witch-Hunt in Early Modern Europe*. 3d ed. London: Pearson, 2006.

Lewalski, Barbara Kiefer. *Milton's Brief Epic: The Genre, Meaning, and Art of Paradise Regained*. Providence, R.I.: Brown University Press, 1966.

Linafelt, Tod. "The Undecidability of Brk in the Prologue to Job and Beyond." *Biblical Interpretation* 4 (1996): 154–72.

Lindberg, Bo. *William Blake's Illustrations to the Book of Job*. Abo: Abo Akademi, 1973.

Lochrie, Karma. *Covert Operations: The Medieval Uses of Secrecy*. Philadelphia: University of Pennsylvania Press, 1999.

Long, Helen Beecher. *Janice Day at Poketown*. Cleveland: Goldsmith, 1914.

Low, Katherine. "The Sexual Abuse of Lot's Daughters: Reconceptualizing Kinship for the Sake of Our Daughters." *Journal of Feminist Studies in Religion* 26, no. 2 (2010): 37–54.

Lowth, Robert. *A Letter to the Right Reverend Author of the Divine Legation of Moses*. 4th ed. London: Millar & Dodsley, 1766.

Lubac, Henri de. *Medieval Exegesis*. Vol. 3, *The Four Senses of Scripture*. Translated by
E. M. Macierowski. Grand Rapids: Eerdmans 2009.

Lüdecke, Heinz. *Albrecht Dürer*. Translated by Richard Rickett. New York: G. P.
Putnam's Sons, 1972.

Luther, Martin. *Luther's Works*. Vol. 7, *Lectures on Genesis, Chapters 38–44*. Translated
by Paul D. Pahl. Saint Louis: Concordia, 1965.

———. *Luther's Works*. Vol. 42, *Devotional Writings*. Translated by Martin H. Bertram.
Philadelphia: Fortress, 1955.

Lydgate, John. *The Minor Poems of John Lydgate*. Vol. 2, *The Secular Poems*. The Early
English Text Society. New York: Oxford University Press, 1961.

Magdalene, F. Rachel. "Job's Wife as Hero: A Feminist-Forensic Reading of the Book of
Job." *Biblical Interpretation* 14 (2006): 209–58.

———. *On the Scales of Righteousness: Neo-Babylonian Trial Law and the Book of Job*.
Brown Judaic Studies 348. Providence, R.I.: Brown Judaic Studies, 2007.

Makdisi, Saree. *William Blake and the Impossible History of the 1790s*. Chicago:
University of Chicago Press, 2003.

Malbon, Elizabeth Struthers. *The Iconography of the Sarcophagus of Junius Bassus*.
Princeton, N.J.: Princeton University Press, 1990.

Mangan, Celine. "The Attitude to Women in the Prologue of Targum Job." Pages 100–
110 in *Targumic and Cognate Studies*. Edited by Kevin J. Cathcart and Michael
Maher. Sheffield: Sheffield Academic, 1996.

———. "Some Observations on the Dating of Targum Job." Pages 67–78 in *Back to the
Sources: Biblical and near Eastern Studies in Honour of Dermot Ryan*. Edited by K.
J. Cathcart and J. F. Healey. Dublin: Glendale, 1989.

———. "The Targum of Job." Pages 1–98 in *The Aramaic Bible: The Targums*. Edited
by Kevin Carthcart et al. Collegeville, Minn.: Liturgical, 1991.

Martin, John Jeffries. *Myths of Renaissance Individualism*. New York: Palgrave
Macmillan, 2004.

Marx, C. W. *The Devil's Rights and the Redemption in the Literature of Medieval
England*. Cambridge: Brewer, 1995.

Marx, Steven. *Shakespeare and the Bible*. New York: Oxford University Press, 2000.

May, James E. "Early Eighteenth-century Paraphrases of the Book of Job." Pages 151–61
in *Man, God, and Nature in the Enlightenment*. Edited by Donald Charles Mell and
Theodore E. D. Braun. East Lansing, Mich.: Colleagues Press, 1988.

McCarthy, Cormac. *The Road*. New York: Vintage, 2006.

McGinnis, Claire M. "Playing the Devil's Advocate in Job: On Job's Wife." Pages 121–
41 in *Whirlwind: Essays on Job, Hermeneutics and Theology in Memory of Jane
Morse*. Edited by Jane Morse et al. New York: Sheffield Academic, 2001.

McKay, Heather A. "She Said to Him, He Said to Her: Power Talk in the Bible or
Foucault Listens at the Keyhole." *Biblical Theology Bulletin* 28, no. 2 (1998):
45–51.

McLaren, Margaret A. *Feminism, Foucault, and Embodied Subjectivity*. Albany, N.Y.:
SUNY Press, 2002.

Meiller, Albert, ed. *La Pacience de Job*. Paris: Klincksieck, 1971.

Mellinkoff, Ruth. *Outcasts: Signs of Otherness in Northern European Art of the Late
Middle Ages*. Vol. 1, *Text*. Berkeley: University of California Press, 1993.

Mellor, Anne K. "Blake's Portrayal of Women." *Blake: An Illustrated Quarterly* (Winter
1982–83): 148–55.

Merian, Matthaeus. *Great Scenes from the Bible: 230 Magnificent 17th-century Engravings*. Mineola, N.Y.: Dover, 2002.

Meyer, Kathi. "St. Job as a Patron of Music." *The Art Bulletin* 36 (1954): 21–31.

Meyers, Carol L., Toni Craven, and Ross Shepard Kraemer. *Women in Scripture: A Dictionary of Named and Unnamed Women in the Hebrew Bible, the Apocryphal/ Deuterocanonical Books, and the New Testament*. Boston: Houghton Mifflin, 2000.

Meyers, Walter E. "Typology and the Audience of the English Cycle Plays." Pages 261–88 in Keenan, ed., *Typology and English Medieval Literature*.

Miles, Margaret R. *Carnal Knowing: Female Nakedness and Religious Meaning in the Christian West*. Vintage Books ed. New York: Vintage, 1991.

Millett, Bella, ed. *Ancrene Wisse: A Corrected Edition of the Text in Cambridge, Corpus Christi College, Ms 402*. Early Text Society. Oxford: Oxford University Press, 2005.

———, ed. *Ancrene Wisse: Guide for Anchoresses, a Translation*. Exeter: University of Exeter Press, 2009.

Morey, James H. *Book and Verse: A Guide to Middle English Biblical Literature*. Illinois Medieval Studies. Chicago: University of Illinois Press, 2000.

———. "Peter Comestor, Biblical Paraphrase, and the Medieval Popular Bible." *Speculum* 68 (1993): 6–35.

Morgan, David. *The Sacred Gaze: Religious Visual Culture in Theory and Practice*. Berkeley: University of California Press, 2005.

Morris, David. *The Culture of Pain*. Berkeley: University of California Press, 1991.

———. *The Religious Sublime: Christian Poetry and Critical Tradition in 18th-century England*. Lexington: University Press of Kentucky, 1972.

Morris, Desmond. *Bodywatching: A Field Guide to the Human Species*. New York: Crown, 1985.

Morris, Desmond, Peter Collett, Peter Marsh, and Marie O'Shaughnessy. *Gestures: Their Origins and Distribution*. New York: Stein & Day, 1979.

Morris, W. "On the Artistic Qualities of the Woodcut Books of Ulm and Augsburg in the Fifteenth Century." *Bibliographica* 1 (1895): 437–55.

Morrow, William S. "Toxic Religion and the Daughters of Job." *Studies in Religion/ Sciences Religieuses* 27, no. 3 (1998): 263–76.

Mounsey, Christ, and Rictor Norton, eds. *Eighteenth-century British Erotica*, vol. 1. London: Pickering & Chatto, 2002.

Muchembled, Robert. *A History of the Devil: From the Middle Ages to the Present*. Translated by Jean Birrell. Malden, Mass.: Polity, 2003.

Muckle, J. T. "The Personal Letters between Abelard and Heloise." *Mediaeval Studies* 15 (1953): 47–94.

Muessig, Carolyn, ed. *Preacher, Sermon and Audience in the Middle Ages*. Leiden: Brill, 2002.

Muggleton, Lodowick. "A True Interpretation of the Witch of Endor." In vol. 2 of *The Works of John Reeve and Lodowicke Muggleton*. London: Joseph & Isaac Frost, 1831.

Mulvey, Laura. *Visual and Other Pleasures*. Theories of Representation and Difference. Bloomington: Indiana University Press, 1989.

Murdoch, Brian. *The Medieval Popular Bible: Expansions of Genesis in the Middle Ages*. Cambridge: Brewer, 2003.

Murphy, Kathleen Middleton. "'All the Lovely Sex': Blake and the Woman Question." Pages 272–75 in Bogan and Goss, eds., *Sparks of Fire*.

Murray, Gilbert. "Prometheus and Job." Pages 56–65 in *Twentieth Century Interpretations of the Book of Job*. Edited by Paul Sanders. Englewood Cliffs, N.J.: Prentice–Hall, 1968.

Muscatine, Charles. *Chaucer and the French Tradition*. Berkeley: University of California Press, 1957.

Mustanoja, Tauno F., ed. *The Good Wife Taught Her Daughter*. Helsinki: Suomalaisen Kirjallisuuden Seuran, 1948.

Nash, David. *Blasphemy in the Christian World: A History*. New York: Oxford University Press, 2007.

Nees, Lawrence. *Early Medieval Art*. Oxford: Oxford University Press, 2002.

New, Melvyn. "Job's Wife and Sterne's Other Women." Pages 55–74 in *Out of Bounds: Male Writers and Gender (ed) Criticism*. Edited by Laura Claridge and Elizabeth Langland. Amherst, Mass.: University of Massachusetts Press, 1990.

News, BBC. "100 Great British Heroes." BBC News, World Edition. No pages. Online: http://news.bbc.co.uk/2/hi/entertainment/2208532.stm.

Newsom, Carol A. *The Book of Job: A Contest of Moral Imaginations*. Oxford: Oxford University Press, 2003.

———. "Job." Pages 138–44 in *Women's Bible Commentary*. Edited by Carol A. Newsom and Sharon H. Ringe. Louisville, Ky.: Westminster John Knox, 1998.

Nichols, Lawrence W. "'Job in Distress,' a Newly-Discovered Painting of Hendrick Goltzius." *Simiolus: Netherlands Quarterly for the History of Art* 13, no. 3/4 (1983): 182–88.

Nickelsburg, George W. E. *Jewish Literature Between the Bible and the Mishnah: A Historical and Literary Introduction*. Philadelphia: Fortress, 1981.

Noble, Richmond. *Shakespeare's Biblical Knowledge*. New York: Octagon, 1970.

Noggle, James. *The Skeptical Sublime: Aesthetic Ideology in Pope and the Tory Satirists*. New York: Oxford University Press, 2001.

Noot, Jan Van Der. *Theatre of Voluptuous Worldlings*. New York: Scholars' Facsimiles & Reprints, 1569.

Norris, Pamela. *Eve: A Biography*. Washington Square: New York University Press, 1998.

Nuttall, A. D. *The Alternative Trinity: Gnostic Heresy in Marlowe, Milton, and Blake*. Oxford: Clarendon, 1998.

O'Connor, Donal. " 'Bless God and Die' (Job 2:9): Euphemism or Irony?" Pages 48–65 in *Proceedings of the Irish Biblical Association*. Edited by Martin McNamara. Dublin: The Irish Biblical Association, 1996.

———. *Job, His Wife, His Friends and His God*. Dublin: Columba, 1995.

Oberman, Heiko A. *Luther: Man Between God and the Devil*. Translated by Eileen Walliser-Schwarzbart. New Haven, Conn.: Yale University Press, 1989.

Oldcorn, Anthony. "Notes." Pages 403–406 in *Dante: Inferno*. Indianapolis, Ind.: Hackett, 2009.

———. "The Perverse Image: Canto Xxv." Pages 328–47 in *Lectura Dantis, Inferno*. Berkeley: University of California Press, 1998.

Omerzu, Heike. "Women, Magic and Angels: On the Emancipation of Job's Daughters in the Apocryphal *Testament of Job*." Pages 57–70 in *Bodies in Question: Gender, Religion, Text*. Edited by Yvonne Sherwood and Darlene Bird. Burlington, Vt.: Ashgate, 2005.

Orgel, Stephen, and Jonathan Goldberg, eds. *John Milton*. New York: Oxford University Press, 1991.

Osten, G. Von der. "Job and Christ: The Development of a Devotional Image." *Journal of the Warburg and Courtauld Institutes* 16, no. 1/2 (1953): 153–58.

Pächt, Otto. *The Rise of Pictorial Narrative in Twelfth-century England*. Oxford: Clarendon, 1962.

Pagels, Elaine. *Adam, Eve, and the Serpent*. New York: Random House, 1988.

Paley, Morton D. *The Traveller in the Evening: The Last Works of William Blake*. Oxford: Oxford University Press, 2003.

————, ed. *William Blake's Jerusalem*. Princeton, N.J.: Princeton University Press, 1991.

Palmer, Barbara D. "The Inhabitants of Hell: Devils." Pages 20–40 in *The Iconography of Hell*. Edited by Clifford Davidson and Thomas H. Seiler. Kalamazoo, Mich.: Medieval Institute Publications, Western Michigan University, 1992.

Panofsky, Erwin. *The Life and Art of Albrecht Dürer*. Princeton, N.J.: Princeton University Press, 1955.

Peacock, Martha. "*Hoorndragers* and *Hennetasters*: The Old Impotent Cuckold as 'Other' in Sixteenth- and Seventeenth-century Netherlandish Art." Pages 485–516 in Classen, ed., *Old Age in the Middle Ages and the Renaissance*.

Perdue, Leo G. "Job's Assault on Creation." *Hebrew Annual Review* 10 (1987): 295–315.

————. *Wisdom Literature: A Theological History*. Louisville, Ky.: Westminster John Knox, 2007.

Perdue, Leo G., and W. Clark Gilpin, eds. *The Voice from the Whirlwind: Interpreting the Book of Job*. Nashville: Abingdon, 1992.

Peters, Charles. *A Critical Dissertation on the Book of Job, Wherein the Account Given by That Book by the Author of the Divine Legation of Moses Demonstrated*. London: Johnston, in St. Paul's Church-Yard, 1757.

Petrarch. *The Triumphs of Petrarch*. Translated by Ernest Hatch Wilkins. Chicago: University of Chicago Press, 1962.

Pettys, Valerie Forstman. "Let There Be Darkness: Continuity and Discontinuity in the 'Curse' of Job 3." *Journal for the Study of the Old Testament* 98 (2002): 89–104.

Pfeiffer, Franz, ed. *Deutsche Mystiker Des Vierzehnten Jahrhunderts*. Vol. 2, *Hermann Von Fritslar, Nicolaus Von Strassburg, David Von Augsburg*. Göttingen: Vandenhoeck & Ruprecht, 1907.

Phillips, Kim M. *Medieval Maidens: Young Women and Gender in England, 1270–1540*. Manchester Medieval Studies. New York: Palgrave, 2003.

Pigler, A., ed. *Barockthemen: Eine Auswahl von Verzeichnissen zur Ikonographie des 17 und 18 Jahrhunderts*. 3 vols. Budapest: Akadémiai Kiadó, 1974.

Pollard, Graham. "The Pecia System in the Medieval Universities." Pages 145–61 in *Medieval Scribes, Manuscripts, and Libraries: Essays Presented to N. R. Ker*. Edited by M. B. Parkes and Andrew G. Watson. London: Scolar Press, 1978.

Poole, Matthew. *A Commentary on the Holy Bible*, vol. 1. London: Banner of Truth Trust, 1962.

Pope, Alexander. *The Art of Sinking in Poetry: Martinus Scriblerus*. Edited by Edna Leake Steeves. New York: King's Crown, 1952.

Power, Kim. *Veiled Desire: Augustine on Women*. New York: Continuum, 1996.

Pui-lan, Kwok. *Discovering the Bible in the Non-Biblical World*. Maryknoll, N.Y.: Orbis, 1995.

———. *Postcolonial Imagination and Feminist Theology*. Louisville, Ky.: Westminster John Knox, 2005.

Raine, Kathleen. *Blake and the New Age*. London: George Allen & Unwin, 1979.

———. *The Human Face of God: William Blake and the Book of Job*. London: Thames & Hudson, 1982.

Reeser, Todd W. "Moderation and Masculinity in Renaissance Marriage Discourse and in Rabelais's Tiers Livre." *The Romanic Review* 90 (1999): 1–25.

Régnier-Bohler, Danielle. "Literary and Mystical Voices." Pages 457–82 in Klapisch-Zuber, ed., *A History of Women in the West*.

Reiss, Edmund. "The Story of Lamech and Its Place in Medieval Drama." *Journal of Medieval and Renaissance Studies* 2 (1972): 35–48.

Renevey, Denis. "Looking for a Context: Rolle, Anchoritic Culture, and the Office of the Dead." Pages 192–210 in *Medieval Texts in Context*. Edited by Denis Renevey and Graham D. Caie. New York: Routledge, 2008.

Renoir, Alain. "Eve's I.Q. Rating: Two Sexist Views of Genesis B." Pages 262–72 in *New Readings on Women in Old English Literature*. Edited by Helen Damico and Alexandra Hennessey Olsen. Bloomington, Ind.: Indiana University Press, 1990.

Richards, Jeffrey. *Consul of God: The Life and Times of Gregory the Great*. London: Routledge & Kegan Paul, 1980.

Rickert, Edith. *The Babees' Book: Medieval Manners for the Young*. New York: Duffield & Co., 1908.

The Riverside Shakespeare. 2d ed. Boston: Houghton Mifflin, 1997.

Robbins, Ruth. "Introduction: Will the Real Feminist Theory Please Stand Up?" Pages 49–58 in *Literary Theories: A Reader and Guide*. Edited by Julian Wolfreys. New York: New York University Press, 1999.

Roberts, Alexander, and James Donaldson, eds. *The Ante-Nicene Fathers*. Vol. 1, *The Apostolic Fathers–Justine Martyr–Irenaeus*. Grand Rapids, Mich.: Eerdmans, 1987.

———, eds. *The Ante-Nicene Fathers: Translations of the Writings of the Fathers Down to A.D. 325*. American ed. 10 vols. Grand Rapids, Mich.: Eerdmans, 1996.

Roberts, Jeanne Addison. "Types of Crone: The Nurse and the Wise Woman in English Renaissance Drama." *Renaissance Papers* 2000 (2000): 71–86.

Roberts, Phyllis B. "The Ars Praedicandi and the Medieval Sermon." Pages 41–62 in Muessig, ed., *Preacher, Sermon and Audience in the Middle Ages*.

Roe, Albert. "Blake's Symbolism." Pages 67–90 in Bogan and Gross, eds., *Sparks of Fire*.

Rogers, Katharine M. *The Troublesome Helpmate: A History of Misogyny in Literature*. Seattle: University of Washington Press, 1966.

Rohrbaugh, Richard L., and Robert A. Kugler, "On Women and Honor in the *Testament of Job*." *Journal for the Study of the Pseudepigrapha* 14 (2004): 43–62.

Roper, Lyndal. *Oedipus and the Devil: Witchcraft, Sexuality and Religion in Early Modern Europe*. New York: Routledge, 1994.

Rowland, Christopher. *Blake and the Bible*. New Haven: Yale University Press, 2010.

———. *"Wheels Within Wheels": William Blake and the Ezekiel's Markabah in Text and Image*. The Père Marquette Lecture in Theology. Milwaukee, Wisc.: Marquette University Press, 2007.

Rowlands, Alison. "Witchcraft and Old Women in Early Modern Germany." *Past & Present*, no. 173 (2001): 50–89.

Rubin, Gayle. "The Traffic in Women: Notes on the 'Political Economy' of Sex." Pages 27–62 in *The Second Wave: A Reader in Feminist Theory*. Edited by Linda Nicholson. New York: Routledge, 1997.

Runions, Erin. "Ms Job and the Problem of God: A Feminist, Existentialist, Materialist Reading." Pages 1:174–89 in Hawkins and Stahlberg, eds., *From the Margins*.

Russell, Archibald G. B. *The Engravings of William Blake*. New York: Blom, 1968.

Russell, Jeffrey Burton. *Lucifer: The Devil in the Middle Ages*. Ithaca, N.Y.: Cornell University Press, 1984.

———. *Mephistopheles: The Devil in the Modern World*. Ithaca, N.Y.: Cornell University Press, 1986.

Salomon, Nanette. "Positioning Women in Visual Convention: The Case of Elizabeth I." Pages 64–95 in Travitsky and Seeff, eds., *Attending to Women in Early Modern England*.

Sasson, Victor. "The Literary and Theological Function of Job's Wife in the Book of Job." *Biblica* 79 (1998): 86–90.

Sawyer, Deborah F. "Gender Criticism: A New Discipline in Biblical Studies or Feminism in Disguise?" Pages 2–17 in *A Question of Sex? Gender and Difference in the Hebrew Bible and Beyond*. Edited by Deborah W. Rooke. Sheffield: Sheffield Academic, 2007.

Scarry, Elaine. *The Body in Pain: The Making and Unmaking of the World*. New York: Oxford University Press, 1985.

Schearing, Linda S., Valarie H. Ziegler, and Kristen E. Kvam, eds. *Eve and Adam: Jewish, Christian, and Muslim Readings on Genesis and Gender*. Bloomington: Indiana University Press, 1999.

Schindler, Audrey. "One Who Has Bourne Most: The Cri de Coeur of Job's Wife." *Australian Biblical Review* 54 (2006): 24–36.

Schreiner, Susan E. *Where Shall Wisdom Be Found? Calvin's Exegesis of Job from Medieval and Modern Perspectives*. Chicago: University of Chicago Press, 1994.

Schroer, Silvia, and Christl Maier. "What About Job? Questioning the Book of 'the Righteous Sufferer'." Pages 175–204 in *Wisdom and Psalms: A Feminist Companion to the Bible, Second Series*. Edited by Athalya Brenner and Carole F. Fontaine. Sheffield: Sheffield Academic, 1998.

Scott, Kathleen L. "Four Early Fifteenth-century English Manuscripts of the *Speculum Humanae Salvationis* and a Fourteenth-Century Exemplar." *English Manuscript Studies, 1100–1700* 10 (2002): 177–203.

Sears, Elizabeth. "'Reading' Images." Pages 1–7 in *Reading Medieval Images: The Art Historian and the Object*. Edited by Elizabeth Sears and Thema K. Thomas. Ann Arbor, Mich.: University of Michigan Press, 2002.

Sedgwick, Eve Kosofsky. *Between Men: English Literature and Male Homosocial Desire*. New York: Columbia University Press, 1985.

———. *Epistemology of the Closet*. Berkeley: University of California Press, 1990.

———. *Touching Feeling: Affect, Pedagogy, Performativity*. Durham, N.C.: Duke University Press, 2003.

Seow, Choon Leong. "Christian Consequences of Job." Paper presented at the Ministers Week, The McFadin Lectures, Brite Divinity School, Fort Worth, Tex., 2009.

————. "Job's Wife." Pages 141–50 in *Engaging the Bible in a Gendered World: An Introduction to Feminist Biblical Interpretation in Honor of Katherine Doob Sakenfeld*. Edited by Linda Day and Carolyn Pressler. Louisville, Ky.: Westminster John Knox, 2006.

————. "Job's Wife, with Due Respect." Pages 351–73 in *Das Buch Hiob und seine Interpretationen*. Edited by T. Krüger, M. Oeming, K. Schmid and C. Uehlinger. Zurich: Theologischer Verlag, 2007.

————. "Reflections on the History of Consequences: The Case of Job." Pages 561–86 in *Method Matters: Essays on the Interpretation of the Hebrew Bible in Honor of David L. Peterson*. Edited by Joel M. LeMon and Ken Harold Richards. Atlanta: Society of Biblical Literature, 2009.

Shahar, Shulamith. *The Fourth Estate: A History of Women in the Middle Ages*. Translated by Chaya Galai. New York: Methuen, 1983.

————. "The Middle Ages and Renaissance." Pages 71–111 in Thane, ed., *A History of Old Age*.

Shepard, Alexandra. *Meanings of Manhood in Early Modern England*. New York: Oxford University Press, 2003.

Shepherd, David. "'Strike His Bone and His Flesh': Reading Job from the Beginning." *Journal for the Study of the Old Testament* 33 (2008): 81–97.

————. *Targum and Translation: A Reconsideration of the Qumran Aramaic Version of Job*. Assen: Royal Van Gorcum, 2004.

Shilling, Chris. *The Body and Social Theory*. London: Sage, 1993.

Shuffelton, George, ed. *Codex Ashmole 61: A Compilation of Popular Middle English Verse*. Middle English Texts Series. Kalamazoo, Mich.: Western Michigan University, Medieval Institute Publications, 2008.

Silber, Evelyn. "The Reconstructed Toledo Speculum Humanae Salvatonis: The Italian Connection in the Early Fourteenth Century." *Journal of the Warburg and Courtauld Institutes* 43 (1980): 32–51.

Simpson, James. *Piers Plowman: An Introduction to the B-Text*. New York: Longman, 1990.

Singer, June. *The Unholy Bible: Blake, Jung and the Collective Unconscious*. Boston: Sigo, 1986.

Skemp, Vincent T. M. *The Vulgate of Tobit Compared with Other Ancient Witnesses*. Atlanta: Society of Biblical Literature, 2000.

Smith, Kathryn A. *Art, Identity and Devotion in Fourteenth-Century England*. Toronto: University of Toronto Press, 2003.

Smith, Susan L. *The Power of Women: A Topos in Medieval Art and Literature*. Philadelphia: University of Pennsylvania Press, 1995.

Snart, Jason Allen. *The Torn Book: Unreading William Blake's Marginalia*. Selinsgrove: Susquehanna University Press, 2006.

Speght, Rachel. "Certaine Quaeres to the Bayter of Women." Pages 29–42 in *The Polemics and Poems of Rachel Speght*. Edited by Barbara Kiefer Lewalski. New York: Oxford University Press, 1996.

Spicer, Joaneath. "The Renaissance Elbow." Pages 84–128 in *A Cultural History of Gesture*. Edited by Jan Bremmer and Herman Roodenburg. Ithaca, N.Y.: Cornell University Press, 1991.

Spittler, Russell P. "The Testament of Job: A History of Research and Interpretation." Pages 7–32 in Knibb and van der Horst, eds., *Studies on the Testament of Job*.

Sprenger, Jacobus. *The Hammer of Witches: A Complete Translation of the Malleus Maleficarum*. Translated by Christopher S. Mackay. New York: Cambridge University Press, 2009.

Stathakopoulos, Dionysios Ch. *Famine and Pestilence in the Late Roman and Early Byzantine Empire: A Systematic Survey of Subsistence Crises and Epidemics*. Edited by Anthony Bryer and John Haldon, Birmingham Byzantine and Ottoman Monographs. Burlington, Vt.: Ashgate, 2004.

Stec, David M. *The Text of the Targum of Job: An Introduction and Critical Edition*. Leiden: Brill, 1994.

Sterne, Laurence. *The Sermons of Mr. Yorick*. New York: Taylor & Co., 1904.

Sullivan, Margaret A. "Aertsen's Kitchen and Market Scenes: Audience and Innovation in Northern Art." *The Art Bulletin* 81, no. 2 (1999): 236–66.

Swinnock, George. *The Works of George Swinnock*, vol. 1. London: James Nisbet & Co., 1868.

Terrien, Samuel. *The Iconography of Job Through the Centuries: Artists as Biblical Interpreters*. University Park: Pennsylvania State University Press, 1996.

———. *Job: Poet of Existence*. Indianapolis: Bobbs-Merrill, 1957.

Tertullian. *Disciplinary, Moral and Ascetical Works*. Edited by Roy Joseph Deferrari. The Fathers of the Church: A New Translation. New York: Fathers of the Church, Inc., 1959.

Thane, Pat, ed. *A History of Old Age*. London: Thames & Hudson, 2005.

Thompson, E. P. *Witness Against the Beast: William Blake and the Moral Law*. New York: The New Press, 1993.

Tilney, Edmund. *The Flower of Friendship: A Renaissance Dialogue Contesting Marriage*. Edited by Valerie Wayne. New York: Cornell University Press, 1992.

Tobin, John. *Handel's "Messiah": A Critical Account of the Manuscript Sources and Printed Editions*. London: Cassell, 1969.

Todd, Margo. *Christian Humanism and the Puritan Social Order*. Cambridge: Cambridge University Press, 1987.

Tours, Gregory of. *History of the Franks*. Translated by E. Bréhaut. New York: Columbia University Press, 1916.

Travitsky, Betty S., and Adele F. Seeff, eds., *Attending to Women in Early Modern England*. Newark: University of Delaware Press, 1994.

Treharne, Elaine, ed. *Old and Middle English C. 890–C. 1450: An Anthology*. 3d ed. Malden, Mass.: Wiley-Blackwell, 2010.

Trible, Phyllis. "Biblical Theology as Women's Work." *Religion in Life* 44, no. 1 (1975): 7–13.

———. "The Effects of Women's Studies on Biblical Studies: An Introduction." *Journal for the Study of the Old Testament* 22 (1982): 3–5.

Turner, Bryan S. *The Body and Society: Explorations in Social Theory*. 3d ed. Theory, Culture & Society. London: Sage, 2008.

Underdown, D. E. "The Taming of the Scold: The Enforcement of Patriarchal Authority in Early Modern England." Pages 116–36 in *Order and Disorder in Early Modern England*. Edited by Anthony Fletcher and John Stevenson. Cambridge: Cambridge University Press, 1985.

Utterson, Edward Vernon, ed. *Select Pieces of Early Popular Poetry*. 2 vols. London: Pickering, 1825.

Vicchio, Stephen J. *Job in the Ancient World*. The Image of the Biblical Job: A History. vol. 1. Eugene, Ore.: Wipf & Stock, 2006.

————. *Job in the Medieval World*. 3 vols. The Image of the Biblical Job: A History. Eugene, Ore.: Wipf & Stock, 2006.

Vicchio, Stephen, and Lucinda Dukes Edinberg. *The Sweet Uses of Adversity: Images of the Biblical Job*. Baltimore, Md.: IPP, 2002.

Vives, Juan Luis. *The Education of a Christian Woman*. Translated by Charles Fantazzi. Chicago: University of Chicago Press, 2000.

Vogler, Thomas A. "Eighteenth-century Logology and the Book of Job." *Religion & Literature* 20, no. 3 (1988): 25–47.

Voragine, Jacobus de. *The Golden Legend: Readings on the Saints*. Translated by William Granger Ryan. 2 vols. Princeton, N.J.: Princeton University Press, 1993.

————. *The Golden Legend: Selections*. Translated by Christopher Stace. New York: Penguin Putnam.

Vrudny, Kimberly. "Scribes, Corpses, and Friars: Lay Devotion to the Genetrix, Mediatrix, and Redemptrix Through Dominican Didactic Use of the *Speculum Humanae Salvationis* in Late Medieval Europe." Ph.D. dissertation. Luther Seminary, 2001.

Warburton, William. *The Divine Legation of Moses Demonstrated*. 2 vols. London: Tegg & Son, 1837.

Warner, Marina. *Monuments and Maidens: The Allegory of the Female Form*. Berkeley: University of California Press, 1985.

Warren, Samuel M., ed. *A Compendium of the Theological Writings of Emanuel Swedenborg*. New York: Swedenborg Foundation, 1974.

Warton, John. *Death-Bed Scenes and Pastoral Conversations*. 4th ed. 3 vols. London: Murray, 1860.

Waters, Claire M. "Talking the Talk: Access to the Vernacular in Medieval Preaching." Pages 31–42 in *The Vulgar Tongue: Medieval and Postmedieval Vernacularity*. Edited by Fiona Somerset and Nicholas Watson. University Park, Pa.: Pennsylvania State University Press, 2003.

Watson, Thomas. *A Body of Practical Divinity: In a Series of Sermons on the Shorter Catechism*. Philadelphia: James Kay, Jun. & Co., 1833.

Wayne, Valerie. "Advice for Women from Mothers and Patriarchs." Pages 56–79 in *Women and Literature in Britain 1500–1700*. Edited by Helen Wilcox. Cambridge: Cambridge University Press, 1996.

Webster, Brenda. "Blake, Sex and Women Revisited." Pages 254–60 in Bruder, ed., *Women Reading William Blake*.

————. "Blake, Women, and Sexuality." Pages 188–206 in *New Casebooks: William Blake*. Edited by David Punter. New York: St. Martin's, 1996.

Weisbach, W. "L'histoire de Job dans les Arts: A Propos du Tableau du Georges de la Tour au Musee d'epinal." *Gazette des beaux-arts* 78 (1936): 102–12.

Weitzmann, Kurt John. *Die Byzantinische Buchmalerei Des Ix. Und X. Jahrhunderts*. Berlin: Mann, 1935.

————. *The Miniatures of the Sacra Parallela, Parisinus Graecus 923*. Princeton, N.J.: Princeton University Press, 1979.

West, Gerald. "Hearing Job's Wife: Towards a Feminist Reading of Job." *Old Testament Essays* 4 (1991): 107–31.

Whately, William. *A Care-Cloth, or the Cumbers and Troubles of Marriage*. Norwood, N.J.: Johnson, 1976.

Wheelock, Arthur K. *Jan Lievens: A Dutch Master Rediscovered*. New Haven: Yale University Press, 2008.

Whittaker, Jason. "From Hell: Blake and Evil in Popular Culture." Pages 192–204 in *Blake, Modernity and Popular Culture*. Edited by Steve Clark and Jason Whittaker. New York: Palgrave Macmillan, 2007.

Wicksteed, Joseph H. *Blake's Vision of the Book of Job*. New York: Haskell House, 1971.

Wielandt, Ulf. "Hiob in der Alt- und Mittelhochdeutschen Literatur." Ph.D. dissertation. Albert-Ludwigs-Universität zu Freiburg, 1970.

Williams, Nicolas M. *Ideology and Utopia in the Poetry of William Blake*. Cambridge: Cambridge University Press, 1998.

Wills, Lawrence M., ed. *Ancient Jewish Novels: An Anthology*. New York: Oxford University Press, 2002.

Wilson, Adrian, and Joyce Lancaster Wilson. *A Medieval Mirror: Speculum Humanae Salvationis 1324–1500*. Berkeley: University of California Press, 1984.

Wiltenburg, Joy. *Disorderly Women and Female Power in the Street Literature of Early Modern England and Germany*. Charlottesville: University Press of Virginia, 1992.

Wittig, Monique. *The Straight Mind: And Other Essays*. Boston: Beacon, 1992.

Wolde, E. J. van. "The Development of Job: Mrs Job as Catalyst." Pages 201–21 in *A Feminist Companion to Wisdom*. Edited by Athalya Brenner. Sheffield: Sheffield Academic, 1995.

———. *Mr and Mrs Job*. London: SCM, 1997.

Wong, Wai-Ching Angela. *"The Poor Woman": A Critical Analysis of Asian Theology and Contemporary Chinese Fiction by Women*. New York: Lang, 2002.

Worthington, William. *An Essay on the Scheme and Conduct, Procedure and Extent of Man's Redemption... To Which Is Annexed a Dissertation on the Design and Argumentation of the Book of Job*. London: Edward Cave at St. John's Gate, 1743.

Wright, Andrew. *Blake's Job: A Commentary*. Oxford: Clarendon, 1972.

Xenophon. *Oeconomicus: A Social and Historical Commentary*. Translated by Sarah B. Pomeroy. Oxford: Clarendon, 1995.

Yaffe, Martin D. "Providence in Medieval Aristotelianism: Moses Maimonides and Thomas Aquinas on the Book of Job." Pages 111–28 in Perdue and Gilpin, eds., *Voice from the Whirlwind*.

Yeats, W. B. "William Blake and the Imagination." Pages 84–87 in *The Collected Works of W. B. Yeats*. Edited by George Bornstein and Richard J. Finneran. New York: Scribner, 2007.

Young, Edward. *Night Thoughts, and a Paraphrase on Part of the Book of Job*. London: Chiswick, 1812.

Ziegler, Joseph. *Beiträge zum griechischen Job*. Göttingen: Vandenhoeck & Ruprecht, 1985.

———, ed. *Iob*. Septuaginta: Vetus Testamentum Graecum. Göttingen: Vandenhoeck & Ruprecht, 1982.

INDEXES

INDEX OF REFERENCES

Index of Authors